Food & Drink

The Cultural Context

Edited by
Donald Sloan

(G) Goodfellow Publishers Ltd

(G) Published by Goodfellow Publishers Limited,
Woodeaton, Oxford, OX3 9TJ

http://www.goodfellowpublishers.com

British Library Cataloguing in Publication Data: a catalogue record for
this title is available from the British Library.

Library of Congress Catalog Card Number: on file.

ISBN: 978-1-908999-04-7

First published 2013

Design and typesetting by P.K. McBride, www.macbride.org.uk

Cover design by Cylinder, www.cylindermedia.com

Printed by Marston Book Services, www.marston.co.uk

Contents

Case Studies

Foreword from Ken Hom OBE

I never stop learning. It's what has fuelled my life-long passion for food and drink. Every trip I take gives me new opportunities to seek out unfamiliar ingredients, sample indigenous dishes and try new cooking methods. And when I am writing about the cuisines of China, and other Asian nations with which I'm closely associated, I continue to make new discoveries.

I also consider myself to be an educator. I have dedicated my career to engaging the public with food and drink, and their place in culture. I truly believe there is no better way to understand those from other countries or communities than by immersing yourself in their culinary heritage. It speaks of power structures, family relations, agricultural and industrial practices, and historical patterns of migration. Most importantly, it reveals their collective identity. This is what I have always tried to convey in my books, articles and television series.

So it felt like a natural progression to become formally involved with higher education, as a Founding Patron of *Oxford Gastronomica* at Oxford Brookes University. It is life-affirming to get to know young people who have natural curiosity, genuine desire to learn and endless enthusiasm. For me it has reinforced the value of engaging students, not only with challenging academic theory, but also by learning through experience. This reflects the content of this text. In addition to chapters from established academics, there are case studies from influential writers, journalist and broadcasters, many of whom provide inspirational support to our students in Oxford. It is the first in what will be a series of texts under the banner of *Oxford Gastronomica*, which we hope will support students who share our fascination for food, drink and culture.

Ken Hom OBE
Paris, August 2013

Acknowledgements

I am immensely grateful to all of the contributors to this text; to my students, colleagues and friends who shape food studies at Oxford Brookes University; and to Sally North and Tim Goodfellow, of Goodfellow Publishers, for their patience.

Donald Sloan

Oxford, August 2013

An Agenda for Food Studies

Donald Sloan

Co-founder and Chair of Oxford Gastronomica, Donald Sloan is also Head of the Oxford School of Hospitality Management at Oxford Brookes University, a position he has held since 2003. In 2003 he was the first recipient of the Martin Radcliffe Fellowship in Gastronomy, funded by the Savoy Educational Trust. In 2008 Donald was appointed a Trustee of the Jane Grigson Trust.

There are many possible approaches to constructing university level educational programmes in food studies. Some encourage historical analysis, others are firmly grounded in the social sciences and an increasing number are focused on political and ethical issues.

This is a somewhat personal agenda. It reflects a framework adopted at one university that might stimulate consideration of the value of studying food and drink from cultural perspectives. At Oxford Brookes University our approach continues to evolve. It is built upon exploration of our relationships with food and drink – what shapes them and what are their consequences, both positive and negative, for individuals and society? It is interdisciplinary and, I hope, challenging and engaging. We aim to provide students with ample opportunity to apply their theoretical knowledge through regular interaction with influential and thoughtful practitioners.

Our relationship with food and drink is increasingly complex. The soaring popularity of celebrity chefs who dominate our television schedules; glossy magazines that reinforce the merits of local and seasonal ingredients; and beautifully produced cookbooks that rise to the top of best-seller lists, might suggest that we live in a culinary utopia. Yet our reliance on mass-produced, pre-packaged meals, pandemic health crises that have catastrophic consequences, the devastation of our natural environment through industrialised production, and the contamination of our lengthy and opaque food supply chain, present a very different version of reality. Such complexity makes it an ideal time to be involved in food and drink studies, and it ensures an audience predisposed to learn.

This chapter provides contextual information about the development of food studies programmes. It then outlines the approach adopted at Oxford Brookes University, which rests on the principles of *interdisciplinarity*, *integrity* and *learning through experience*. The chapters and case studies have been written by academics, food and drink writers, journalists, broadcasters and activists, most of whom make direct contributions to the learning experience of our students. By cross-referencing to each, I will show how their input supports our educational objectives and enriches our learning environment.

The context

Outside of the sciences, food studies is a relatively new area of focus for universities. Given that it draws on numerous academic disciplines, something that does not rest well within established academic structures, it is perhaps not surprising that it is still an emerging field. While intense media attention may fuel interest, it also ensures that what is considered in vogue can change on a regular basis.

Atkins and Bowler (2001) provide a useful overview of dominant approaches to food studies that have been adopted over the years, reflected not only in academic publications, but also in a limited number of university degree programmes worldwide. Theses are:

- *Historical approaches.* Work of this nature is largely focused on the study of food at particular points in time or on the nature of production and consumption over periods of history. The common goal is to provide evidence-based social commentary on issues such as diet and nutrition, poverty and wealth, and lifestyles. Contributors to the 'developmental' school have gone further by exploring food habits in the context of broader influences such as social interplay and class hierarchies. For example, Elias (1939) proposed that increasingly complex and inter-connected 'figurations' (social networks) have a continuously civilising impact on individuals and communities. He argued that the imposition of self-restraint, manifest through dining etiquette, is a necessary prerequisite for the effective operation of society. The work of Mennell, most notably *All Manners of Food* (1985), has greatly influenced such approaches to food studies. While using historical works on food and drink as his source material, Mennell goes beyond the cataloguing of behaviour or the observation of social change. Instead, he adopts the developmental or 'process' approach of Elias to analyse how conflict and competition between social groups has shaped food habits in England and France, through the ages.

■ *Cultural and sociological approaches.* Anthropologists from the functionalist school have examined the role of food customs in maintaining stable societies. While their work has been criticised for underplaying societal change and progression, it has contributed to our understanding of how apparently esoteric and anachronistic rituals surrounding food production and consumption carry valuable symbolic significance and are part of broader cultural frameworks. Less concerned with the functional use of food in our daily lives, structural sociologists have focused on the way in which our culinary taste and food-related behaviour are products of social conditioning derived from the contexts in which we exist. One of the most influential contributors in this field was Pierre Bourdieu, a Marxist structuralist, whose work has had a profound impact on food studies. In *Distinction: a social critique on the judgement of taste* (1984), he argued that taste is not only an expression of class, but that it also shapes and reinforces class distinctions. He explored class as a construct of cultural and social capital, in addition to occupation and income, and in doing so revealed much about how food is used to communicate 'legitimate' social standing.

■ *Post-modern and post-structuralist approaches*. Applied to the study of food, postmodernism has focused on the fall of eternal, largely class-based influences on the construction of taste, and the consequent rise of individualism. For example, Beck (1992) proposed that individuals have been required to create their own biographies and identities as the influence of embedded cultural frameworks has diminished. Bauman (2002) suggested that individuals' sense of identity and meaning were increasingly being constructed on a self-assembly basis through willing and conscious membership of relatively autonomous habitats. The work of Ritzer (1993) has featured highly within the study of food in post-modern contexts. He established the concept of McDonaldization, a process through which mass-produced, standardised products are reaching beyond traditional class and taste boundaries to deaden the experience of consumers. Post-modernists do not necessarily argue that as the influence of class has diminished we have witnessed the democratisation of culinary taste, but rather that the basis of social differentiation has changed.

■ *Food systems*. Traditionally, the study of food systems has focused on the supply chain, encompassing production, supply and consumption. This 'vertical' analysis contrasts with structuralist and post-modern perspectives which seek to determine 'meanings' of consumption across the whole of society. More recently, powerful commentary on modern food systems has focused on ethical issues, including the potentially damaging impacts of dominant business practices. This includes growing concerns over the increased commodification of food, the ownership of food production and supply by complex multi-national companies, and the perceived lack of rigorous impact analysis. For example, Blythman (2004) has explored the power of large-scale retailers, Pollan (2008) questioned the connection between food systems and health crises, and Steel (2008) highlighted the precarious nature of food supply to urban locations.

The framework

Interdisciplinary learning

One of the most significant challenges in constructing coherent and robust academic programmes in food studies is that it is not in itself an academic discipline. It is instead a domain of application to which those from a variety of academic backgrounds contribute their diverse perspectives. Even if a programme were to lie clearly within one of the four approaches previously identified – historical, cultural and sociological, postmodern or food systems – it is likely that the learning experience would still have to cross academic boundaries.

It is worth considering why the traditional (and still ubiquitous) organisational structure adopted by universities can maintain academic separatism and mitigate against collaborative approaches to teaching. It is built around academic disciplines that have their own theoretical frameworks and curriculum content. Disciplines rest within specialist academic departments. Members of faculty are socialised into discipline-specific conventions with respect to focus of research and approaches to teaching. Further, the means by which the value of contributions to knowledge is assessed may differ markedly between disciplines. Davies and Devlin (2007: 1) provide a useful summary of the constituent elements of academic disciplines:

- the presence of a community of scholars;
- a tradition or history of inquiry;
- a mode of inquiry that defines how data is collected and interpreted;
- defining the requirements for what constitutes new knowledge;
- the existence of a communications network.

One of the many potential problems with this well-established approach is that it might not acknowledge the manner in which boundaries of academic disciplines should change over time, possibly as a result of external contextual issues. For example, within the social sciences, prevailing political or moral climates may necessitate a change in focus of teaching and research, which would benefit from the integration of different perspectives. In addition, it does not necessarily recognise, and therefore encourage, the debt owed by particular disciplines to others. For example, research methodologies used in sciences are now widely adopted in social sciences.

Support for higher education that draws on multiple disciplines is nothing new. The mathematician and moral philosopher Dugald Stewart, a forefather of liberal education and a key figure in the Scottish Enlightenment, which came to define that country's educational philosophy. Broadie (2011) notes Stewart's belief that, '…we should not expect to find the highest cultivation of the human mind among those of confined pursuits.' In Stewart's own words:

> 'But is it perfectly consistent with the most intense application to our favourite pursuit, to cultivate that general acquaintance with letters and with the world which may be sufficient to enlarge its mind, and to preserve it from any danger of contracting the pedantry of a particular profession. In many cases, the sciences reflect light on each other; and the general acquisitions which we have made in other pursuits, may furnish us with useful helps for the farther prosecution of our own. (1797, in Broadie, 2001: 109).

In a contemporary context, the terms *multi-disciplinary*, *cross-disciplinary* and *interdisciplinary* are often used interchangeably to signify approaches to teaching that integrate different academic subject areas, yet they do have different definitions. Multi-disciplinary education points to several discrete disciplines co-existing within one academic programme, without crossover. This limits the possibility of applying a variety of perspectives to a single complex issue. Cross-disciplinary learning encourages students to explore areas that lie outside the established frame of reference of their dominant or base academic discipline. This could encompass programmes such as the History of Medicine or Financial Management for the Charity Sector.

Newell (2010) provides a definition of interdisciplinary learning as, '…a process of answering a question, solving a problem, or addressing a topic that is too broad or complex to be dealt with adequately by single discipline or profession…[it] draws on disciplinary perspectives and integrates their insights through the construction of a more comprehensive perspective.' (p14). Davies and Devlin (2007) describe various interpretations of interdisciplinary studies that lie on a continuum. At one extreme, the integrity of discrete disciplines is maintained and they are applied to one particular topic (e.g. Women's Studies). At the other, boundaries are merged and the re-imagined disciplines are used to address specific challenges, often medical or scientific.

Despite such positive definitions, the challenges of constructing coherent interdisciplinary curricula that ensure appropriate academic experiences for students are well documented. For example, if programmes are too broad in their focus, and numerous disciplines are being utilised, how can sufficient depth be achieved? How can students be expected to engage with the academic 'languages' of disparate disciplines in addition to different theoretical frameworks. Students often have a natural affinity with particular subject areas. Can this be maintained if they are drawing on a variety of disciplines?

Spelt et al (2009) undertook a comprehensive review of academic literature relating to interdisciplinary education. They note the rise in the number of interdisciplinary programmes, and their distinctive characteristics: 'In comparison with traditional higher education, which focuses on domain-specific knowledge and general skills, this kind of higher education also aims to develop boundary-crossing skills. Boundary-crossing skills are, for instance, the ability to change perspectives, to synthesize knowledge of different disciplines, and to cope with complexity'. (p366). Their research is focused on identifying optimal conditions for achieving effective interdisciplinary learning. Using as a base Biggs' principle of 'constructive alignment' (2003), which emphasises coherence between teaching strategies, assessment and intended learning outcomes, they provide a model of the sub-skills required to achieve the ideal learning experience for students (Table 1). There are four categories of sub-skills: interdisciplinary thinking (pedagogic knowledge), student, learning environment and learning process. While no one model could be applicable within all circumstances, work of this nature does provide a planning framework that can be used, within the context of the particular challenges inherent in interdisciplinary teaching, for curriculum development, the broader student experience and staff development. Its emphasis on the outcomes of the overall learning experience contrasts with much of the literature on interdisciplinarity, which focuses purely on pedagogic practice.

Table 1: Potential sub-skills and conditions for interdisciplinary higher education

Interdisciplinary thinking	
Having knowledge	Knowledge of disciplines
	Knowledge of disciplinary paradigms
	Knowledge of interdisciplinarity
Having skills	Higher-order cognitive skills
	Communication skills
Student	
Personal characteristics	Curiosity
	Respect
	Openness
	Patience
	Diligence
	Self regulation
Prior experiences	Social
	Educational
Learning environment	
Curriculum	Balance between disciplinary and interdisciplinary
	Disciplinary knowledge inside or outside courses on interdisciplinarity
Teacher	Intellectual community focused on interdisciplinarity
	Expertise of teachers on interdisciplinarity
	Consensus on interdisciplinarity
	Team development
	Team teaching
Pedagogy	Aimed at achieving interdisciplinarity
	Aimed at achieving active learning
	Aimed at achieving collaboration
Assessment	Of students' intellectual maturation
	Of interdisciplinarity
Learning process	
Pattern	Phased with gradual advancement
	Linear
	Iterative
	Milestones with encountering questions
Learning activities	Aimed at achieving interdisciplinarity
	Aimed at achieving reflection

From Spelt et al (2009)

Interdisciplinary learning – welcome to new domains

Taken together, and in the context of a broader curriculum, Chapter 2 by Lugosi and Chapter 3 by Ritzer and Galli, highlight the opportunities and challenges of constructing interdisciplinary programmes in food studies. They tackle, from social and cultural perspectives, the construction of taste and food habits. Lugosi explores the use of food and drink in the formation of individual and collective identity and the impact on relationships with food and drink of variables such as gender, class and ethnicity. Ritzer and Galli take a fresh look at globalisation, in particular to assess its influence on choice and availability of food and drink, as well as its influence on the distinctiveness of cultures.

In the context of this framework for food studies, these chapters provide base theoretical perspectives that will shape students' engagement with a range of additional topics, including those informed by other academic disciplines. For example, in Chapter 5, in which Harris discusses the foodways of the African American Diaspora from historical perspectives, the concept of *identity* is key. Students' comprehension of her proposition that foodways can sustain a sense of cohesion amongst those from 'scattered' communities, as well shaping the character of the new communities in which they settle, will be informed by their prior learning. Similarly, they should be able to apply Ritzer's insights on the impact of globalisation when considering the means by which displaced populations can maintain a sense of belonging.

In case study 2, McCarthy reflects upon the role of the food community – producers, chefs, restaurateurs and retailers – in re-shaping the identity of New Orleans, after the city was devastated by Hurricane Katrina.

As noted by Spelt (Table 1), this approach is dependent upon commitment and consensus of academic staff (possibly through team-teaching and cross-referencing) and on successful induction of students, not only to the concept of inter-disciplinarity, but also to the language and conventions of unfamiliar disciplines.

Interdisciplinary learning – diverse resources

In Case Study 3, Geraldene Holt discusses the contribution of Jane Grigson, widely regarded as one of the United Kingdom's most influential food writers. In doing so, Holt reveals the broader contribution of cookery books to our cultural life, documenting social history, recording characteristic recipes, maintaining traditions and stimulating regional and national pride.

Jane Grigson's private collection of food and cookery books, research notes and travel diaries – all the rich source material for her publications – is now held on permanent loan by Oxford Brookes University. There it has joined the collections of, amongst others, Prue Leith, Ken Hom and John Fuller, as well as the national brewing library, to form one of the world's most substantial libraries focused solely on food, drink and culture.

The resource delivers value to students by:

- providing historical and applied data that supports their interdisciplinary research; and
- enriching their conceptual study of food literature by linking them directly with the private collections and personal artefacts of influential contributors.

Integrity in educational delivery

The study of food and drink from cultural perspectives inevitably requires learners to engage with a range of highly controversial issues. For example, we are witnessing intense debate about the power of multi-national companies in the food sector – their impact on our natural environment, their control over our global food system and their responsibility for health crises. As educators, we have to consider how best to explore such issues with students who may hold a diverse range of views and come from many different cultural backgrounds. Should we be concerned about the potential for accusations of (liberal) bias, cultural insensitivity or even ideological indoctrination?

There is evidence that values-based education is in vogue, which might fuel concerns that academics are predisposed to adopt particular views on ethical issues. For example, we are operating in an environment that requires students to develop 'graduate attributes' – a range of skills that it is hoped will enhance their life chances. Amongst them is 'global citizenship' (variations exist internationally) which, although different definitions are adopted, implies the need for responsible practice and care for the impact of our actions. Applied within a business environment this has ethical implications.

One option is to adopt a neutral and impartial stance. Challenge students to consider alternative and opposing standpoints and encourage them to develop their own informed opinions. This would also require careful balance in the nature of co-curricular activities. Certainly, denials by academics in the face of accusations of bias might suggest that this is a favoured approach.

But having spent years developing depth of knowledge and possibly becoming 'champions' of particular stances, is it realistic or desirable to require academics to simply present balanced arguments? As Hickey and Brecher (1990) suggest, is it not healthier to embrace bias and to accept that stating and defending points of view is a necessary prerequisite to developing students' critical and intellectual capacities? To conceal opinions that have been shaped through careful analysis not only undermines honesty and academic integrity, it also assumes little or no ability on the part of students to recognise the legitimacy of alternative views.

Problems might only arise if bias is hidden, or if a particular political or ideological agenda is presented as the universal truth. This is worth considering in the context of food studies, a field in which we are seeing the rise of special interest groups as higher education providers. Take for example, the University of the Gastronomic Sciences in Pollenzo, Italy, which is formally linked to the worldwide Slow Food movement. Note – I precede my comments by declaring my support for Slow Food, which at its best articulates an appealing defence against corporate dominance of our global food system, and for widespread access to good food. Founded by journalist Carlo Petrini as a reaction against perceived damage being inflicted on Italian heritage through the rise of fast food, Slow is now a worldwide political movement. A charismatic orator, Petrini delvers his message about the value of Slow Food in unequivocal terms. And the official Slow Manifesto leaves us in no doubt about the supposed legitimacy of the organisation's case: 'We are enslaved by speed and have all succumbed to the same insidious virus: Fast Life, which disrupts our habits, pervades the privacy of our homes and forces us to eat Fast Foods. ...So Slow Food is now the only progressive answer.' (2003, xxiii). I am not questioning the integrity of the distinguished academics who contribute to the range of undergraduate and masters programmes offered at the University of the Gastronomic Sciences. Rather I am posing a question. Is it possible for an academic institution that is aligned to a political organisation to deliver education that is untainted by ideology? To attempt to transmit particular values to students is something quite different from presenting them with particular arguments as a means of enhancing their critical faculties.

Ensuring integrity – tackling controversy head-on

In Chapter 4, Hawkins tackles highly controversial ethical issues. She explores why there is increasing scrutiny of the global food system, driven by media coverage of inequalities in access to food, health crises, food security and the environmental impacts of production and waste. She does not shy from presenting her own (well-informed) views, particularly on what she sees as popular yet misguided assumptions about the motives and influence of multi-national companies, free trade and a lack of food literacy amongst consumers.

Hawkins could not be accused of adopting a neutral stance, built only on an exposition of contrasting views. Instead, she is laying out her own case, confident in the knowledge that it is well-considered, and hopeful that it will stimulate discussion and debate amongst students.

Learning through experience

It seems inconceivable that food studies programmes could fail to integrate experiential dimensions. To theorise on taste, without tasting, would be a tragedy. But what kind of experiences should be constructed that ensure valuable outcomes for students: that extend their theoretical understanding, enhance their knowledge of 'practice', make their learning experience as enjoyable as possible, enable them to develop their own networks of professional and personal contacts, and provide opportunities for civil engagement?

Dominant theories on experiential learning are still built around models of personal reflection, originally conceptualised by Dewy (1938). David Kolb's work (1984) remains the most influential and it is still used extensively in adult education, particularly that which has focused on management and leadership. As Bergsteiner et al note, 'Kolb's theory posits that learning is a cognitive process in constant adaptation to and engagement with one's environment. Individuals create knowledge from experience, rather than just from received instruction.' (2010: 30). He presents a cyclical model that contains four sequential steps: concrete experience, reflective observation, abstract conceptualisation and active experimentation. Through conscious reflection on real-life situations learners are encouraged to draw conclusions and to consider future actions. Their hypotheses are tested through implementation and through reference to theory, which results in additional learning.

Despite its persistence, Kolb's work has received criticism. Seaman (2008) suggests that theories on experiential learning were, understandably, shaped by the historical period in which they were developed. Those who use them to inform contemporary educational practice are failing to challenge their currency and relevance. For example, during the 1970s, when work of this nature was being developed, there were two contrasting forces. One was to meet the needs of an adult education system that was seeking ways to formally accredit learners' prior work experience. The other was more idealistic, and reflected a movement to promote self-realisation through holistic approaches to education. The imposition of bureaucratic educational procedures does not seem to sit well alongside flexible and relatively experimental approaches to teaching. Some have also questioned whether this form of reflective, or 'constructivist', experiential learning is too focused on the individual, rather than the collective, in ways that resonate with somewhat tainted forms of western capitalism.

A re-conceptualisation of learning through practice (or experience) by Lave and Wenger (1991) rejects the notion that effective learning occurs through formal and conscious reflection on a series of discrete, identifiable, 'concrete' experiences. Their concept of *legitimate peripheral participation* focuses on knowledge and skills acquisition through membership of 'communities of practice'. The term 'peripheral' does not, as one might assume, mean that learners are afforded little consideration by established members of such communities. Rather, it is empowering, indicating a level of participation that is appropriate given variables such as prior experience, the structure of the learning community and power relations. Through the process of participation, learners not only develop knowledge and skills, but also assign meaning to activities and establish their own identities, as well as shaping the nature of communities for those who follow. Legitimate peripheral participation is not presented as a pedagogic technique, but more as a means of understanding how learning occurs through interaction in social contexts. Yet it can inform approaches to the structuring and development of learning environments.

Accepting our aims of engaging students, through experience, with the dynamic nature of food and drink and their place in culture, and of exploring interdependent relationships, such as between agriculture and foodservice, the work of Lave and Wenger provides a useful platform. We can assume that the 'community of practice', containing established and peripheral members, is built from within the university environment. A learning curriculum (as opposed to a teaching curriculum) can be developed, which avoids formal knowledge transmission and assessment being the sole drivers of motivation to engage (for both learners and educators). Educators' responsibility for providing ongoing access to additional activities that support learning through interaction, including to experienced practitioners, becomes another essential element of a thriving community of practice. As students grow in confidence, as their relationships strengthen and as they move towards a central position in the community, they are continuously developing knowledge and skills, attaching meaning to their activities, developing their identity and character, and becoming 'co-creators' of that community. Their understanding of complex theory, and of its value, is also enhanced through continuous application to a variety of real-life experiences.

Gastronomic field trips

In case study 5, Marc Millon focuses on Devon, a region that boasts one of the United Kingdom's most vibrant and diverse culinary cultures. Once a year, he hosts a field trip for around fifty students, during which they meet and interact with organic farmers, cheese-makers, brewers, retailers, restaurateurs and chefs, all of whom are shaping the area's reputation and driving its economy. The highlight of the experience is a dinner, incorporating a wide array of local ingredients, at which Michael Caines, one of the UK's leading chefs, outlines his personal philosophy.

Students are also regular visitors to Burgundy, where colleagues from the Burgundy School of Business introduce them to local vineyard owners, chefs and restaurateurs. They learn, as discussed by Chapuis and Lecat in Chapter 6, what combination of factors result in a region having an embedded and defining culinary and wine heritage.

The experience of field trips delivers value to students by:

- connecting them with those responsible for constructing communities of practice;
- exposing them to issues they have studied from a theoretical perspective, including local food systems and the potential for food tourism to drive local economies, community cohesion and pride; and
- strengthening their learning community, focused around a common area of interest – food and drink.

Sunday Times Oxford Literary Festival

Through *Oxford Gastronomica*, Oxford Brookes University's centre for food and cultural studies, we construct a series of talks focused on food and food literature for the annual Sunday Times Oxford Literary Festival. Chapter 7, by Fred Plotkin, and Case Study 4, by Yasmin Alibhai-Brown, both recent contributors to the festival, reflect the focus of their presentations. Alibhai-Brown tells a personal story about her family leaving their native Uganda after the tyrannical Idi Amin assumed power. She describes how food and food literature have helped maintain a sense of belonging for those forced to leave their homeland. Plotkin explores the role of food and drink in opera – the tastes and food habits of leading composers, performers and fictional operatic characters.

Students attend the sessions at the literary festival; organise and host 'fringe' events, including discussions, lectures and literary lunches; and host individual speakers. The experience delivers value to students by:

- encouraging them to consider the role played by food and drink in diverse cultures, by reflecting on their representation in the arts; and
- broadening the scope of their educational experience.

Volunteering in Transylvania

In Case Study 6, Pamela Ratiu and Rareş Crăiuţ focus on Transylvania Fest, an annual celebration of the region's culinary culture and architectural heritage. They outline the historical context that inspired the festival and their ambitions to use it as the base for enhancing community cohesion, national and international tourism and local economic activity. Since 2008, students from Oxford Brookes University have been providing voluntary support for Transylvania, during the summer months. They live and work in the region, helping to conceptualise and stage the event. Responsibilities include event planning, engaging local food and drink producers, building on-line marketing platforms, organising fund-raising activities and hosting VIP receptions.

The experience delivers value to students by:

- giving them practical exposure to issues they have studied from a theoretical perspective, including the maintenance of distinct food cultures and food tourism as a means of developing local economies;
- providing opportunities to learn about a particular culinary culture, and how it reflects the characteristics of the region; and
- giving them membership of a productive (sub) community of practice, to learn through interaction and to shape that community's impact on others.

Shaping the character of destinations?

Case studies 7, 8 and 9, explore the changing role of food and drink in particular destinations. Robinson discusses the 'coming out' of Australian food and drink, focusing on the impact it has had on the country's self identity, international reputation and place in the world. Campion explores British cuisine, tracking the forces that have transformed its quality, enhanced its image and fuelled national pride. Bloomfield focuses on one particular location, London's Soho, and considers the concentration of diverse cultures that have shaped the culinary scene of this Bohemian quarter of the city.

The content of these case studies reflects a series of expert-led discussions with students, each one addressing the food, drink and culture of specific destinations.

The experience delivers value to students by:

- expanding their knowledge of specific culinary cultures;
- enabling them to apply theoretical knowledge, on issues of identity and cultural development, to particular destinations; and
- exposing them to leading food and drink writers and academics.

Conclusion

As demand for food studies grows, there will inevitably be more debate and discussion about how best to construct formal educational programmes. This chapter has provided one possible framework, specifically focused on the determinants and consequences of food and drink production and consumption. It rests on three broad principles:

- *Interdisciplinary learning.* Food studies is a domain of application which requires contributions from a variety of academic disciplines. Accepting that with comprehensive planning we can overcome challenges inherent in delivering interdisciplinary programmes, we can then focus on the opportunities they present. By drawing on different academic disciplines, students can synthesise knowledge and tackle complex issues from multiple perspectives.

- *Integrity in educational delivery*. Inevitably, food studies requires participants to engage with controversial issues, many of which have ethical and moral dimensions. Academics should not undermine their integrity by masking their personal views. Instead, they should state and defend their positions, in part to create a challenging and engaging learning environment, but also as a means of enhancing students' intellectual capacity.

- *Learning though experience*. To study food, drink and culture, without exposure to 'real life' scenarios and without meeting talented practitioners, is unimaginable. Students should be growing as members of vibrant communities of practice, focused not only meeting prescribed outcomes of formal curriculum, but also on learning through continuous interaction.

References

Atkins, P. and Bowler, I. (2001) *Food in Society*, London: Arnold

Bauerlein, M. (2006) 'How academe short changes conservative thinking', *Chronicle of Higher Education*, **53** (17), B6-B8

Bergsteiner, H., Avery, G., Neumann, R. (2010) 'Kolb's experiential learning model: critique from a modelling perspective', *Studies in Continuing Education*, **32** (1), 29-46

Blythman, J. (2004) *Shopped: the shocking power of British supermarkets*, London: Fourth Estate

Broadie, A. (2007) *The Scottish Enlightenment*, Edinburgh: Birlinn Limited

Davies, M. and Devlin, M. (2007) 'Interdisciplinary higher education for teaching and learning', Melbourne: CSHE, University of Melbourne Press

Fenwick, T. and Tara, J. (2000) 'Expanding perceptions of experiential learning: A review of the five contemporary perspectives on cognition', *Adult Education Quarterly*, **50** (4), 243-272

Hickey, T. (1990) 'In defence of bias', *Studies in Higher Education*, **15** (3), 1587-1598

Krometis, H., Clark, E.P., Gonzalez, V., and Leslie, M, (2011) 'The death of disciplines: Developing a team-taught course to provide interdisciplinary perspectives for first year students', *College Teaching*, **59** (2), 73-78

Lave, J. and Wenger, E. (1991) *Situated Learning: legitimate peripheral participation*, New York: Cambridge University Press

Petrini, C. (2003) *Slow Food: The Case for Taste*, New York: Columbia University Press

Pollan, M. (2008) *In Defence of Food*, London: Penguin

Newell, W.H. (2010) 'Educating for a complex world', *Liberal Education*, **96** (4), 6-11

Quay, J. (2003) 'Experience and participation: relating theories and learning', *Journal of Experiential Education*, 26 (2), 105-112

Seaman, J. (2008) 'Experience, reflect, critique: The end of the learning cycles era', *Journal of Experiential Education*, **31** (1), 3-18

Spelt, E., Biermans, H., Tobi, H., Luning, P. And Mulder, M. (2009) 'Teaching and learning in interdisciplinary higher education: a systematic review', *Educational Psychology Review*, **21** (4), 365-378

Squires, G. (1992) 'Interdisciplinarity in higher education in the United Kingdom', *European Journal of Education*, **27** (30), 201-210

Steel, C (2008) *Hungry City: How Food Shapes our Lives*, London: Chatto and Windus

Turesky, E. and Wood, D.R. (2010) 'Kolb's experiential learning as a critical frame for reflective practice', *Academic Leadership*, **8** (3), 1-21

Food, Drink and Identity

Peter Lugosi

Peter is a Reader at the Oxford School of Hospitality Management. His work draws on sociology, geography and anthropology in examining contemporary hospitality. He has researched and published on a wide range of subjects including customer experience management, co-creation in consumer experiences, hospitality and urban regeneration, migrants' experiences of hospitality work, research ethics, entrepreneurship and organisational culture.

Identity refers to who we think (or feel) we are, but also to who others think we are. Identities are closely tied to our values, attitudes, beliefs, preferences, behaviours and personality characteristics that distinguish us from others around us. However, none of us are unique in our values, beliefs or our characteristics, and our identities often reflect those of others. Our identities are inevitably shaped by the people we interact with, the environments in which we live, and the cultures that we encounter. Therefore, to best understand how identities emerge, it is important to consider the social and cultural contexts in which people live.

Eating and drinking are universal to all cultures; but, the beliefs and practices surrounding food and drink reflect the particular characteristics of cultures alongside the identities of the people who are part of those cultures. Food, drink and identity interact in multiple ways. This chapter considers these interactions in commercial hospitality and social settings. It examines the relationship between food, drink and identity from the consumption perspective, i.e. how foods and drinks influence and communicate identities in social and domestic settings; and how identities and the desire to articulate our sense of selves shape when, how and what foods and drinks we consume. The chapter also incorporates the production point of view, particularly within commercial contexts. It discusses how notions of identities are exploited through marketing and in the creation of commercial hospitality experiences. It also considers the ways staff's identities are involved in creating food and drink related experiences.

The chapter is split into five sections: the first examines different conceptions of identity. The second part focuses on the way identities are performed in different social spaces. The third, fourth and fifth sections focus specifically on gender, class and ethnicity, as particular aspects of identity.

Identity, identification and belonging

Before we continue it is important to address three problematic assumptions that can restrict our understanding of identity and its relationship with culture.

- First, it may be assumed that identity is something innate, and that we are born with genetic traits that largely predetermine our values, attitudes, beliefs, preferences and characteristics. We cannot ignore the fact that genetics and inherited traits influence behaviours and identities. However, it is not possible or particularly useful, in this chapter, for us to dwell on the genetic factors underpinning identity. It is also important to bear in mind that biological determinism ignores the importance of socialisation and culture in shaping our identities. Indeed many scientists have attempted to account for the way environmental factors interact with genetics in shaping personality traits (Reimann, Angleitner and Strelau, 1997).

- Second, it may be assumed that the emphasis on values, attitudes, beliefs, preferences and characteristics places identity in the realm of the mind, and it is thus reduced to a cognitive process. As Burkitt (1999) suggests, the danger with this is that it separates the mind from the body, i.e. thinking from doing and feeling. It is important to stress that we see, touch, smell, hear and taste. We process experiences and sensations through our brains, but engage with the world through our bodies. The multi-sensual nature of human experience, particularly surrounding food and drink, means we cannot ignore the body and physicality in shaping our identities (Bell and Valentine, 1997).

- Third, it may also be assumed that identities are fixed, stable aspects of our psychology. Marketing and advertising frequently invite us to discover or know our 'real' selves – implying that there is an authentic, real self to be revealed. However, this view appears to ignore the dynamic nature of identity and the way our sense of self changes in different stages of our lives or in different domains of activity.

An alternative approach to identity recognises that identities change and that they are shaped by our environment and our relationships with others. Social scientists argue that we continually 'construct' our identities (Hall and Du Gay, 1996). In short, we are different people in different social contexts. For example, we may act or speak differently when eating a family meal than when we are eating with friends or partners. We may also behave differently when in a formal setting, than we do eating or drinking at home or in a more casual venue. Furthermore we prioritise different values, thoughts or behaviours at different stages in our lives. A young, single person may have different priorities than someone older, married with children and various family obligations. The implication of this is that how we think or act, and who we are, constantly shifts.

Writers suggest that rather than thinking of identity as something concrete and stable, it is more useful to think about selves through the notion of *identification* (e.g. Bhabha, 1990, 1996; Hall, 1996). Who we think or feel we are is shaped by how we identify with or against an 'other', or others. We may be more or less like other people in terms of values, characteristics, behaviours, etc. We therefore position ourselves as belonging to a group of people, or being a certain type of person; and in the same way others identify with us. More importantly, belonging to a group or identifying with certain individuals also positions people as being different from numerous others. In other words, as Bourdieu (1986) and Barth (1969) argued, boundary maintenance and the articulation of difference become central to defining individual, group and cultural identity.

Similarity and difference are articulated through food and drink in two main ways: first, the foods and drinks that are consumed; and second, the rituals associated with their transformation and consumption. Particular foods featuring in people's diets often reflect social and cultural values. Serving and consuming them thus comes to highlight social and cultural identification with specific group norms. These can be on religious grounds, for example, in the distinction of kosher or halal foods among Jews and Muslims, and adhering to rules governing what can be consumed. Secular examples of food reflecting social and cultural values include the consumption of offal, including feet, the face, ears, beaks, testicles, brains, hearts, livers, etc. These feature in many diets and their consumption reflects people's socialisation into cultures where these are part of established food norms (Lugosi *et al.*, 2012). In contrast, markets have developed for 'sanitised' cuts of meat, for example, boneless, white chicken meat. It is also possible to detect counter-trends among individuals who celebrate offal (See e.g. Helou, 2011). Rather than being a signifier of impoverishment, the consumption of such 'cheap' cuts of offal meat may act as a declaration of sophistication. Consumers of offal thus identify with values that reject the sanitisation of food and hence, cheap, industrially produced food.

Affiliation and identification with group norms and values are also reflected in contemporary concerns about sustainability, provenance and the ethical dimensions of foodstuffs. For example, studies show how consumers may express various levels of enthusiasm for, and commitment to, local, organic or fair-trade (e.g. Long and Murray, 2012). People may criticise and attack food manufacturers and retailers who engage in unethical or unsustainable practices; they may boycott particular foodstuffs or organisations, while staying loyal to others, or opt out of existing systems altogether, creating alternative food supply networks, for example, farmers' markets, vegetable box schemes and community food growing (See e.g. Goodman *et al.* 2011; Leitch, 2003; Trauger and Passidomo, 2012). It may also be reflected in people's willingness to pay a premium for sustainable and ethical foods and drinks (McGoldrick and Freestone, 2008).

Beyond the foods themselves, the methods of transformation, whether cooking, preparation or service, and the rituals associated with consumption also become signifiers of identity and acts of identification. This may include fasting as part of religious observance, for example, during Ramadan; or feasting to celebrate special occasions such as weddings (Selwyn, 2000). Most rituals associated with eating and drinking, whether it is consuming with some people, but not others, prioritising certain individuals over others when distributing foods, eating meals according to specific courses, using particular vessels and cutlery, toasting, and wishing people a 'good appetite' all have a cultural basis (See e.g. Cole, 2007; Counihan and Van Esterik, 2008; Douglas, 1982; Finkelstein, 1989; Goody, 1982; Visser, 1992; Wilson, 2005, 2006). Observing such conventions reflects socialisation into the values of social groups or classes, and thus identification with that group or class. However, it is important to recognise that just as notions of identity have become more unstable and fluid, so have the groups or communities that people come to identify with or against. It is therefore useful to reconsider the groups and networks with which people associate and thus identity.

Traditional conceptions of communities or groups suggest stable entities, characterised by physical proximity, ongoing interaction, shared values and a strong sense of affiliation among members (Jones, 1998). Such communities may still exist but changes in economic conditions, patterns of work and global movements of people and information have given rise to alternative forms of group and belonging. Rather than being united through 'strong ties' underpinned by shared heritage and territory, people are connected through informal, 'weak ties' to a wider network of geographically dispersed people (Urry, 2007).

Wittel (2001) has suggested that contemporary society has given rise to a 'networked sociality'. Within networked sociality, relationships may be functional, for example, for work purposes, social causes or information exchange; however, people are often brought together by shared emotions or aesthetics, related experiences, imaginations, or desires to form 'neo-tribes' (Maffesoli, 1996). Neo-tribes reflect the blurring of individual and shared identity as people are united by feelings of affiliation and identify with a loose collection of others in defining themselves and their values. Interactions may be temporary and superficial, which are facilitated by technology, communication devices and social media in particular. However, these interactions may extend into the 'real' world and develop into ongoing relationships.

Consumption is often at the heart of such networked sociality and neo-tribalism. Historically, identities were shaped much more by stable social institutions, traditions and heritage, but as those have become increasingly fragmented, people look for alternative markers or points of reference in constructing their identities. The consumption of products, services or experiences, including those related to food and drink, help to shape who we are. Consumption also communicates our values to others (Cova *et al.*, 2007), though not all consumption should be thought of as purposive attempts to communicate with others. This link between consumption and the construction and communication of self rests on the assumption that people's identities change in different social contexts. To better understand this contextual shifting of selves, it is useful to examine how identities come to be articulated, or performed, and the spaces in which such performances take place.

Identity, performance and space

The idea of 'identity as performance' draws on a theatrical metaphor (Goffman, 1990) and suggests that people play 'roles', which are shaped by the 'audience' and expectations of how someone should behave in particular social situations. The physical environment is the 'stage', shaping behaviours; people employ 'props', and interactions can be seen as 'social dramas' that frequently follow patterns as if they were scripted.

This 'dramaturgical' approach to identity developed by Goffman (1990) foregrounds several issues in our thinking about the self. First, it sensitises us to the importance of interaction and to the roles that others play in shaping our behaviours and identities. Second, it helps us to appreciate the importance of the material aspects of our world in shaping identities. For example, it highlights how something as ordinary as an item of food or drink helps to define and communicate who we are to others. Third, the dramaturgical approach also stresses the importance of the body in shaping identities. Our bodies become vehicles for expression of our values and attitudes through our gestures and movements. Body shapes and forms of body modification, whether clothing, hairstyles, facial hair, tattoos or piercings also reflect who we are and who we identify with.

The dramaturgical approach may suggest that any expression of identity is merely an act that masks some true self. However, others have gone further in rejecting the existence of a real authentic self; arguing instead that identity exists only as far as it is continuously performed (Butler, 1993). Rather than a finished product, identity is perpetually reinvented as it is reconstructed (Fuss, 1991; Hall and du Gay, 1996). This highlights the importance of context and the role of space. Spaces are not neutral backdrops or empty containers in which people construct or perform identities. Spaces are loaded with symbolic meaning, and power relationships shape how people perceive, interact in, or relate to, particular spaces. People may be excluded from certain spaces, for example, because of their sex, gender, age, sexuality, ethnicity or their lack of various sorts of capital. Others may be welcomed in certain spaces and feel included precisely because of some aspect of their identity. More importantly, individuals and groups can project their power or authority over spaces through their embodied expressions of identity.

Performances of self, and inclusion and exclusion, are evident in domestic settings as well as the commercial ones (i.e. bars, restaurants and cafes), but also in public spaces such as parks, squares, streets and beaches. Performances of self also extend to the virtual spaces of social media sites, internet forums and chat rooms. During domestic hospitality, there are culturally specific expectations of how good hosts and guests should behave (Telfer, 2000). This includes the various rituals referred to earlier; however, roles and rituals extend to include, for example, the presentation of gifts from the guest to the host as a mark of appreciation. In return the host is expected to perform his or her duties and anticipate the guest's needs, demonstrate hospitableness alongside some level of culinary expertise (see e.g. Mellor, *et al.*, 2010). Failure to perform these roles, and to adhere to the social conventions of a group, therefore suggests either incompetence or a deliberate attempt to challenge the identity norms of a group which is linked to the space they inhabit.

Within commercial spaces, the relationship between identity and belonging has further complex implications. Organisations utilise specific aspects of their commercial propositions, including the physical design, marketing, the products they sell, the services they provide and the experiences they offer, to engage with consumers' sense of identity. Commercial propositions often draw on references to cultural identity from a specific national or ethnic group, for example, in foodservice contexts, Italian (Albrecht, 2011), Chinese (Lu and Fine, 1995) or Thai (Germann Molz, 2004); and in drinking venues, Irish (O'Mahony *et al.*, 2006) and Australian (West, 2006). Operators seek also to appeal to numerous different values consumers identify with, including nationality (Andrews, 2005), ethnicity and religion (Berris and Sutton, 2007), ethical, environmental or health consciousness (Poulston and Yiu, 2011); sexuality (Lugosi, 2009) and cultural activities (Lugosi *et al.*, 2010). This also includes an array of other lifestyle values, for example fashionableness (Cuthill, 2007), community (Erickson, 2009), collective safety (Lugosi, 2009) or gastronomic refinement (Tressider, 2011). It is also important to stress that commercial operators exclude individuals whose values and expressions of identity do not match the commercial propositions on offer. So, for example, dress codes, decorations, printing menus in French in non-French speaking countries, displaying menus using pictures, serving ales rather than lagers, or vice versa, excludes people because these reflect values they do not identify with. Consumers come to define and communicate their social statuses and values through their patronage of venues, and in the venues they avoid (Bell and Valentine, 1997; Berris and Sutton, 2007; Warde and Marteens, 2000).

Consumption in venues also enables consumers to experiment with new roles, where temporary expressions of self can be explored and indulged (Cuthill, 2007; Lugosi, 2008).

The identities of frontline staff are also implicated in the production of commercial hospitality. 'Customer facing' employees are expected to perform service roles, which requires them to adapt their bodies, for example, through uniforms, adopt appropriate behaviours and display particular emotions, i.e. friendliness, patience and care (cf., Erickson, 2009; Gibbs and Ritchie, 2010; Seymour and Sandiford, 2005; Sherman, 2007). A further implication of this is that organisations are selective about which types of people look and sound appropriate, and whose performances of self are aligned with the organisation's desired self image and propositions of hospitality (McDowell, 2009; Nickson and Warhurst, 2007). Staff in hospitality organisations therefore have to engage in 'aesthetic labour' (Nickson and Warhurst, 2007) and 'emotional labour' (Seymour and Sandiford, 2005) alongside the physical labour their jobs entail. It is also useful to highlight that in some organisations, particularly small, owner-operated, entrepreneurial business, operators also try to communicate their identities to consumers with the aim of making the encounter seem more unique and personal (Di Domenico and Lynch, 2007).

Public spaces also become sites where individual and collective identities are formed and displayed. However, who and what identities are expressed are highly contested, and different groups attempt to territorialise spaces, with mixed consequences. For example, parks are occupied during picnics and barbeques, becoming social spaces where groups gather to strengthen ties and express solidarity (Danesi, 2011; Jacobs, 2003). Such gatherings may be seen to be healthy assertions of group identity. Street foods may also be considered as positive and vibrant expressions of culture. The local, entrepreneurial nature of street food contributes to economic wellbeing (Tinker, 1997) and the sights, sounds and smells of street foods may enhance the appeal of a destination for tourists (Hsieh and Chang, 2006). However, drinking on the street is often more contentious. For the people involved, street drinking can reflect expressions of belonging to a group (Hunt *et al.*, 2005) and during festivities, street drinking may be considered an acceptable expression of collective sentiment (Mitchell and Armstrong, 2005). However, authorities often view street drinking as antisocial expressions of individual or group identity, which undermine the values of a broader culture and the 'civilised' values they represent (Jayne *et al.*, 2011).

Finally, it is important to consider the importance of food and drink related performances of identity in virtual spaces. This includes people posting images of food and drink to social networking sites such as Facebook or Twitter, while discussing the experiences associated with their consumption. Text or pictures showing gastronomic triumphs, experimentation or excessive indulgence and the resulting deviant behaviours again serve to communicate identities and connect individuals within networks. Food and drink manufacturers and distributors have responded to this by using data from social media sites to refine their promotional tactics and to turn consumers into advocates for brands. Contemporary examples include the growing presence of 'Like' functions and social media links now included on company websites, which enable visitors to highlight their approval of a brand or organisation and to embed their preferences into their social networking profiles. Other examples include the targeted display of paid-for adverts on social networking platforms. The interaction of consumer identities, marketing and social media is likely to continue to expand in both size and sophistication. Whatever form they take, a continuing feature will be that organisations attempt to create links between the cultural values associated with foods and drinks and the identities of their consumers.

Some users of social media develop their interest in food and drink into sophisticated and sustained constructions of identity. Food blogging becomes a form of 'serious leisure' (Stebbins, 1992), which drives individuals to invest significantly in developing their knowledge and in communicating their experiences (Watson *et al.*, 2008). Moreover, blogs and websites run by such amateur food and drink enthusiasts become focal points for other like-minded individuals. Their ongoing interactions through these virtual spaces reinforce their neo-tribal identities, for example as 'foodies' (Lugosi, *et al.*, 2012; Watson *et al.*, 2008).

The previous sections have considered the fluid nature of identity and its relationship to food and drink in different social domains. The discussion has highlighted that numerous key factors shape who we (think or feel we) are, whom we identify with and how we act. These include sex and gender, age, class, ethnicity, religion, sexuality, culture, socialisation and life experiences. However, it is useful to examine in further detail three areas: gender, class and ethnicity, which are often key to understanding the interaction of food, drink and identity in contemporary cultures.

Food, drink and gender

Sex and gender, are interrelated, but it is useful to differentiate between the two: sex refers to a biological category, principally male and female; gender is culturally defined. There are social conventions that shape our understanding of what is male/female or masculine/feminine. For example, a person can be considered more or less masculine or feminine because of the clothes they wear, the activities they like to do and they way they speak or gesture. People thus assume certain gendered identities often because they conform to certain social norms concerning how men or women are expected to behave. Gender roles and identities are frequently projected on to individuals or groups. In other words people categorise others because they (are seen to) adopt certain gender-related attitudes and behaviours. For example, stereotypically, being caring, emotional or gentle are considered female traits so people displaying those characteristics are considered feminine. This becomes an important factor shaping people's identities.

Gender interacts with the production and consumption of food and drink in multiple ways. Within commercial contexts, jobs and work related performance expectations are often shaped by sex and preconceptions of gender identities. For example, studies have repeatedly shown that certain occupations such as that of chef are considered masculine and are male dominated, while many other service and back-of-house supporting jobs, such as cleaning, are considered feminine and are often done by women (cf., Erickson, 2009;

Fine, 2008; McDowell, 2009; Sherman, 2007). The gendering of jobs creates expectations for how people perform their identities while assuming those occupational roles. This may be evident in the pressure placed upon kitchen staff to adopt masculine roles when working intensively for long hours in demanding physical settings within macho cultures. People may also be expected to assume feminine, caring, often subservient, roles in service settings. Access to and success in these occupational roles is thus dependent upon people's ability and willingness to perform those gendered identities.

Within domestic settings, gendered identities continually shape the production of food and drink, with males and females often taking different roles (Beagan *et al.*, 2008). While some areas of cooking, for example barbeques, may be considered male domains, studies have shown that the provision of food for family members, control over the household food supplies, and domestic competence (e.g. in cooking ability) are assumed to be part of a woman's role in the household (Charles and Kerr, 1988; DeVault, 1991; Valentine, 1999). Gendered identities and associated expectations are thus continually reaffirmed as being the norm. This may be because people are socialised into accepting gender roles. Gender norms may also be reinforced by the male being the principal household income provider, a woman's existing knowledge in the area, or just by a woman finding it easier to continue to carry out those domestic responsibilities rather than trying to share it with others in the household (Beagan *et al.*, 2008). However, it is also important to recognise that, in some cultural contexts at least, men may be taking larger roles in domestic food preparation (Meah and Jackson, 2012). Contemporary changes to household composition, for example, single and various forms of shared occupancy, may encourage further changes in existing gender norms, with males performing more of the roles previously assumed by women.

Food and drink consumption is also highly gendered (Gal and Wilkie, 2010). As an obvious example, meat is often considered masculine; whereas pulses and leafy foods, feminine (O'Doherty Jensen and Holm, 1999; Sobal, 2005). Similar patterns can be detected with drinks. This also extends to eating and drinking behaviours. Dieting and concern for health and body image, for example, may be considered feminine (Gough, 2007); excessive consumption, masculine (O'Doherty Jensen and Holm, 1999). Such gendered assumptions impact upon food and drink choices, and the consumption of specific items thus reproduces gendered identities (Dienhart and Pinsel, 1984; Gal and Wilkie, 2010; O'Doherty Jensen and Holm, 1999; Wilson, 2005). However, it is also important to stress that notions of gender are not absolutely fixed (Rogers, 2008). For example, men are increasingly concerned with health and body image (Grogan, 2008) and women have been seen to be emulating male patterns of alcohol consumption (Berridge *et al.*, 2009).

Gender identities and gender values also influence how food and drink products and services are marketed. Gender-based appeals become evident in numerous ways; but some are more obvious than others. Certain adverts overtly target women, and use female characters, for example, portraying them indulging in chocolate or drinking sparkling wine as part of a fun social occasion. Other forms of gender-based marketing are more subtle. For example, labelling products as 'low-calorie' or 'diet' stresses product characteristics that have traditionally appealed to women. More specifically, the product appeal draws on assumptions about female body conscious-ness. Gender associations are also embedded in product names, packaging design and in their marketing representations (Moss, 2009). Coca-Cola Light, for example, is sold in a red and white can; whereas Coca-Cola's alternative low-calorie drink Coke Zero is sold in a black can and positioned to appeal to males. The gendered nature of the two Coke products is reflected in their advertisement: Coca-Cola Light featuring women; Coke Zero, men. It is also important to appreciate how product placement and sponsorship reinforces products' gender appeal. For example, Coke Zero sponsored largely male activities, including computer gaming, American football and soccer based events and television programs.

Gender also extends to commercial propositions and is reflected in product range, menu descriptions and offers. The coding of gender reflects the themes highlighted earlier: some of it is overt; others are more subtle, involving culturally accepted gender norms. In practice, hot spicy dishes, large portions or heavy, red-meat based calorific dishes can often be considered masculine, and this is reflected in their names and descriptions e.g. 'hearty'. In contrast, dishes based on green leaves, non-meat items like tofu, labelled lighter, or involving colours or fruits in their description have feminine values associated with them (Gal and Wilkie, 2010). Experiments on menu descriptions reflect these associations. For example, Gal and Wilkie (2010) gave dishes masculine and feminine names, for example the 'Rutherford Ribeye' versus 'Filet Paulette' and participants chose dishes that matched gender expectations. Similar patterns were noticed in their experiments with beverages.

Finally, gender values and identities are also relevant when thinking about venue design and the construction of the overall service experience. In the UK, as elsewhere in the world (Douglas, 1987; Pratten and Lovatt, 2007; Wilson, 2005), drinking venues were primarily male domains. Women were and often continue to be excluded because venues' layout, facilities and general commercial propositions reinforced male values. For example, studies show that women resent entering venues if they feel they will be scrutinised by males or subjected to their advances. Moreover, vertical drinking or stools by the bar does not address women's desire to socialise or be comfortable, and the food and drink choices for them are limited (Pratten and Lovatt, 2007; Schmitt and Sapsford, 1995). These studies also suggest that the venue's cleanliness, the dominant presence of men, perceived lack of general safety and sense of care towards them from staff reinforced their exclusion.

The bar and pub market has evolved, partly as demand among males and females has changed, but also as operators have specifically targeted female consumers. Many venues now have glass fronts, contemporary design features and comfortable seating. Beyond offering natural light and the ability to view others outside the venue, using large glass fronts rather than brickwork also means women can see into the venue before entering. The ability to assess the venue and its patrons helps to lessen the pressure caused by entering a space where they could not see inside. These were complemented by the extension of product lines that appealed to women, for example, greater and higher quality food choice and wines (Pratten and Carlier, 2012; Pratten and Lovatt,

2007; Moss *et al.*, 2009). Such operational features can be seen as attempts to broaden the appeal of drinking venues; and redefining the gendered nature of hospitable space can attract more female clientele to eat, drink and socialise in these settings.

Food, drink and class

Social class is another important factor that has significant influence on identities. Social class refers to hierarchically distinguished groups in society. Differences in class are reflected in the types of work that people do, their education, and in the values and attitudes they are likely to adopt. Class values and positions often manifest themselves in behaviours, most obviously in how people speak, but also in the sort of leisure activities they participate in, and of course in the food and drinks they consume (See e.g. Bourdieu, 1986; Hunt, 1991; Seymour, 2004). Class laden values, attitudes and behaviours are constantly reproduced through a variety of social institutions including the family and home life, education, friendship networks and workplace cultures. Individuals are socialised to accept certain norms and particular values, beliefs, and behaviours thus become naturalised. Bourdieu (1986) attempted to explain this processes of ongoing socialisation and adoption through the notion of 'habitus'. The existence of a habitus does not suggest we all blindly accept the class values we encounter through our lives; but Bourdieu (1986) argued that we are more likely to adopt certain values and rules because they are normalised, which is key to shaping our sense of identities and the people we identify with (See Bourdieu, 1986 and Seymour, 2004 for discussion of habitus and how it influences food and drink related behaviours).

Class influences on identities are closely linked to access to capital. There are different forms of capital: for example, eco nomic, cultural and social capital (Bourdieu, 1986). Put simply, economic capital refers to the money you have available to purchase goods, services and experiences. Cultural capital refers to knowledge that you have, including etiquette, taste and other culturally specific experience and expertise. Social capital refers to your rela-tionships and networks and the resources you can access or mobilise through your connections with people and groups. These three types of capital may seem different, but they have something in common: they all provide power and access. Power and access in this context simply means that people with greater capital resources at their disposal can have greater choices over what they do, where they go, who they can interact with and what activities they can get involved in (See Bourdieu, 1986 for a further discussion of capital and its implications). A central theme within writing on culture is distinction. Access to and the ability to mobilise cultural capital enables people of different classes to differentiate themselves from people in other classes. Eating and drinking are just two domains of social activity which reinforce and communicate distinctions in status and identity.

Class, like gender and other factors influencing notions of identity, is not stable (Roberts, 2001); nor are matters of class equally important in all cultures. However, its relevance is often evident when considering the production and consumption of food, in commercial and non-commercial contexts (Goody, 1982). Class values are often coded into commercial propositions, for example, in the dishes available in restaurants, or even how dishes are described on menus. The use of exotic foreign names to describe foods and cooking methods often suggests attempts to appeal to particular class values. It implies that those reading the menus, and consuming the foods, are likely to be appropriately knowledgeable and equipped with the cultural capital to appreciate how particular ingredients or preparation techniques enhance the eating experience. It also implies that those people have a wider gastronomic repertoire. Certain foods and descriptions of foods thus appeal to some people, reinforcing that a venue complements their values and identities. Moreover, it can also exclude consumers who do not appreciate those cultural values.

Some venues serve easily recognisable, unpretentious, sometimes traditional, foods, and use generally understandable descriptions that have broad appeal. Within affordable, casual-dining, family-oriented venues, including branded chain restaurants such as Red Lobster, TGI Friday's or Harvester, accessible descriptions reject certain ('higher') class values and the pretentions associated with them. However, it is also possible to argue that using traditional ingredients and dishes, simple preparation methods and menu descriptions in relatively expensive restaurants directly targets educated, middle-class consumers, who valorise notions of tradition, locality and simplicity (See Blythman, 2012 for discussion on 'what to eat', which reflects the championing of such values).

Beyond the product range and menus, class values are also entangled in the broader commercial proposition. The venue's design, the uniform that staff are expected to wear, the service they are expected to provide, and by extension, the identity performances of frontline staff, often have class dimensions. Historically, in contexts emulating Western and European class culture, the use of tablecloths, a large variety of dishes, cutlery and silverware, suited (male) waiting staff and elaborate rituals of service and dining were characteristic of higher class values (Finkelstein, 1989; Visser, 1992). Again, frontline staff's ability to perform class values, for example, through their use of language, gestures and behaviours, also reinforces the class dimension of the hospitality experience on offer (Sherman, 2007).

Many contemporary venues in Western-centric contexts often use atmospheric spot lighting, natural wood or polished metal surfaces, and forego tablecloths and complicated rituals in favour of a more casual dining experience (Cuthill, 2007). The staff are often dressed in stylish, less formal, but smart uniforms. Such venues thus make reference to alternative (middle) class values and taste. Contrast this with self-service eateries or establishments where service is reduced to a minimum; venues where staff are casually dressed or wear a standard company uniform, for example a branded T-Shirt or top; and venues where furnishing is focused on efficiency, cost effectiveness and the accommodation of a high volume of visitors. Such commercial hospitality propositions also reference class values, even if it is only through the absence of objects that reflect middle or higher class values of cultural refinement. These examples represent crude oversimplifications of class-based commercial propositions. Yet, it is through such subtle signifiers of identity that venues communicate with their clientele.

Class relations also permeate the production and consumption of food and drink in social and domestic contexts. Academics have discussed at considerable length the differences in the eating and drinking habits of people from different classes (Bell and Valentine, 1997; Bourdieu, 1986; Goody, 1982; Hunt, 1991; Seymour, 2004; Visser, 1992; Warde and Martens, 2000) and I do not intend to rehearse their arguments at length here. Suffice to say, this body of work stresses the importance of capital, habitus and social distinction highlighted previously. Socialisation, habitus and access to various forms of capital shape what types of food and drink people consume and how. Moreover, they shape expectations and desires to consume particular types of food and drink. Foods, drinks and the rituals associated with their preparation and consumption are used to reinforce differences between classes. Commercial food and drink producers, marketers and distributors exploit class differences, alongside people's desire to demonstrate distinction. They develop products that appeal to specific class segments; and, as stated previously, consuming those foods and drinks becomes part of the processes through which people construct their own sense of identities.

Once again, class values associated with foods and drinks are not always overt; rather they are implicit in their production, marketing and distribution. For example, some products are widely distributed and marketed through a variety of mass media. The marketing may stress value for money rather than the inherent quality or special feature of the foods or drinks themselves. Contrast this with emphasis on organic, regionally produced, fair-trade, economically sustainable, authentically sourced food and drinks, or on exclusivity, uniqueness and artisan characteristics rather than on price. Stressing such aspects of foods and drinks highlights several aspects of class identity. Firstly, it suggests that consumers are willing and able to pay extra for the higher quality and value of the food – thus stressing that they have access to economic capital. Secondly, it demonstrates that consumers are aware of the significance of different ingredients, places of origin and production methods. In other words, they have the appropriate cultural capital, in the form of education, gastronomic experience and refinement of taste. Thirdly, it suggests that they have a desire to invest in what they consume, whether it is because those foods and drinks are of superior quality, ethically produced or simply because consuming them communicates to others their access to capital.

Food, drink and ethnicity

Another concept which deserves further clarification is ethnicity. Ethnicity refers to groups of people who identify with each other through a common language or dialect alongside shared customs, heritage, religious beliefs, and various other social and political institutions (Cashmore, 1994). Ethnicity is not the same as race, although the terms are often interlinked when thinking about particular social groups. Race is itself a very complicated concept, the meaning of which has changed over centuries. Contemporary social scientists use 'race' to distinguish between people according to specific physical features, for example, skin pigmentation or hair texture (Cashmore, 1994), but it is no longer considered a useful way to categorise people in term of genetic lineage (American Anthropological Association, 1998). Ethnicity is more useful concept when thinking about the social and cultural distinctiveness of groups. Similarly to class, ethnicity and ethnic differences are normalised because they continue to be reproduced by groups and their social institutions, for example, the church or the family. As with class identities, they are not fixed and they evolve over time as people incorporate multiple social and cultural influences into ethnic identities. Moreover, as with the perpetuation of class, new generations do not adopt ethnic influences wholly but may also simultaneously adapt them in constructing hybrid identities.

The interactions of food, drinks and ethnicity echo the themes highlighted previously in this chapter insofar as they continually interact with the production and consumption of food and drink in commercial and non-commercial settings. Ethnicity influences employee experiences in commercial foodservice environments and ethnic identity can have positive and negative consequences. Ethnic entrepreneurs and hospitality operators frequently employ people from their own ethnic groups in their businesses (Ram *et al.*, 2001;

Wahlberg, 2007). The employment of people from particular ethnic groups may add to the authenticity of the overall experience (Muñoz *et al.*, 2006). Furthermore, migrants from certain ethnic groups may actually be employed because of positive stereotypes concerning their perceived work ethic and organisational commitment (Anderson, 2010). However, ethnic minorities may actually be marginalised in hospitality and foodservice organisations – forced to endure poor working conditions and to engage in low-paid, low-status, back-of-house jobs. Marginalisation and exploitation may stem from poor language skills, de-recognition of existing experience and qualifications, undocumented or unauthorised status in a country, but also because of skin colour, where whites and those with lighter complexions are given higher status, customer-facing roles (McDowell, 2009; Watt, 2011; Wright, 2007). It is also important to stress the interaction of ethnicity, gender and class. Women from ethnic minorities, and those with limited access to social and cultural capital often encounter multiple pressures to endure such poor working conditions and rewards (Adib and Guerrier, 2003; McDowell, 2009).

Various aspects of ethnic identity are entangled in commercial propositions through the products offered, the terms used to market dishes and drinks, and in the construction of the servicescape (See e.g. Germann Molz, 2004; Lu and Fine, 1995; O'Mahony *et al.*, 2006). A venue's ethnic links may come from their owners and operators who have migrated from another country or have personal ties to ethnic or national cultures. Running these venues, working in them and patronising them provides opportunities for people with a shared sense of heritage to reconnect with their culture, form social ties, articulate their sense of identities, generate income and enter the labour market (See e.g. Brown and Mussell, 1984; Kim, 2009, Wahlberg, 2007). However, the theming of venues using ethnicity may not involve any actual links with people from that culture and may simply be a commercial invention (See Brown and Patterson, 2000).

Themed venues make reference to specific aspects of ethnic identity and culture and bring them together in the creation of an experiential offering. This involves a certain level of selection by operators – often highlighting stereotypical dimensions of a culture, and using venue decorations, staff and uniforms, food and drinks offerings and music to communicate those values to consumers (Beardsworth and Bryman, 1999; Brown and Patterson, 2000; Robinson, 2011). The commercial mobilisation of ethnic and cultural values raises a number of questions concerning the authenticity of the food, drink and hospitality experiences. More specifically, do ethnically themed venues offer authentic experiences of ethnic foods and cultures? What aspects of ethnic identity are foregrounded or remain hidden from consumers? Are consumers aware of the contrived nature of some themed hospitality venues? Is there a single authentic representation or recreation of any ethnic group or culture? Is authenticity equally important for all consumers? Some consumers may invest considerable effort into trying to find authentic experiences; others may accept that themed venues are inaccurate reflections of national or ethnic identity, although such venues may still offer authentically enjoyable experiences (Lego et al., 2002; Muñoz et al., 2006; Muñoz and Wood, 2009). Moreover, consumers' ability to judge what is or is not authentic is likely to be determined by their previous experiences of particular cultures (see e.g. Ebster and Guist, 2004). The answers to the questions raised above will inevitably vary across different contexts and among different consumers. Nevertheless, authenticity and the authentication of food and drink will continue to be the subject of debate among academics, food and drink producers, commercial operators, consumers and members of ethnic groups for whom particular foods and drinks are tied to their interests and identities (cf. Beer, 2008; Gilmore and Pine, 2007).

The interaction of food, drink and ethnic identity within commercial contexts extends beyond venues, especially when there is a clustering of venues and they are located in neighbourhoods, or even regions, inhabited by sizeable ethnic groups. Restaurants, cafes, bars and retail outlets selling foodstuffs for and by members of particular national and ethnic groups become particularly visible when places start to be ethnically branded, for example, Chinatown, Koreatown or Banglatown (cf. Shaw, 2011; Lee and Park, 2008). Within these zones or regions, food and drink are used as one of many markers to signify and demarcate ethnic communities. This may extend to purposive attempts to market places as tourist destinations based on the foods and drinks of groups residing there (Okumus, *et al.*, 2007), who may use these representations to reinforce a sense of local, regional or ethnic identity (Everett and Aitchison, 2008;).

Attempts to control an ethnic group's ability to sell and consume their foods may also be a way to assert power over places and to exclude certain ethnic groups. For example, in 2009 the Italian city of Lucca banned the opening of new business that sold foods that differed from the city's ethnic tradition, which followed an earlier campaign: 'Yes to polenta, no to couscous: Proud of our traditions' by the Northern League political party (Nowak, 2012). Nowak (2012) questioned the legitimacy of such claims of cultural and culinary heritage, pointing to the changing nature of regional foods and foodways. More importantly, his discussion demonstrates how conflicts over food are manifestations of broader social and political tensions.

Food and drink can thus be used positively or negatively in assertions of identity, but both scenarios reflect the powerful relationship food and drink has with ethnicity. As numerous studies show, the transformation and trans-action of foods and drinks, as well as their avoidance, become ways to reaffirm ethnicities, while asserting boundaries between ethnic groups (cf. Brown and Mussell, 1984; Beriss and Sutton, 2007; Wilson, 2006). Food and drink connects individuals to their places of origin, which reinforces ethnic ties and identities. This may also inhibit adjustment to or acceptance of the 'other' and therefore reinforce social separation. Finally, it is worth noting that political and economic interests are always likely to be entangled in the interaction of food, drink and ethnicity. More specifically, political and religious groups, producers, marketers, intermediaries and retailers may encourage the repro-duction of food and drink related behaviours to generate income, reassert particular ideologies or norms, or demonstrate the distinctiveness of a group.

Conclusion

Whatever the social context, examining food and drink practices reveals a great deal about the identities of those involved. This chapter has discussed how identities are entangled in food and drink related activities in commercial and social contexts. It has suggested that identities are shaped by and mobilised in the production of food and drink. Identity was implicated in food and drink marketing, preparation and service, and in the construction of the environment in which they are consumed. Matters of identity also permeate the consumption of food and drink. People's social statuses and sense of selves shape what, when, where and how they consume. Eating and drinking can also shape people's identities by providing opportunities to discover new cultural experiences, engage with different people and grow as a result. Food and drink related practices thus have a stabilising effect, helping to reproduce cultural norms, values and practices; but they also have a potentially transformative effect.

The chapter also considered a number of different factors that influence food and drink related practices, particularly gender, class and ethnicity. These intersect with countless other factors, including sexuality, age, life-stage, family status and (dis)ability to shape people's experiences and thus their identities. People may choose to consider the interaction of food, drink and identity for a number of reasons: academics may do so to understand the dynamics of cultures, while commercial operators may seek to gain a deeper understanding of their consumers, staff and the experiences they provide. Whatever the motivation, it is important to remain sensitive to how these personal and cultural factors continue to influence people's relationship with food and drink.

Finally, as this chapter has emphasised, it is important stress the fluid, mobile nature of identity and culture. The increasing global circulation of goods, people and information, which is fuelled by technological developments, will inevitably change people's relationship with food and drink. History has demonstrated that this mobility will help create new, hybrid food and drink related social practices that borrow from multiple cultures. These emerge alongside new hybrid identities as people move and encounter new cultures, thus incorporating new cultural influences alongside existing ones. However, history also suggests that there will be counter-movements as people, driven by a sense of loss, displacement or nostalgia, try to recapture traditional cultural values. The production and consumption of food and drink are likely to be central to reasserting stable notions of identity.

References

Adib, A. and Guerrier, Y. (2003) The interlocking of gender with nationality, race, ethnicity and class: The narratives of women in hotel work, *Gender, Work and Organization*, **10** (4), 413-432.

Albrecht, M.M. (2011) 'When you're here, you're family': Culinary tourism and the Olive Garden restaurant, *Tourist Studies*, **11** (2), 99-113.

American Anthropological Association (1998) American Anthropological Association Statement on 'Race' (May 17, 1998), Available from: http://www.aaanet.org/stmts/racepp.htm (Last accessed 09 January 2012).

Anderson, B. (2010) British jobs for British workers?: Understanding demand for migrant workers in a recession, *The Whitehead Journal of Diplomacy and International Relations*, **XI** (1), 103-114.

Andrews, H. (2005) Feeling at home: Embodying Britishness in a Spanish charter tourist resort, *Tourist Studies*, **5** (3), 247-266.

Barth, F. (ed.) (1969) *Ethnic Groups and Boundaries*, Oslo: Norwegian University Press.

Beagan, B., Chapman, G. E., D'Sylva, A. and Raewyn Bassett, B. (2008) "It's just easier for me to do it": Rationalizing the family division of foodwork, *Sociology*, **42** (4), 653–671.

Beardsworth, A. and Bryman, A. (1999) Late modernity and the dynamics of quasification: The case of the themed restaurant, *The Sociological Review*, **47** (2), 228–257.

Beer, S. (2008) Authenticity and food experience – commercial and academic perspectives, *Journal of Foodservice*, **19** (3), 153–163.

Bell, D. and Valentine, G. (1997) *Consuming Geographies*, London: Routledge.

Beriss, D. and Sutton, D. (eds) (2007) *The Restaurants Book*, Oxford: Berg.

Berridge, V., Herring, R. and Thom, B. (2009) Binge drinking: A confused concept and its contemporary history, *Social History of Medicine*, **22** (3), 597-607.

Bhabha, H.K. (1990) Interview with Homi Bhabha: The third space, in J. Rutherford (ed.), *Identity: Community, Culture, Difference*, London: Lawrence and Wishart, pp. 207-221.

Bhabha, H.K. (1996) Culture's in-between, in S. Hall and P. du Gay (eds), *Questions of Cultural Identity*, London: Sage, pp. 53-60.

Blythman, J. (2012) *What to Eat*, London: Fourth Estate.

Bourdieu, P. (1986) *Distinction*, London: Routledge.

Brown, L.K. and Mussell, K. (eds) (1984) *Ethnic and Regional Foodways in the United States*, Knoxville: University of Tennessee Press.

Brown, S. and Patterson, A. (2000) Knick-knack paddy-whack, give a pub a theme, *Journal of Marketing Management*, **16** (6), 647-662.

Burkitt, I. (1999) *Bodies of Thought*, London: Sage.

Butler, J. (1993) *Bodies that Matter*, New York: Routledge.

Cashmore, E. (1994) *Dictionary of Race and Ethnic Relations, 3rd ed.* London: Routledge.

Charles, N. and Kerr, M. (1988) *Women, Food and Families*, Manchester: Manchester University Press.

Cole, S. (2007) Hospitality and tourism in Ngadha: An ethnographic exploration, in C. Lashley, P. Lynch and A. Morrison (eds.), *Hospitality: A Social Lens*, Oxford: Elsevier, pp. 61-72.

Counihan, C. and Van Esterik, P. (eds.) (2008) *Food and Culture, 2nd edn*, Abingdon: Routledge.

Cova, B, Kozinets, R.V. and Shankar, A. (2007) *Consumer Tribes*, Oxford: Butterworth-Heinemann.

Cuthill, V. (2007) Consuming Harrogate: Performing Betty's café and Revolution vodka bar, *Space and Culture*, **10** (1), 64-76.

Danesi, G. (2011) Commensality in French and German young adults: An ethnographic study, *Hospitality and Society*, **1** (2), 153-172.

DeVault, M. (1991) *Feeding the Family*, Chicago: University of Chicago Press.

Di Domenico, M. and Lynch, P. (2007) Commercial home enterprises: Identity, home and setting, in C. Lashley, P. Lynch and A. Morrison (eds.), *Hospitality: A Social Lens*, Oxford: Elsevier, pp. 117-128.

Dienhart, L. and Pinsel, M. E. (1984) *Power Lunching*, Chicago, Ill: Turnbull and Willoughby.

Douglas, M. (ed.) (1987) *Constructive Drinking*, Cambridge: Cambridge University Press.

Ebster, C. and Guist, I. (2004) The role of authenticity in ethnic theme restaurants, *Journal of Foodservice Business Research*, **7** (2), 41-52.

Erickson, K.A. (2009) *The Hungry Cowboy*, Mississippi: University of Mississippi Press.

Everett, S. and Aitchison, C. (2008) The role of food tourism in sustaining regional identity: A case study of Cornwall, South West England, *Journal of Sustainable Tourism*, **16** (2), 150-167.

Fine, G.A. (2008) *Kitchens*, Berkeley: University of California Press.

Finkelstein, J. (1989) *Dining Out*, Oxford: Polity Press.

Fuss, D. (ed.) (1991) *Inside/Out*, London: Routledge.

Gal, D. and Wilkie, J. (2010) Real men don't eat quiche: Regulation of gender-expressive choices by men, *Social Psychological and Personality Science*, **1** (4), 291-301.

Germann Molz, J. (2004) Tasting an imagined Thailand: Authenticity and culinary tourism in Thai restaurants, in L. M. Long (ed.), *Culinary Tourism*, Lexington, KY: UPK, pp. 53-75.

Gibbs, D. and Ritchie, C. (2010) Theatre in restaurants: Constructing the experience, in: M. Morgan, P. Lugosi and J.R.B. Ritchie (eds.), *The Tourism and Leisure Experience*, Bristol: Chanel View, pp. 181-201.

Gilmore, J. H. and Pine, J.B. (2007) *Authenticity*, Boston, MA: Harvard Business School Press.

Goffman, E. (1990) *The Presentation of Self in Everyday Life*, London: Penguin.

Goodman, D., DuPuis, M.E. and Goodman, M.K. (2011) *Alternative Food Networks*, Abingdon: Routledge.

Goody, J. (1982) *Cooking, Cuisine and Class*, Cambridge: Cambridge University Press.

Gough, B. (2007) Real me don't diet: An analysis of contemporary newspaper representations of men, food and health, *Social Science and Medicine*, **64** (2), 326-337.

Grogan, S. (2008) *Body Image*, 2nd edn, Hove: Routledge.

Hall, S. (1996) Introduction: Who needs identity?, in S. Hall and P. du Gay (eds.), *Questions of Cultural Identity*, London: Sage, pp. 1-17.

Hall, S. and du Gay, P. (eds.) (1996) *Questions of Cultural Identity*, London: Sage.

Helou, A. (2011) *Offal*, Bath: Absolute Press.

Hsieh, A. and Chang, J. (2006) Shopping and tourist night markets in Taiwan, *Tourism Management*, **27** (1), 138-145.

Hunt, G. (1991) The middle class revisited: Eating and drinking in an English village, *Western Folklore*, **50** (4), 401–420.

Hunt, G. P., MacKenzie, K. and Joe-Laidler, K. (2005) Alcohol and masculinity: The case of ethnic youth gangs, in T. Wilson (ed.), *Drinking Cultures*, Oxford: Berg, pp. 225-254.

Jacobs, M. (ed.) (2003) *Eating Out in Europe*, New York, NY: Berg.

Jayne, M., Valentine, G. and Holloway, S. L. (2011) *Alcohol, Drinking, Drunkenness*, Aldershot: Ashgate.

Jones, S. G. (1998)'Information, internet, and community: Notes toward an understanding of community in the information age, in S.G. Jones (ed.), *Cybersociety 2.0*, London: Sage, pp.1-35.

Kim, E. C. (2009) 'Mama's family': Fictive kinship and undocumented immigrant restaurant workers, *Ethnography*, **10** (4), 497-513.

Lee, Y. and Park, K. (2008) Negotiating hybridity: Transnational reconstruction of migrant subjectivity in Koreatown, Los Angeles, *Journal of Cultural Geography*, **25** (3), 245-262.

Lego, C., Wood, N., McFee, S. and Solomon, M. (2002) A thirst for the real thing in themed environments: Consuming authenticity in Irish pubs, *Journal of Foodservice Business Research*, **5** (2), 61–74.

Leitch, A. (2003) Slow Food and the politics of pork fat: Italian food and European identity, *Ethnos*, **68** (4), 437-462.

Long, M.A. and Murray, D. L. (2012) Ethical consumption, values convergence/divergence and community development, *Journal of Agricultural and Environmental Ethics* (In-press).

Lu, S. and Fine, G.A. (1995) The presentation of ethnic authenticity: Chinese food as a social accomplishment, *The Sociological Quarterly*, **36** (3), 535-553.

Lugosi, P. (2008) Hospitality spaces, hospitable moments: Consumer encounters and affective experiences in commercial settings, *Journal of Foodservice*, **19** (2), 139-149.

Lugosi, P. (2009) The production of hospitable space: Commercial propositions and consumer co-creation in a bar operation, *Space and Culture*, **12** (4), 396-411.

Lugosi, P., Bell, D. and Lugosi, K. (2010) Hospitality, culture and regeneration: Urban decay, entrepreneurship and the 'ruin' bars of Budapest, *Urban Studies*, **47** (14), 3079-3101.

Lugosi, P., Janta, H. and Watson, P. (2012) Investigative management and consumer research on the Internet, *International Journal of Contemporary Hospitality Management*, **24** (6), 838-854.

Maffesoli, M. (1996) *The Time of the Tribes*, London: Sage.

McDowell, L. (2009) *Working Bodies*, Chichester: Wiley.

McGoldrick, P. J. and Freestone, O. M. (2008) Ethical product premiums: Antecedents and extent of consumer's willingness to pay, *The International Review of Retail, Distribution and Consumer Research*, **18** (2), 185-201.

Meah, A. and Jackson, P. (2012) Crowded kitchens: The 'democratisation' of domesticity?, *Gender Place and Culture*, In–press. Published online 18 July 2012, DOI: 10.1080/0966369X.2012.701202.

Mellor, J., Blake, M. and Crane, L. (2010) "When I'm doing a dinner party I don't go for the Tesco cheeses": Gendered class distinctions, friendship and home entertaining, *Food, Culture and Society*, **13** (1), 115-134.

Mitchell, J.P. and Armstrong, G. (2005) Cheers and booze: Football and *Festa* drinking in Malta, in T. Wilson (ed.), *Drinking Cultures*, Oxford: Berg, pp.179-200.

Moss, G. (2009) *Gender, Design and Marketing*, Farnham: Gower.

Moss, G., Parfitt, S. and Skinner, H. (2009) Men and women: Do they value the same things in mainstream nightclubs and bars?, *Tourism and Hospitality Research*, **9** (1), 61-79.

Muñoz, C.L. and Wood, N.T. (2009) A recipe for success: Understanding regional perceptions of authenticity in themed restaurants, *International Journal of Culture, Tourism and Hospitality Research*, **3** (3), 269-280.

Muñoz, C.L., Wood, N.T. and Solomon, M.R. (2006) Real or blarney? A cross-cultural investigation of the perceived authenticity of Irish pubs, *Journal of Consumer Behaviour*, **5** (3), 222 – 234.

Nickson, D. and Warhurst, C. (2007) Opening Pandora's box: Aesthetic labour and hospitality, in C. Lashley, P. Lynch and A. Morrison (eds.), *Hospitality: A Social Lens*, Oxford: Elsevier, pp. 155-171.

Nowak, Z. (2012) Italian stuffed vs. Maghreb wrapped: Perugia's Torta al Testo against the Kebab, Paper presented at the Oxford Symposium on Food and Cookery, 6-8th July, Oxford.

O'Doherty Jensen, K. and Holm, L. (1999) Preferences, quantities and concerns: Sociocultural perspectives on the gendered consumption of foods, *European Journal of Clinical Nutrition*, **53** (5), 351–359.

Okumus, B., Okumus, F. and McKercher, B. (2007) Incorporating local and international cuisines in the marketing of tourism destinations: The cases of Hong Kong and Turkey, *Tourism Management*, **28** (1), 253–261.

O'Mahony, G.B., Hall, J. and Binney, J. (2006) A situational model of development in hospitality retailing: The case of Irish pubs, *Journal of Services Research*, **5** (2), 77-95.

Poulston, J. and Yiu, A. (2011) Profit or principles: Why do restaurants serve organic food?, *International Journal of Hospitality Management*, **30** (1), 184-191.

Pratten, J. D. and Carlier, J.-B. (2012) Women and wine in the UK: A business opportunity, *Journal of Food Products Marketing*, **18** (2), 126-138.

Pratten, J.D. and Lovatt, C. (2007) Women customers in pubs: Still a business opportunity, *International Journal of Wine Business Research*, **19** (2), 90-97.

Ram, M., Abbas, T., Sanghera, B., Barlow, G. and Jones, T. (2001) 'Apprentice entrepreneurs'? Ethnic minority workers in the independent restaurant sector, *Work, Employment and Society*, **15** (2), 353-372.

Reimann, R., Angleitner, A. and Strelau, J. (1997) Genetic and environmental influences on personality: A study of twins reared together using the self- and peer report NEO-FFI scales, *Journal of Personality*, **65** (3), 449-475.

Roberts, K. (2001) *Class in Modern Britain*, Houndmills: Palgrave.

Robinson, S. (2011) Inventing Australia for Americans: The rise of the Outback Steakhouse restaurant chain in the USA, *Journal of Popular Culture*, **44** (3), 545-562.

Rogers, R.A. (2008) Beasts, burgers, and hummers: Meat and the crisis of masculinity in contemporary television advertisements, *Environmental Communication*, **2** (3), 281-301.

Schmitt, R. and Sapsford, R. (1995)'Issues of gender and servicescape: marketing public houses to women, *International Journal of Retail Distribution and Management*, **23** (3), 34-40.

Selwyn, T. (2000) An anthropology of hospitality, in C. Lashley and A. Morrison (eds.), *In Search of Hospitality*, Oxford: Butterworth-Heinemann, pp. 18-37.

Seymour, D. (2004) The social construction of taste, in D. Sloan (ed.), *Culinary Taste*, Oxford: Elsevier, pp. 1-22.

Seymour, D. and Sandiford, P. (2005) Learning emotion rules in service organizations: Socialization and training in the UK public house sector, *Work, Employment and Society*, **19** (3), 547-564.

Shaw, S. (2011) Marketing ethnoscapes as spectacles of consumption: 'Banglatown – London's Curry Capital', *Journal of Town and City Management*, **1** (4), 381-395.

Sherman, R. (2007) *Class* Acts, Berkeley: University of California Press.

Sobal, J. (2005) Men, meat, marriage: Models of masculinity, *Food and Foodways*, **13** (1), 135–158.

Stebbins, R.A. (1992) *Amateurs, Professionals and Serious Leisure*, Montreal: McGill-Queens's University Press.

Telfer, E. (2000) The philosophy of hospitableness, in C. Lashley and A. Morrison (eds.), *In Search of Hospitality*, Oxford: Butterworth-Heinemann, pp. 38-55.

Tinker, I. (1997) *Street Foods*, New York: Oxford University Press.

Trauger, A. and Passidomo, C. (2012) Towards a post-capitalist-politics of food: Cultivating subjects of community economies, *ACME: An International E-Journal for Critical Geographies*, **11** (2), 282-303.

Tresidder, R. (2011) Reading hospitality: The semiotics of Le Manoir Aux Quat'Saisons, *Hospitality and Society*, **1** (1), 67-84.

Urry, J. (2007) *Mobilities*, Cambridge: Polity Press.

Valentine, G. (1999) Eating in: Home, consumption and identity, *The Sociological Review*, **47** (3), 491–524.

Visser, M. (1992) *The Rituals of Dinner*, London: Viking.

Wahlbeck, Ö. (2007) Work in the kebab economy: A study of the ethnic economy of Turkish immigrants in Finland, *Ethnicities*, **7** (4), 543-563.

Warde, A. and Martens, L. (2000) *Eating Out*, Cambridge: Cambridge University Press.

Watson, P. Morgan, M. and Hemmington, N. (2008), Online communities and the sharing of extraordinary restaurant experiences, *Journal of Foodservice*, **19** (6), 289-302.

Watt, P. (2011), Work-life mobility and stability: The employment histories of immigrant workers at a unionized Toronto hotel, *Hospitality and Society*, **1** (2), 117–136.

West, B. (2006) Consuming national themed environments abroad: Australian working holidaymakers and symbolic national identity in 'Aussie' theme pubs, *Tourist Studies*, **6** (2), 139-155.

Wilson, T.M. (ed.) (2005) *Drinking Cultures, Oxford:* Berg.

Wilson, T.M. (ed.) (2006) *Food, Drink and Identity in Europe,* Amsterdam: Rodopi.

Wittel, A. (2001) Toward a network sociality, *Theory, Culture and Society,* **18** (6), 51-76.

Wright, T. (2007) The problems and experiences of ethnic minority and migrant workers in hotels and restaurants in England, *Just Labour: A Canadian Journal of Work and Society,* **10**, 74-84.

Food and Drink:
The declining importance of cultural context?

George Ritzer and Anya Galli

George Ritzer is a Distinguished Professor at the University of Maryland. In the application of social theory to the social world, his many books include The McDonaldization of Society *and* The Globalization of Nothing.

Anya Galli is a Graduate Fellow at the Program for Society and the Environment at the University of Maryland.

When we pop open a can of Coca Cola or reach into a bag of potato chips, we are most-likely consuming a product available to consumers in many locations across the globe and made of ingredients produced in multiple countries. While food and drink remain an integral part of cultural practices and identities today, very few of the products we purchase at the supermarket or in chain restaurants are actually local. What processes have contributed to the seemingly limitless availability of out-of-season produce, the global spread of name-brand food and drink, and the prominence of low cost 'convenience' foods and fast food restaurants in cities across the globe?

There is no question that national and 'local' social structures and cultures continue to be important throughout the world. Similarly, today's global citizens continue to have agency through which they make an array of choices and, more importantly, construct their social and cultural worlds. In other words, the dialectics between culture and agency (Archer, 1988), and structure and agency (Giddens, 1984) continue to be of great importance. This is true globally, as well as nationally and locally.

While we acknowledge all of that, much of the senior author's (Ritzer, 2013; 2007) work is focused on the idea that these dialectics have been greatly affected by a variety of global forces which have been either set in motion, or greatly amplified, since the end of WW II. In this essay we will focus on how these changes affect food and drink. Among other things, we will argue that those changes have tended to both expand and reduce social and cultural differences in food and drink throughout much of the world. This perspective is in line with Giddens's argument that larger structural and cultural changes are both enabling and constraining. On the one hand, many people around the world now have access to a wider variety of food and drink than they ever had before (Belasco, 2008). For example, products and brands once limited to local markets are available globally, allowing consumers in the global North to eat tomatoes and peaches, grown in warmer climates, year-round. On the other hand, many of the changes associated with globalization detailed in this essay have served to limit, at least in some ways, individual choice in food and drink consumption. The increasing dominance of multi-national corporations in the production and marketing of food and drink products threatens smaller-scale, locally-based products, production and consumption practices in developing countries, changing not only what is available, but how it is consumed (Wilk, 2006). The availability of what we consider today to be the most essential food commodities – coffee and sugar, for example – is directly tied to the political and economic forces associated with global capitalism (Mintz, 1986). More generally, these forces tend to greatly alter, if not undermine, the social, cultural and agential dialectics that existed in the realm of food and drink prior to their ascendancy.

What are these forces? First, there is globalization (Ritzer, 2010; 2012), which we define here as 'a transplanetary process or set of processes involving increasing liquidity and the growing multidirectional flows of people, objects, places and information as well as the structures they encounter and create that are barriers to, or expedite, those flows' (Ritzer, 2010: 2). It is possible to trace globalization back thousands of years, or at least several centuries, and there are many different views on the beginnings of globalization. We will adopt the view here that what we now think of as globalization can be traced to the end of the end of World War II. Many other changes after the war – for example, the fall of the Soviet Union and the Communist bloc – contributed to globalization and its expansion, but we will take the end of WW II as a watershed in the history of globalization.

The emergence of a second important force – Americanization – can be thought of as the spread of a particular type of globalization involving largely one-way flows from the US rather than the multi-directional flows that define globalization in general (Kuisel, 1993; Crothers, 2010). Like globalization, Americanization can be seen as pre-dating WW II (for example, US entry into WW I in 1917), although the former significantly pre-dates America's rise as a global superpower. America's dominant role in WW II spurred the process of Americanization as other major world powers were either decimated by the war and/or mired in communist regimes which greatly hindered economic development (see Vogel [2011] on Mao's responsibility for destroying the Chinese economy in the 1950s and 1960s and Deng's role, beginning in the late 1970s, in its current efflorescence). America's increasing power coincided with increasing globalization. The US and its corporations took advantage of structural and cultural changes to further enrich their wealth and influence. While globalization is inherently multi-directional, the hegemony of the US meant that in the second half of the 20th century more information, products, and services flowed out of its borders than in. As a result of this imbalance, monetary flows poured into the US making it by far the richest country in the world. Today, this economic predominance is on the wane. Massive amounts of money now flow out of the US, especially to China, which is on the rise as a competitor and becoming the probable successor to the US (Naughton, 2006).

Nevertheless, the imprint of Americanization, especially in terms of culture, continues to manifest itself and remain strong in many parts of the world (Antonio & Bonnano, 2000).

A third force is the rise of consumer society (Baudrillard, 1970/1998; Galbraith, 1958). Pre-existing infrastructure allowed the US to rapidly expand its production facilities after WW II, and production dominated the American economy, fueled by demand from other parts of the world which needed to rebuild their factories. As wealth flowed into the country, the focus began to shift in the US, especially in the wake of wartime deprivations, in the direction of consumption. Accelerating consumption in ensuing decades, what Baudrillard (1970/1998) later heralded as the arrival of 'consumer society', meant that the US quickly became the world leader in consumption even as its industrial base was showing the first signs of the decline (the emergence of the 'rust belt'). The US compensated for increasing industrial decline at the transition of the 20th and 21st centuries by both expanding consumer society within its borders and by exporting much of it (shopping malls [Ritzer, 2010], credit cards [Ritzer, 1995], iPhones and iPads) to the rest of the world. Thus, American consumer culture, exported by the US and in many cases eagerly embraced outside its borders, is central to the global impact of Americanization in general.

At a more abstract level, the fourth force is the expansion and global proliferation of the process of rationalization, through which economies and their components strive for greater efficiency and productivity (Weber, 1921/1968). The rise of rationalized production is another domain in which the US took the lead following WW II. Early on, US advances were in realm of production: for example, Ford's automobile assembly line, Taylor's scientific management of labor, Sloan's divisional system at General Motors, automation, robotization, and so on. However, as production began to decline in the late 1940s and 1950s, companies began to shift their focus to the rationalization, or 'McDonaldization' (Ritzer, 1993; 2013), of consumption. The significance of the McDonald's model was the fact that it adopted rational principles – efficiency, calculability, predictability and control – from the factory and brought them into the consumption-focused setting of the fast-food restaurant. From there, the application of these principles expanded into many other consumption sites, as well as virtually every other sector of society including the church (Drane, 2001/2008) and education (Hayes and Wynyard, 2002). Like Americanization, rationalization and McDonaldization are global processes. Both McDonald's and, more importantly, its principles, have been widely exported: McDonald's alone has locations in around 120 countries throughout the world, and McDonaldized processes are increasingly popular within and beyond the global food industry.

Finally, and at least in some eyes most importantly, is the expansion of capitalism, especially with the demise of what once seemed to be a viable alternative – communism. As Marx detailed early on, capitalism must continuously expand or die (1884/1991): once it has begun to exhaust opportunities to grow within a given country, it turns outward and seeks to expand globally (Harvey, 2001). In the post WW II era, the US was the leading capitalist society in the world. At first, giant American production companies, so powerful that Servan-Schreiber (1968) worried that they were overwhelming European competitors, sought to spread their market-dominance throughout the globe. But American industry was already beginning to decline and the American capitalist system was beginning to shift its focus to the domain of consumption: after first concentrating on expansion in the US, American companies (very successfully) shifted their sights to the global market.

What does all of this mean for food and drink at a global level? While there certainly remains great variation in food and drink around the world, perhaps even greater variation with the addition of globalized products to local consumption traditions, the aforementioned processes also contribute to varying levels of global homogenization in these domains. When it comes to food and drink, there is no single, nor simple, relationship between the global and the local: this is a realm in which national identity may be constructed in relation to increasing global influence and where global and local interact not as polar opposites, but as interrelated forces (Wilk, 2006). However, it seems likely that those homogenizing, global elements will continue to expand in the future further reducing in significance, but certainly not eliminating, local food and drink.

Let us look at each of the forces mentioned above and what they mean for global food and drink. Central to the operating definition of globalization is the increasing fluidity, or increasing mobility, of almost everything, including food and drink, and the increasing degree to which they flow throughout the world in all directions (Ritzer 2010: 2). In this context, the global food industry can be described in terms of the decreasing association of specific origins with specific foods, increasing interaction and dispersion of food cultures, and the decline of barriers that exist to certain flows of food products, foodways, and modes of production. This definition of globalization allows us to consider how the availability and popularity of commodities like sugar (Mintz, 1986) and bananas (Koeppel, 2008) are linked to the expansion and spread of global superpowers; once considered in terms of national dominance on the global market, food and drink are increasingly controlled by powerful multinational corporations. Among the most notable examples today are Chilean fruits and vegetables, New Zealand lamb, Australian beef, coffee from many parts of the world, and many of the industrialized, brand-name foods and drinks, often American in origin, to be discussed below.

However, the definition of globalization also highlights the importance of barriers to global flows, which are especially important to consider in the case of food and drink. Perhaps the most important barrier to the global homogenization of food and drink is the continuation of the importance of local (and individual) tastes and traditions. Such tastes go to the heart of many cultures and are therefore highly likely to be adhered to and protected from flows of global food and drink. Dietary restrictions associated with religious or cultural traditions include not only what people consume (such as limitations on the consumption of pork or alcohol), but how some food and drink are produced (guidelines for the slaughter of animals and the separation of certain foods from others). Further, the mere availability of new, global products does not necessarily imply that food habits will shift to include them to a significant effect. While consumers may try these products as a treat or novelty, their everyday consumption practices may be harder for grobal products to infiltrate. Traditions such as meals (number of times per day, size of meals, when certain foods are to be consumed, etc.), the feeding of children (what babies and children are to eat early in their lives), and the historical availability of certain staple foods (rice, potatoes, etc.) also pose barriers to multinational marketing of food and drink.

Nevertheless, the increasing availability of non-local foods that accompanies global flows of consumer culture means that in some cases, local tastes are becoming more global. Consumers are developing tastes for specific 'American' products sold by multi-national companies that have established brand recognition in the global market. For example, when Taco Bell opened a location in Mexico, customers were disappointed to find that the menu had been altered to be more similar to local cuisine, demanding the more processed, 'American' versions (Pilcher, 2008).

In some cases, global food products, such as palm oil (an ingredient in many processed foods that comes largely from Indonesia) and honey produced in China, are less expensive than locally produced products. Lower costs associated with free trade agreements and government subsidies, bulk production, lower wages for workers, and market loopholes make some globally-sourced ingredients cheaper for producers and consumers alike (Barndt, 2008). Further, the costs of transporting food and drink, especially by air, have been declining and are likely to decline still further with the advent of new massive airplanes (e.g. the Airbus 380) and containerized cargo ships, as well as the emerging 'aerotropoli' and their associated shipping centers (e.g. for FedEx and UPS) (Kasarda and Lindsay, 2011). However, the additional distribution costs of fresh and non-subsidized foods mean that such products are only available to those who can afford them – it is unlikely that they will be affordable for the global lower classes, let alone the global poor, especially the 'bottom billion' (Collier, 2007). When it comes to tastes today, the upper reaches of the global class system have their pick of the very best (and most expensive) of global food and drink and they are also be able to dip into the best of the local products. The middle classes will also follow this pattern, although they may consume many globally-sourced foods due to the lower cost at the supermarket. However, the lower classes and especially the global poor will be largely, if not entirely, excluded from this world of consumption, although many of them will produce that which they themselves will be unable to afford.

The selectivity of the globalization of food and drink is analyzable through the lenses of a series of concepts developed in *The Globalization of Nothing* (Ritzer, 2007). 'Grobalization' in this context involves the imposition by powerful nations and their corporations of their food and drink, and even their manner of consuming them, on other, less powerful parts of the world. Among the major examples are the global export of American colas (Coca colonization [Foster, 2008]), breakfast cereals, and fast food (McDonaldization). 'Glocalization' involves the integration of global exports with local practices producing phenomena that combine the global and the local (Robertson, 2001). The term 'glocal' is meant to imply that in the global age it is difficult to find much, if anything, that is not influenced in some way by the global (as well as the local). Culinary traditions that were once uniquely local now incorporate global products, and products and brands that were once considered to be foreign, like American fast food, has been adapted to fit local customs. For example, the McDonald's menu in the Phillipines has been glocalized in that it includes 'McSpaghetti', an item that mimics local cuisine (Watson, 2006). However, it is important to underscore the fact that while the food may at least in some cases be glocalized, the overall systems by which fast food restaurants operate have been grobalized: as we see in the case of McDonald's in Israel, the local falafel industry remains a successful competitor, in part because it has taken on many of the characteristics of McDonald's (uniformity, industrial standardization, efficiency, etc.) (Ram, 2010).

Then there are the concepts of *nothing* and *something*. In the case of the concerns of this paper, *nothing* is food and drink that is centrally conceived, centrally controlled and lacking in distinctive content. Coca Cola, Kellogg's Corn Flakes and Big Macs are paradigmatic examples of nothing as the term is used here: their branding, ingredients, and consumption practices are largely the same regardless of the location in which they are consumed, and they carry little, if any, local cultural significance to consumers. In contrast, food and drink that is *something* is that which is indigenously conceived, controlled and rich and distinctive content. Any food or drink that is truly local in character – produced and consumed in accordance with local traditions – would be categorized as something.

The intersections and interactions of these four concepts (grobal, glocal, something, nothing), really two continua, yield four categories of great relevance to this analysis.

- The first is the *grobalization of nothing* or the export of food and drink that meet the definition of nothing and their imposition on local cultures throughout the world. The significant effect of grobalization of nothing on food and drink is the declining impact of indigenous cultural context: grobal products are part of a global culture and are minimally affected by the nature of local culture (Tomlinson, 2012). Overall, the grobalization of nothing poses significant threats to regional cuisines and local products (Miele & Murdoch, 2007).

- The *grobalization of something* as far as food and drink are concerned involves the exportation of products that meet the definition of something. These are largely local products that have acquired a receptive global audience. Exports such as Parmigianio cheese or Champagne fall into this category and are increasingly found in higher-end shops and liquor stores, especially throughout the global North. These products, which tend to be costly because of high production and shipping costs and relatively low demand, are a much smaller global presence and have an infinitesimal market in comparison to the grobal forms of nothing.

- The *glocalization of nothing* involves glocal food and drink that meet the definition of nothing even though they are produced locally. Examples would be food and drink that, while they are (g)local in character, have been affected by grobal processes and products in terms of how they made, sold, marketed and so forth. Mecca Cola, an alternative to Coca Cola, would be one example, as would mass-produced Jamaican jerk chicken sold in Jamaican restaurants that look much like American fast-food restaurants.

- Finally, the *glocalization of something* would be food and drink that, in spite of being influenced by grobal processes, continue to be more a reflection of g(local) realities. Examples would be most food and drink that we usually think of as local (for example, British fish and chips, French baguettes), although here they are categorized as glocal because of the increasing impossibility of totally escaping grobal influences even if they only involve attempts to resist them. The Slow Food movement, founded in Italy and formally established in 1985 when a McDonald's opened in Rome, upholds 'glocal somethings' (foods with rich and distinctive content linked to local culture), and seeks to protect them in the face of increasing grobal homogenization of food and drink (Sassatelli & Davolio 2010).

All of these combinations of grobal/glocal and something/nothing co-exist and interpenetrate conceptually (see Ritzer, 2007: 120) as well as in the world today. For example, while the Slow Food movement stands for 'somethingness' and defends the glocal in the face of eradication by grobal 'nothingness', it has become increasingly grobal itself as it attempts to push 'slow' products on the global market (Ritzer, 2007: 214). Food and drink virtually everywhere in the world reflect the global influence of these processes and their interpenetration. However, the impact of globalization is differentially distributed and there are places where one or more of these possibilities are absent. For example, all four possibilities are likely to be found in the wealthy areas of the global North, while the grobalization of both nothing and something is likely to be virtually absent in the poor areas of the global South. On the one hand, these areas are so poor that they are usually deemed not worth the efforts of the purveyors of the grobalization of nothing (the other 75 or so countries in the world that do not have a McDonald's) even though these are generally considered low-priced items in the global North. Of course, to the poor in the global South they are likely to be prohibitively expensive. In many ways the poor in the global South are 'doomed to something' in terms of food and drink; with grobal forms of nothing largely absent and prohibitively expensive, the 'bottom billion' must eat and drink that which is indigenously conceived, controlled and rich in distinctive content, even as the availability of these foods is severely limited by climate changes, political unrest, or other factors. While we might think that is desirable in many ways, many of those doomed to something would readily surrender such food and drink in return for more grobal forms of nothing. At the same time, the food and drink that can be considered grobal forms of something – generally 'gourmet' products sold in high end stores – are far beyond the budgets of all but the elites in the global South.

The US is the world leader in the creation of various forms of nothing, and it also leads the world in the creation, exportation and imposition of food and drink that meet the definition of nothing. It is no accident that Coca Cola, Kellogg's and McDonald's, as well as the other dominant leaders of the food industry, are American firms. However, there are a number of less visible players such as those involved in giant agribusinesses such as the 30,000 people who work at Archer Daniels Midland. They are devoted to many different aspects of turning agricultural products into products for the home, especially food and drink. The 21,000 employees at Monsanto focus, among other things, on seeds. Conversely, the United States is *not* a leader in the grobalization of food and drink that meet the definition of something. While there are certainly high-quality American wines and cheeses, to take two examples, the US still lags far behind countries like France and Italy in these markets. The US certainly has its share of glocal somethings in food and drink (New Orleans cuisine, various beers from micro-breweries throughout the country), but they are of little consequence on the global market.

The same is true of America's glocal nothings, for example, the food and drink at most local diners and 'greasy spoons', which consist of generic, industrially-produced ingredients in a distinctly 'American' setting, but lack distinctive cultural content. How do we account for US domination of the grobalization of food and drink that meet the definition of nothing? A major factor is the early success of Fordist mass production. The success of Fordism had a wide range of effects, including the industrialization of the production of food (including industrial farming). Huge corporations came to dominate food production through the application of mass production and assembly-line techniques, the implementation of which was made less costly by subsidies and trade agreements. Producing massive quantities of inexpensive food and drink, these corporations became dominant in the American market and quickly turned their attention to the global market, aided by the creation and eventual global dissemination of supermarkets and superstores (e.g. Wal-Mart and Costco in the US and Carrefour in France), as well as fast food restaurant chains. The spread of these consumption sites expanded the market for American products, at the same time as serving as spaces of grobalized consumption aimed to 'Americanize' global shopping habits and popularize the taste for industrialized food and drink. In fact, in Beijing, China, the notion of 'fast food' (including eating manners, environment, social interaction patterns, and the packaging and production of foods) refers specifically to Western chains and its Chinese imitations (Yan, 2008). Rationalization and its associated processes are well-attuned to the production and sale of nothing; conversely they are ill-suited to producing and selling something.

A third force, consumer society, can be thought of as consisting of four basic elements, all of which encourage the consumption of goods that meet the definition: objects of consumption, sites of consumption, the consumption process, and consumers themselves (Ritzer, Goodman and Weidenhoft, 2001).

■ First, food and drink exist as *objects* of consumption in all societies whether or not consumer society is a dominant force. However, when consumption defines a society, food and drink become commodities, sold widely and consumed beyond what is necessary for survival. Basic necessities are turned into brands that are made to seem more desirable than non-branded food and drink (Holt, 2004; Arvidsson, 2006). Among other things, this means that a higher price can be charged for them than for their generic competitors. The most successfully branded of these products become objects of conspicuous consumption (Veblen, 1899/1994). For example, designer waters Perrier (France) and San Pellegrino (Italy), both owned by Nestlé corporation, are popular in expensive American restaurants. As objects of consumption, food and drink may serve as symbols of class and status, further elevating prices (and potential profits). Organic and 'natural' food products, especially popular amongst wealthier consumers for whom 'eating healthy' is a symbol of status, are part of a wider trend initiated by environmentally-concerned consumers and now part of a hugely successful marketing campaign driven by the same corporations responsible for most of conventional, processed food production in the US (Pollan, 2006).

■ The rise of consumer society is also marked by the proliferation of *sites* of consumption. Shops offering food and drink have existed for thousands of years, but in recent decades the sites involved in the consumption of food have undergone a number of revolutionary developments including the rise of the supermarket and the fast food restaurant. Today, many of the dominant players in the supermarket (Wal-Mart, Koninklijke Ahold, Sainsbury) and fast food restaurant sectors (Yum! brands, which includes KFC and Pizza Hut; Starbucks) have become powerful multi-national corporations. Originating in the United States – and hence major examples of Americanization – these sites have also been grobalized, becoming major consumption sites in many other parts of, especially, the developed world. The *sites* of fast food restaurants themselves are an example of the grobalization of nothing as is much of the food and drink on offer in them: walking into a Starbucks restaurant in Texas, consumers see similar décor and purchase similar drinks to those purchased in Hong Kong. Marketing familiarity and predictability, grobal consumption sites have no need to adapt to local tastes and habits, although local businesses may adapt to fit the grobal model. Consumers in Beijing were found to enjoy dining at Kentucky Fried Chicken (KFC) not for the food itself, but for the consumption process – the setting, food presentation, and atmosphere of the fast food restaurant: local businesses attempting to compete with KFC failed to a large degree despite the fact that they offered similar, if not identical menus, because they could not compete with the novel setting and environment provided by Western fast food chains (Yan, 2008).

■ Third, the consumption *process* itself has changed dramatically as objects and sites of consumption have been grobalized. Shopping at 'big box' stores for bulk brand name products differs dramatically from more personalized shopping at a neighborhood grocery store, liquor story, or butcher shop. Eating and drinking at a fast food restaurant, especially if it is done in one's car after leaving the drive-through window, is radically different from a sit-down meal at a traditional restaurant, diner, or pub. These differences, motivated by low prices in the supermarket aisles and convenience foods have their roots in the United States economic system and its emphasis on speed and efficiency. As a result of grobalization, as well as Americanization, similar consumption processes are now practiced in many other parts of the world. Thus, it is not just American objects of consumption and consumption sites that have been disseminated around the world, but perhaps more profoundly, they have brought with them a process of obtaining and consuming food and drink.

■ In many ways, a new, global type of *consumer* has been brought into being by the changes associated with the rise of consumer society. Today, consumers in the US and across the globe are consuming very different types of food and drink, are doing so in radically different consumption sites, and consuming them in very different ways. There is increasing global similarity not only in the behavior of consumers, but also in their thought processes and even their identities. While no one has consciously grobalized or Americanized the global consumer, the export of grobalized objects, settings and consumption processes originally conceived in the US has, in effect, grobalized the consumers themselves.

The process of rationalization is central to the rapid rise of consumer society and the grobalization of food and drink. More specifically, in terms of the four elements of consumption, we have experienced the rationalization of the objects of consumption (the foods and drinks themselves), the consumption process (drive-through windows; self-checkout lines), the sites of consumption (fast food restaurants and supermarkets, in particular), and the consumer (the 'McConsumer' of food and drink). While McDonaldization often coexists with local tastes and consumption habits, it is also of potential danger to local traditions. Because literally everyone is a consumer of food and drink, their cultural significance is often more susceptible to McDonaldization (and commoditization) than other aspects of the local.

Of particular interest here are the objects; the foods and drinks themselves. First, they are increasingly *efficient* to consume: Chicken McNuggets, prepared meals at the supermarket, microwaveable meals, five-hour energy drinks, juice boxes, bottled water, and so on. Second, food and drink are increasingly *predictable* in the sense that they look and taste the same from one time and place to another time and place. This is particularly true of branded food and drink and fast food sold globally, such as Coca Cola and Starbucks coffees. *Calculability* is most notable in this case because of the 'race to the bottom', whereby suppliers offer large quantities of products at low prices. Supermarkets are well-stocked with large packages and bottles that offer lower prices in comparison to smaller packages and bottles. Warehouse stores like Costco take this to an extreme by offering even larger sizes as well as multi-packs of various products, all intended to attract customers while still guaranteeing a profit for the supplier. Of course, the corporations that produce McDonaldized food and drink exercise great *control* over them so that they are pretty much the same wherever and whenever they are sold. The most important aspect of the McDonaldization thesis in general, and as it applies to food and drink, is the *irrationality of rationality*. Fundamentally, emphasis on the efficiency and predictability of food products and the focus on controlling quantitative factors (price and profit margins) over quality and nutrition fails to take into account local tastes and differences in consumer habits. Tied closely to the grobalization of nothing, the McDonaldization of food produces and sells products that are centrally conceived and controlled and lacking in distinctive content, even if they are marketed within different cultural contexts.

Of course, we cannot discuss McDonaldization and consumer society without discussing capitalism, as the vast majority of food and drink are produced and consumed within global markets dominated by capitalism. While globally influential food and drink could be, and have been, produced in other types of economies (the socialist economies of the Soviet Union and China are examples, although they had notable failures in this regard), today, in part due to free trade agreements, capitalism has no significant competitors when it comes to food production. Under capitalism, food and drink have become commodities, wherever possible low-priced commodities, that can be sold in great volume in much the same form in many different places. While high-priced food and drink are also often commoditized, and there are great profits to be made from them, the relatively small elite market for them means that the large multi-national corporations focus on the low-priced commodities because the potential clientele, and profits, are virtually limitless.

As Marx recognized from the beginning, capitalism is inherently expansionistic. Once it begins to experience limits in the national market it will seek to globalize, more accurately in the terms used here, it will seek to grobalize, spreading processes of production and consumption as well as the products themselves far and wide. There are, of course, many examples of this in the realm of food and drink. Beyond the obvious American examples, other successful grobalized food and drink include Barilla pasta from Italy, Beck's beer from Germany, Foster's beer from Australia, Fiji bottled water, and so on. Thus, capitalism, especially with the dominance of multi-national corporations, is a force that incessantly pursues and pushes the grobalization of food and drink that fit the definition of nothing, regardless of their cultural origins. As we might expect, there is simply far less profit to be earned from the elite consumers of the world able to afford products that can still be classified as something. The glocal market for food and drink, whether it is something or nothing, is simply too small to interest most multinationals (although they would certainly be of interest to smaller, more capitalistic businesses). Thus, most indigenous street food and drink, as well as local delicacies for the elites, does not attract much interest from the leaders in global capitalism, unless they can be transformed into commodities that can be grobalized.

Consumer capitalism, at least through the last half of the 20th century, has been closely associated with United States; in terms of our interests here, corporations based, at least initially, in the US have been the dominant players in the global food and drink industry. Prior to the end of WW II, most of the focus in capitalism was on production, but in the last half the twentieth century multi-national corporations came to learn increasingly that there was great profit to be made by a focus on consumption in general and of food and drink in particular. US-branded objects of consumption have a long history, including the iconic Campbell's Soup (1869), Heinz Tomato Ketchup (1876), and Oreo Cookies (1912). Of course, other countries have their famous brands, as well. The modern self-service supermarket was created in the United States and dates back to 1916 as does the modern fast food restaurant. Many of the other great innovations, at least in sites of consumption, began in the post WW II era with the McDonald's franchise system beginning in 1955; the first shopping mall food court in 1974; Costco in 1983, and so on. In terms of consumption processes, the first drive-through window was created in 1948 by In-N-Out-Burger and self-checkout began in supermarkets in 1992. It is reasonable to assume that all of the above have profoundly altered the consumption, and the consumer, of food and drink in a variety of significant ways.

This essay has focused on forces that have led to the global homogenization of food and drink – especially multinational brands and fast food restaurants. However, it is important to note that the vast majority of food consumed in the world has seen minimal influence from the changes described above, or has not been affected at all. After all, most food – especially food outside the global North – is derived from local ingredients, and prepared and consumed locally. Much of the global South has little, if any, access to many of the branded food and drink products or outlets that are commonplace in the developed North. In some ways, access to the benefits associated with globalization – conferred mainly on those living in the global North – means access to more products that fit the definition of grobal nothing. While many in the global South are 'doomed' to the consumption of food and drink that fits the definition of something, the poor of the global North are increasingly 'doomed' to the consumption of cheap, processed foods. That is, those that fit the definition of nothing (both in terms of our arguments and in terms of nutrition) and are available as part of fast food dollar menus and in corner convenience stores in neighborhoods where there are no grocery stores.

If the majority of food in the world is still produced and consumed locally, then why devote so much attention to globalization, Americanization, consumer society, rationalization (and McDonaldization) and capitalism? First, there are significant barriers to these global forces within the realm of food and drink. Of greatest importance are the local traditions that continue to play a role in, and serve as a barrier to, the consumption of food and drink defined by these global forces. The perishability of much food and drink is another barrier, as is the fact that many products are only produced in limited regions of the world. Because of their ties to the local, when food and drink *are* significantly influenced by global processes it indicates the power of these forces, and the processes we have described have dramatically affected how food and drink are produced, distributed and consumed. In addition, these processes continue to extend their reach and affect the food and drink in those parts of the world as yet largely unaffected by globalization. Food and drink will never be as globalized, as close to the nothing end of the continuum, as Americanized, as commoditized, and as dominated by capitalism as many other products. However, it is safe to say that food and drink will be increasingly affected by these processes. (G)local food and drink will survive, even prosper, but it will coexist in more locales in the world with the homogenized products that result from these processes. Multinational corporations will continue to extend their reach in other ways, as well. For example, they will reach deeper into societies in which they already exist, seeking new populations for their wares. They will certainly continue to focus on young people, especially children, to ensure that future generations consume their food and drink. And as Foucault (1979) would put it, they will continue to seek to dig ever more deeply into peoples' 'souls', making them lifelong (hyper-) consumers and, more specifically, consumers of brand-name forms of nothing.

References

Antonio, R.J. & Bonanno, A. (2000) A New Global Capitalism? From "Americanism and Fordism" to "Americanization-Globalization." *American Studies*, **41**(2), p.33-77.

Archer, M.S. (1988) *Culture and Agency: The Place of Culture*, Cambridge: Cambridge University Press.

Arvidsson, A. (2006) *Brands: Meaning and Value in Media Culture*, New York: Routledge.

Barndt, D. (2008) Whose "Choice"? "Flexible" Women Workers in the Tomato Food Chain' in C. Counihan & P. Van-Esterik, eds. *Food and Culture: a Reader*. New York: Routledge.

Baudrillard, J. (1970/1998) *The Consumer Society*. London: Sage.

Belasco, W. (2008). *Food : the Key Concepts*. New York: Berg.

Collier, P. (2007) *The Bottom Billion: Why the Poorest Countries are Failing and What Can Be Done About It*, New York: Oxford University Press.

Crothers, L. (2010) *Globalization and American Popular Culture*, Lanham, MD: Rowman & Littlefield.

Drane, J. (2001) *The McDonaldization of the Church: Consumer Culture and the Church's Future*, Macon, Georgia: Smyth & Helwys.

Foucault, M. (1979) *Discipline & Punish: The Birth of the Prison*, New York: Vintage.

Galbraith, J.K. (1958) *The Affluent Society*, New York: Houghton Mifflin.

Giddens, A. (1984) *The Constitution of Society: Outline of the Theory of Structuration*, Berkeley, CA: University of California Press.

Harvey, D.(2001) *Spaces of Capital: Towards a Critical Geography*, New York: Routledge.

Hayes, D. & Wynyard, R. (eds.) (2002) *The McDonaldization of Higher Education*, Charlotte, NC: Information Age Publishing.

Holt, D.B. (2004) *How Brands Become Icons: The Principles of Cultural Branding*, Cambridge, MA: Harvard Business School Publishing Corporation.

Kasarda, J.D. & Lindsay, G. (2011) *Aerotropolis: The Way We'll Live Next*, New York: Farrar, Straus and Giroux.

Koeppel, D. (2008) *Banana: The Fate of the Fruit that Changed the World*, New York: Plume.

Kuisel, R. (1993) *The Seduction of the French: The Dilemma of American* Berkeley, CA: University of California Press.

Marx, K. [1884] (1981) *Capital, Volume Two*, New York: Vintage Books.

Miele, M. & Murdoch, J. (2006) Slow Food. In G. Ritzer (ed.), *McDonaldization : the Reader*. Thousand Oaks, CA: Pine Forge Press, pp. 270-274.

Mintz, S. (1986) *Sweetness and Power: The Place of Sugar in Modern History*, New York: Penguin Books.

Naughton, B.J. (2006) *The Chinese Economy: Transitions and Growth*, Cambridge, MA: The MIT Press.

Pilcher, J.M.(2008) Taco Bell, Maseca, and Slow Food : a postmodern apocalypse for Mexico's peasant cuisine? in Carole Counihan & P. Van Esterik (eds.), *Food and Culture : a Reader*. New York: Routledge, pp. 400-410.

Pollan, M. (2006) *The Omnivore's Delimmma: a Natural History of Four Meals*, 1st Edition, New York: Penguin Group.

Ritzer, G. (1993) *The McDonaldization of Society*, Thousand Oaks, CA: Pine Forge Press.

Ritzer, G. (1995) *Expressing America: a Critique of the Global Credit Card Society*, Thousand Oaks, CA: Pine Forge Press.

Ritzer, G. (2007) *The Globalization of Nothing 2*, Thousand Oaks, CA: SAGE Publications Inc.

Ritzer, G. (2010) *Globalization : a basic text*, West Sussex: Wiley-Blackwell.

Ritzer, G. (2010) *Enchanting a Disenchanted World: Continuity and Change in the Catherdrals of Consumption 3*. Thousand Oaks, CA: Pine Forge Press.

Ritzer, G. (2013) *The McDonaldization of Society: Twentieth Anniversary Edition*, Thousand Oaks, CA: Pine Forge Press.

Ritzer, G., Goodman, D. & Wiedenhoft, W. (2001) Theories of consumption, in G. Ritzer & B. Smart, (eds). *The Handbook of Social Theory*, Thousand Oaks, CA: SAGE Publications Inc, pp. 410-427.

Robertson, Roland. (2001) Globalization Theory 200 Plus: Major Problematics. In George Ritzer and Barry Smart, eds., *Handbook of Social Theory*. London: Sage.

Sassatelli, R. & Davolio, F. (2010) Consumption, Pleasure and Politics: Slow Food and the politico-aesthetic problematization of food. *Journal of Consumer Culture*, **10**(2), p.202-232.

Servan-Schreiber, J.J. (1968) *The American Challenge*, New York: Atheneum.

Veblen, T. [1899] (1994) *The Theory of the Leisure Class*, New York: Penguin Books.

Vogel, E.F. (2011) *Deng Xiaoping and the Transformation of China*, Cambridge, MA: Harvard University Press.

Watson, J.L. (ed.) (2006) *Golden Arches East: McDonald's in East Asia*, Stanford, CA: Stanford University Press.

Weber, M. [1921] (1968) *Economy and Society*, Totowa, NJ: Bedminster.

Wilk, R. (2006) *Home Cooking in the Global Villiage: Caribbean Food from Buccaneers to Ecotourists*, New York: Berg.

Yan, Y. (2008) Of Hamburger and Social Space: Consuming McDonald's in Beijing, in C. Counihan & P. Van-Esterik, eds., *Food and Culture: a Reader*. New York: Routledge, pp. 500-522.

Food Ethics

Rebecca Hawkins

Dr Rebecca Hawkins is a Director of the Responsible Hospitality Partnership, Senior Lecturer at Oxford Brookes University, and a Visiting Professor to the International Centre for Responsible Tourism at Leeds Metropolitan University. She has focused throughout her career on the development of strategies and policies for sustainable tourism, and has contributed to the responsible business agenda in this sector for the last 20 years.

'One cannot think well, love well, sleep well, if one has not dined well.'

Virginia Woolf, *A Room of One's Own*

Food is often described as one of life's simple pleasures. But scratch the surface and it becomes clear that food is far from simple and that the production, preparation, processing and service of food is far from pleasurable for many thousands of people globally. It is because of the intrinsic relationship between people and food that consideration of food ethics is so critical. Ethical dilemmas are evident in almost every aspect of the food production and processing cycle.

The food industry is characterised by its scale. According to Euromonitor, it is the world's largest industry (although figures on the economic contribution of the industry vary according to what is included within the classification of 'food'), (Euromonitor, 2013). It established the first globally integrated markets, it permeates every civilisation and it makes a sizeable contribution towards emissions of carbon dioxide (the key gas implicated in climate change) (FCRN, 2010). Some food brands are universally recognised. Few, in even the most remote societies, will be unfamiliar with the bright red logo of the Coca Cola company or the yellow and red banner of the McDonalds hamburger chain. Others are defined by their localism and use their local credentials as a badge of pride and distinctiveness.

We produce more food at lower prices than at any point in history. It is a perverse fact, therefore, that millions of people live in hunger. In fact perversity permeates throughout any study of food and ethics. Science and technology, for example, have rendered once unproductive land fertile and yet thousands of acres become barren each year from poor agricultural practices. Global distribution systems have combined with refrigeration to facilitate widespread access to fresh produce in all corners of the earth, yet one third of the food that is produced perishes before it gets to market. Developments in genetics have produced super-resistant crops, but consumers are afraid to eat them. Millions go hungry and the health of thousands is threatened by obesity caused by excess. We value freshness, but consume more processed foods than ever before. International trade in food thrives and yet governments covet food security. Genetic biodiversity is considered fundamental to food security and yet monocultures dominate.

These issues are complex and all have ethical dimensions. Food prices, for example, are kept low by regional and international trade agreements, government subsidies, mass production, low wage costs and the dominance of a small number of global companies who are able to utilise supply chains for competitive advantage. The fruits of scientific endeavour are often available only to those who can (or are willing to) pay, even when the roots of that endeavour may originate from developing countries which receive no financial reward. Efficient distribution systems are accessible only to those who can produce at sufficient scale to service the global food supply chain, leaving smaller or poorer farmers with limited access to global and regional markets.

This chapter will introduce key debates on food issues and their implications for those working in and using the services of food businesses.

Defining ethics

Aristotle is generally credited with being to first to write about ethics (probably drawing on earlier verbal work by Socrates and Plato) in his three treatises: *Nicomachean Ethics*, *Eudemian Ethics* and *Magna Moralia*.

Broadly speaking, Aristotle's definition of ethics: 'the study of how individuals should best live', remains unchanged in modern times. This definition and those that have followed, make it clear that the term ethics does not relate to a universally agreed set of behaviours or rules. Instead, it refers to a broad concept about what constitutes good behaviour. The concept of ethics is well rehearsed in most cultures and frequently expressed through axioms, such as, 'doing the right thing'. Ethics thus relates to a way of behaving and this relates to the values of individuals and societies (i.e. what we consider to be right or wrong, good or bad).

Because the concept relates to values, perceptions of what is ethical can differ considerably between individuals and cultures. To quote a few obvious examples:

- In some societies it is considered unethical to have more than one wife. In others polygamy is the expected norm.

- In some societies, it is considered unethical to perform invasive medical procedures even if the result is to save a life. In others, it is considered unethical to fail to save that life regardless of the medical cost.

- In some societies, it is considered unethical to charge interest for the lending of money. In others, money lending and the charging of interest is the expected norm.

In recent years, the concept of ethics as something that is associated with the individual or community has been extended into other spheres. We have seen the use of the term ethics extended to describe a different way of doing business (for example 'ethical business'), a type of consumer ('ethical consumerism'), new types of finance ('ethical investment') and even ways of governing ('ethical government').

We can add to this list the term 'ethical food'. This is generally considered to be food that has been produced by systems that have minimal negative impact on the environment, is produced in a way that respects human welfare and is sold at a price that reflects its true value. Subsets of the ethical food offer are often considered to be food that is of local origin, produced organically, produced using systems that have a high standard of animal welfare, or produced using Fair Trade systems. As a general rule, ethical food is a very small percentage of the total food market by value and is accessible only to the more wealthy elite in societies. From China to the UK and the USA to Russia, there has been an increase in the interest of these wealthy elites in securing access to more ethical food.

Ethical food is not the focus of this chapter. Instead, it discusses the broader issues around ethics as they apply to the mainstream food industry. Because ethics is related to the values of individuals or societies, notions of what is or is not ethical are likely to differ significantly, depending on the perspectives of the readers. For example: their cultural and religious beliefs, and attitudes towards issues such as environmental protection, animal welfare, treatment of communities and technology. This fact makes the study of ethics as they apply to food (as opposed to ethical food) both fascinating and complex. It also means that there are no definitively right or wrong answers, only different perspectives. A few common themes about what constitutes unethical food do emerge across many different cultures.

Why ethics matter in the modern world

The misdemeanours of a few global companies (primarily, but not exclusively in the financial sector), means that ethics has never been more in vogue. No doubt stimulated by the financial crisis, a number of leading thinkers have begun to ask fundamental questions, not only about how the economy is organised, but also about the type of society we want to live in. There is an emerging view, expressed by popular columnist Arianna Huffington, that 'Ethics should precede economics... We know this because we've seen the results of capitalism without conscience: the pollution of the air we breathe, the water we drink, and the food we eat; the endangerment of workers; and the sale of dangerous products - from cars to toys to drugs. All in pursuit of greater and greater profits.' (Huffington Post). Other texts, such as Diane Coyle's *The Economics of Enough*, Naomi Klein's *No Logo* and the New Economic Foundation's *Valuing what matters* echo this sentiment.

This interest in ethics in business may be fashionable, but it is not new, nor is it unique to Western societies. During medieval times, the Roman Catholic church defined legitimate business behaviour in Canon law, including reference to what today would be called ethical issues. The Qur'an makes various references to the principles of ethical business, including 'O you who believe! eat not up your property among yourselves in vanities: but let there be amongst you traffic and trade by mutual good-will ...' [Qur'an, 4:29].

Academics too, have been discussing the concept of ethics in a business context for generations. In more recent times, Archie Carroll's seminal paper 'The Pyramid of Social Responsibility', states that 'economic and legal responsibilities embody ethical norms about fairness and justice, ethical responsibilities embrace those activities and practices that are expected or prohibited by societal members even though they are not codified into law. Ethical responsibilities embody those standards, norms or expectations that reflect a concern for what consumers, employees, shareholders, and the community regard as fair, just or in-keeping with the respect and protection of stakeholders moral rights.' (Carroll, 1991).

Increasingly, ethical practices in business at least are presented as desirable not just (or even necessarily) because they 'do the right thing', but importantly because they are key to building trust. And trust in businesses is a commodity that has been in short supply in recent years (see Figure 1). There are few businesses that would thrive without the trust of political leaders, consumers, employees, shareholders and so on. It is this that gives any discussion of ethics a new potency in modern society. It also underlies the flurry of statements that have been developed by some of the world's largest companies with titles such as *Our Ethics, Our Values* (or something similar).

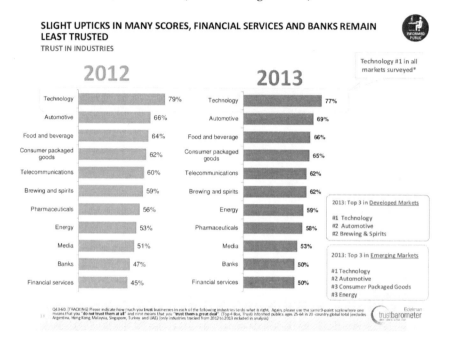

Figure 1: Trust – a commodity that i s sought by all businesses
Source: Edelman Trust Barometer, www.edelman.com/trust-downloads/global-results-2/

The fact that ethics helps to build trust is supported by a wealth of psychological literature that points to people's innate sense of morality (even if they choose not to act on it). See, for example, the works of Jonathan Haidt (2006). He has identified five universal moral themes that apply across cultures (i) avoidance of doing harm, (ii) due respect for authority, (iii) striving for cleanliness or purity, (iv) loyalty to group or community, and (v) a sense of fairness (Haidt, 2006). These universal moral themes should, in theory at least, predicate most people to a preference for ethical choices. One could argue that, in food retail at least, this fact is supported by surveys of public opinion in which respondents claim to make decisions that are based on 'doing the right thing' – see for example (Mintel, 2006). The evidence that they act on their instinct when it comes to actual purchasing behaviour is somewhat less convincing.

Ethical aspects of food

Almost all aspects of food production, processing and service have an ethical dimension, with a large number of overlaps and contradictions (see Figure 2).

Figure 2

The ethical dialogue related to some of these issues is relatively new (for example, chemical pesticides and obesity). But for most, this dialogue has been replayed in multiple guises over the last two centuries or more. Take the issues around employment conditions and particularly those associated with human rights in the food industry. These were played out in another form in the 1830s when the anti slavery movement finally achieved its aim of abolishing slavery. Slaves were a crucial link in the agricultural supply chain. Their labour ensured European markets' access to cheap sugar. The modern human rights movement seeks to ensure that the thousands of farmers who operate on a small scale (who work at or below subsistence levels to provide crops for an international food system that they cannot afford to access) and the workers who are employed in primary food processing factories that offer little in the way of human rights protection (sometimes excluding the right to exercise free will to leave that employment) are protected. In so doing, human rights campaigners bring into question the issue of cheap food in developed countries – pointing out that often it is cheap because those who produce it are poorly paid and badly treated.

A renewed sense of urgency

Consideration of the ethical issues around the modern food industry may not be new. But the urgency to review them has increased. This is because:

- Consumer awareness of the manifestations of unethical food production systems (whether based on health or environmental grounds) has increased significantly, especially among wealthier consumers. This is partly a result of 24 hour newsrooms and social media networks that give campaigners real time unrestrained access to a global audience. Most major food businesses have suffered from some form of consumer backlash in the last two decades (no matter how short lived) based on perceived unethical dimensions of their food production methods.

- Pressure to address inequalities in a food system that is based on ability to pay rather than need. These inequalities may have the highest profile when they are between nations (typically developed and developing), but are also evident within nations. In 2005, for example, Cook and Frank found that 'in the USA, 35 million people (12.1%) lived in food-insecure households, 24.3 million in households without hunger, and 10.8 million with hunger. Subpopulations with the highest prevalence of household food insecurity are blacks (22.4% of households), Latinos (17.9% of households), households with children younger than 6 years (16.7%), and single-mother households (30.8%). (Cook and Frank, 2008)

- The nutritional needs of a growing population. In the last decade, the global population has exceeded seven billion and the balance of rural versus urban dwellers has tipped. More people now live in cities than the countryside and this has significant implications for land ownership and food production. Many commentators consider that there is capacity to feed seven billion people, but whether this can be done within the framework of current production methods, distribution systems and market mechanisms is unclear. The bigger challenge still is feeding the global population of nine billion people that is anticipated by 2050.

- The health burden of a population indulged by diets rich in fat and sugar. Otherwise known as the 'obesity time-bomb', this phenomenon is expected to reverse the sustained increase in life expectancies in some developed countries. It is also forecast to push public health systems to the brink.

- The scale of modern agriculture and fishing. Modern farming and fishing has more in common with large scale manufacturing than the bucolic idyll many western consumers associate with food. As a result,

  □ oceans have been plundered, sometimes using inherently wasteful systems. In Europe, for example, as much as70% of some fish types are thrown back into the sea dead, a consequence of a fisheries policy intended to protect livelihoods and prevent pollution

  □ forests have been flattened. See for example, the encroachment of palm oil plantations in Indonesia, coffee and soya plantations in Latin America

  □ previously fertile lands have been rendered barren. In Australia, for example, farmland is on the decline, with more than 60m hectares - an area the size of Germany and the UK combined - falling out of production over the past two decades. What has been witnessed in Australia is replayed in areas of the USA, Canada and Spain.

- The scale of impacts associated with large scale agricultural production is such that some people are asking whether we are destroying the capacity of future generations to feed themselves.

- The globalisation of the modern food industry. There are just a handful of global corporate food processers and retailers (circa 147) that take crops from millions of farmers and provide food products to billions of consumers (see Table 1). In fact, as noted later in this chapter, the international food system is often described as an hour glass where these global corporate businesses (some still in private ownership) have more control over food production, processing and distribution than any single government.

- The increased vertical integration of food production. This has given multinational companies an unprecedented level of control over the food supply chain. Whether this is a good or bad thing is open to question. The international food system in its current format has probably done a better job of distributing affordable food than any totalitarian government (with the probable exception of Cuba). The multinational companies that drive that system are, however, seen as the cause of many ills – including the addiction to the wrong types of food that lie at the base of the obesity epidemic and the destruction of biodiversity. The potential danger in a vertically integrated food system is the level of power this delivers to a tiny number of companies. The choices made by these companies lie outside of governmental control (they can simply choose to relocate from one regime to another) and the economic power of these monolithic companies (many have balance sheets that exceed the GDP of those governments that seek to regulate them) can have unprecedented impacts on the food choices available to the global population. Ironically, however, when it comes to ethics, the policies of these giants have perhaps the greatest potential to deliver change in global food availability.

Table 1: Where does money go in the UK food system?

Gross value	
UK food processing, manufacture and retailing sector (2002)	£37 billion
UK faming sector (2002)	£6,68 billion
Net Profits	
Top six UK supermarkets (2002)	£2,781 million
All UK farms cobined (2002)	£2,235 million
Profits as % return on capital (2002)	
Tesco	11.0%
UK farmers	0.54%
Incomes	
Terry Leahy (CEO of Tesco) pre-tax salary (2002)	
(Equivalent to the combined income of 243 UK farm households)	£2.46 million
UK average net farm income (pre-tax) (2002)	£10,100

Source: Corporate Watch, 2013 (www.corporatewatch.org)

The ethical issues that permeate the international food industry are many and multi-faceted. They range from over-arching ethical principles: such as securing the fundamental right to a life free from hunger as enshrined in the Universal Declaration of Human Rights, to very specific dilemmas such as the implications of farming with genetically modified plants. Within the popular media, the ethical debate is often presented as clear cut using pre-defined conceptions of deserving and undeserving, good and bad, safe and unsafe.

Take, for example, the highly corrosive debate about genetically modified organisms (GMOs). In the European press, discourse has been couched in the terminology of Frankencrops. Emotive commentary stimulates an immediate reaction from a concerned public. The ethical argument, in reality, has multiple dimensions. There are those who believe that GMOs may be one of a range of technologies that are essential in the arsenal to address global hunger. This is a debate that is rarely included in the press. The debate about whether GMOs can or cannot play a role in reducing world hunger is instead played out in a framework in which the companies that develop and promote these technologies are inevitably the 'villains', and the community groups and campaigners who so vocally object to them, the 'saviours'. GMOs may yet prove to be unsafe (and the author is no defender of them). But they may equally prove to be the solution to global hunger. If the latter, then are concerns of consumers, shaped by ill-informed debate, perpetuating hunger for the masses?

Those involved in and who use the food industry (consumers in particular) make ethical choices every day. In fact, it is often posited that consumer choices can fundamentally change the industry and 'force' it to engage in more ethical behaviours. This would perhaps be true were it easy to understand the ethical issues and if the debate were not so emotive. The complexity of the food supply chain and lack of information from which to assess what is ethical (or even to view the consequences of the unethical) is such that there is little real evidence that consumer choices have significantly resolved many of the underlying ethical dilemmas in the food industry.

Even the major food retailers often cannot trace the precise origins or ethical credentials of many of their products (see for example the recent horse meat scandal in Europe). What has emerged as a proxy to help consumers make ethical choices is a range of logos and standards (such as the Green

Frog of the Rain Forest Alliance, Red Tractor of the Global Gap scheme, and the logo of the Sustainable Restaurant Association). Multiple market research studies demonstrate that few consumers really understand what these logos mean and that they have very limited ability to steer consumers towards choices that are genuinely ethical. It is also an inconvenient truth that most of the organisations that have developed these labels rely on the mainstream food industry's patronage for their survival. This unhealthy dependence has resulted in a watering down of criteria to the extent that few labels are in any way effective at delivering the change that is needed.

Five modern dilemmas

There are five modern dilemmas that indicate the breadth of the debate around food, the ethical judgements that are often implicit and the need to develop solutions that tackle the root causes of problems, rather than that simply target the symptoms. The issues are:

1 Hunger

Probably the most emotive of the five issues is mass hunger. Despite improvements in technology and increases in the amount of food available, the number of people who are undernourished has increased significantly over the last two decades. According to the WTO, 925 million people are 'hungry' or undernourished. That is the equivalent of 1 in 7 of the global population. As demonstrated in Figure 3, the majority, but not all, of these people live outside of so called developed countries.

The increase in hunger is not a direct result of a decline in agricultural productivity. In fact, world agriculture produces 17% more calories per person today than it did 30 years ago. And that is despite a 70% population increase (FAO 2002, p.9).

Moreover, hunger is not necessarily most prevalent in areas where there are poor farming practices, lack of access to productive land, or even poor yields. For example, a 2005 health survey found that chronic malnutrition in Ethiopia was highest in the most agriculturally productive regions (SUN Movement, 2012). The inference of the study is that large-scale production leads directly to export, or simply to a lack of local food diversity. It is a problem that Samuel Hauenstein Swan, Senior Policy Adviser, Action Against Hunger, recognises. 'Malawi promoted corn – it didn't dramatically improve the food security of the people, but it dramatically improved the exports. They are one of the big maize exporters now. But did that reduce the numbers of stunting? Not really ... ministers of agriculture are still focussed on these very few grains [while] nutritious crops like sweet potatoes are not easily commercial.' (www. guardian.co.uk/global-development-professionals-network/2012/dec/03/ food-aid-improving-nutrition). Apparently, therefore, hunger is not necessarily the result of a lack of food productivity, but of a lack of access to the right mix of food, at the right price.

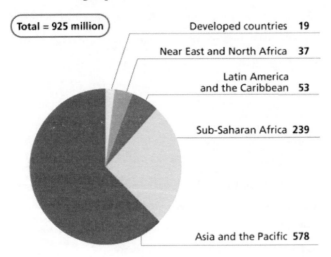

Figure 3: The number of hungry people in the world

Source: World Hunger Education Service (2012), *2012 World Hunger and Poverty Facts and Statistics*

2 Obesity

Perhaps the second most emotive issue in the food debate, especially when viewed against the issue of hunger, is the number of people who are chronically overweight. It is on this issue that ethical judgements are perhaps most obviously made. Images of malnourished children, transmitted from famine-struck regions of Africa, are all too familiar. The emotive appeal of these images (and very real tragedy for those affected) is adequately emphasized by the size of the public response to appeals such as that launched by Bob Geldof in 1984, known as Band Aid.

Contrast this with images of obesity. Characterised by western citizens (often Americans), usually consuming products from branded fast food outlets. They encourage the viewer to make an ethical judgement: malnourishment is a characteristic of the worthy poor who bear no responsibility for their own fate. Obesity on the other hand is a characteristic of the rich world. The images portray a message that those who are obese are greedy, lazy and, through their own negligence, likely to cause a public health crisis.

The reality may be different. It is true that extreme obesity and malnutrition are both tragic. But there is evidence in some countries at least (and especially those with particularly liberal policies towards urban planning and business), both conditions may have their roots in poverty.

According to the World Health Organisation (WHO), 1.6 billion adults worldwide are overweight and at least 400 million adults are obese. By 2015, it is expected that the number of overweight adults will reach 2.3 billion with more than 700 million being obese (WHO, 2009). Obesity is so prevalent in some countries that it is considered the major public health issue. It is a major risk factor for chronic conditions such as cardiovascular disease, diabetes, musculoskeletal disorders and some cancers.

Obesity is mainly a condition of developed countries, but that does not mean that it is a condition of the rich. Data from the USA would seem to demonstrate that obesity is prevalent in poorer communities (National Health and Nutrition Examination Study, 2011). One study revealed that more than one-third of adults who earn less than $15,000 annually were obese, as compared to 25 percent of those who earn more than $50,000 a year (Izzo, 2011). More specifically still, some authors claim that obesity is at its highest in urban communities that have lost their markets and small community based stores, where there is limited public space and typically where there are high proportions of minority populations. Typically, in these communities the density of fast food outlets per head of population is high and access to cheap fresh food is limited (some, for example, Patel 2010, claim that cheap fresh food has been eliminated by the practices of the supermarkets and fast food chains competing for market dominance). These impacts have been exacerbated in recent years by the increase in basic food prices, the practices of major food companies to include cheap fillers (most notably palm oil, sugar and cereal binders), a reduction in access to non-built up space in which to exercise or grow food and the cheapness of fast food. In effect, obesity within some of these communities may not relate to greed, but to poverty, a lack of easy access to the right type of food, combined with heavy promotion of the wrong type of food and poor educational achievement about the characteristics of good nutrition (Patel, 2010, p. 269). In some countries, therefore, obesity may have some roots in common with hunger, most specifically a lack of access to the right types of food at an affordable price.

3 Technology

The advertisements for any supermarket or food service business often contain images of fresh natural products, produced by healthy people living fulfilling lives. In most cases, however, the imagery belies the truth. It is millennia since our food was produced without exploitation, centuries since it was 'as nature intended' and decades since it has been produced without extensive use of chemicals. These facts notwithstanding, developed and increasingly developing countries have benefitted from the technology that underpins our international food system. For the most part, this system has delivered a high volume of safe and cheap food. For many countries access to this food has been pivotal to the urbanisation and development process. It has, however, not been achieved without cost.

Nothing epitomises this cost as aptly as the plight of the humble honey bee. According to Andrew Sims: 'About one in every three mouthfuls of food you eat relies more or less on honeybee pollination. Since 2006, in the USA, beekeepers have been reporting losses of between 30% and 90% of their hives.

The British Beekeepers Association has warned that honeybees could disappear from Britain by 2018.' (Sims, 2008) Speculation about the cause of the decline in bee populations has focussed on everything from chemical pesticides (and particularly the use of a group of pesticides known as neonicotinoids) to climate change, a lack of access to appropriate food and electromagnetic radiation. For some groups, the bee has become a potent symbol of all that is wrong in modern farming and particularly calls into question the use of advanced chemical technology by industrial scale farmers. In particular, it has brought into focus the potentially disastrous consequences of modern chemical processes.

Technology underpins the modern agricultural system and at least in part is the reason that, for many, food is plentiful and cheap. Technology, however, is expensive to develop and to access and is typically developed, owned and controlled by large international companies in developed countries. Table 2 lists the concentration of technology development in agricultural markets.

Table 2: Concentration in the food and agricultural industry

- Ten corporations control 80% of the global agrochemical market, ten companies control 31% of the seed market and four agribusinesses (Syngenta, Du Pont, Monsanto and Bayer) control almost 100% of the transgenic (GM) seed market.

- Three companies (Cargill, Archer Daniels Midland (ADM) and Zen Noh) control 65% of US soybean exports and 81% of corn exports, four companies (Cargill, ADM, Cenex (now in a joint venture with Cargill) and General Mills) control 60% of US grain handling facilities and four companies (Cargill, ADM, Bunge and Ag Processing Inc) control 80% of US soybean crushing facilities.

- In the US, four beef processors slaughter 81% of the cattle and four companies control 50% of broiler chicken production. The biggest beef processors in the US are also the dominant processors in Canada and Australia.

- Six processors (Arla/Express, Dairy Crest, Robert Wiseman, Glanbia, Associated Co-operative Creameries and Nestle) control 93% of UK dairy processing.

- Four supermarkets (Tesco, Asda/Wal-mart, Sainsbury and Somerfield) control 75% of UK food retailing.

Source: http://www.corporatewatch.org

As a rule, the more sophisticated the technology, the greater the initial invest-ment. Inevitably, the victims of this process are smaller farmers who cannot afford to access the technology or who do not farm on a scale to make it viable. It is claimed that some companies have exacerbated this problem, for example, when taking GMOs into developing countries (where their use is already widespread). Raj Patel presents detailed analysis on this topic in his book *Stuffed and Starved* (2010). Mass migration from farms stimulated by a range of factors has resulted in concentration of land into the hands of few very large landowners. What is true of agrochemical technology is true of food processing technology. As illustrated in Figure 5, the vast majority of processing for many core products now lies with a small number of multina-tional companies.

The ethical debate around technology is complex. But the ethical issues revolve around two core tenets: who can gain access to new technology (and at what cost) and the health and environmental costs of implementing that technology. When these issues are viewed in the context of a food production system that is dominated by a small number of companies, they gain added significance.

4 Waste

The greatest perversity in the modern food system relates to levels of food waste. There is disconnect in a world in which 925 million people go hungry and yet one-third to one-half of all food produced (1 – 2.2. billion tonnes) goes to waste annually (Institute of Mechanical Engineers, 2013). Wastage for some crops can be extensive. According to IMechE, for example, losses of rice in South East Asian countries 'can range from 37% to 80% of total production depending on development stage, which amounts to total wastage in the region of about 180 million tonnes annually. In China, a country experiencing rapid development, the rice loss figure is about 45%, whereas in less-devel-oped Vietnam, rice losses between the field and the table can amount to 80% of production' (Institute of Mechanical Engineers, 2013, p. 4).

Food waste arises because: (i) farmers are not able to tend their crops and livestock sufficiently to secure a successful harvest, (ii) farmers are unable to get crops to market post-harvest either because of a lack of infrastructure, preservation technologies or resources, (iii) crops once at market cannot be sold because of an excess of specific types of products or very low prices, (iv) crops are damaged during the food processing/logistics cycle, (v) food is not sold within secondary markets (vi) food is disposed of by consumers. There are some familiar causes underpinning the origins of food waste, not least among them, the domination of a small number of very large companies which exclude small farmers from the global food supply chain (because of their size) and encourage consumers to consume more than they need (if in doubt, think about the real purpose of the popular 'buy-one-get-one-free' promotions).

5 Environmental impacts

Our final modern dilemma relates to the environmental impacts of farming and how these are accounted for. The impacts of farming are such that organisations like WWF believe that the food production and processing sector will shortly be viewed by the NGO community with the suspicion currently reserved for the oil extraction sector. While there is little doubt that the impacts of agriculture can be positive (for example, enhancing habitats), the net ecological balance of impacts at the current time is negative.

In total, it is thought that food production and processing accounts for around one quarter (23%) of the global ecological footprint of humankind (Kleanthouse, 2010). Its impacts include habitat loss, genetic erosion, soil erosion and degradation, water consumption, water course pollution, biodiversity decline and carbon emissions (WWF, 2013). Biodiversity is thought to have diminished significantly. Of more than 50,000 edible plant species in the world, just 15 crops species provide 90% of food energy intake with three – rice, maize and wheat – making up two thirds of this total (UNFAO *in* Hawkins R and Bohdanowicz P, 2011). Within current economic frameworks, the 'farming sector' produces these impacts without financial penalty or need (and in some instances, means) to remedy the damage. In effect, the services of nature are considered to be provided free of charge and when one area of land becomes unproductive, the global food machine simply moves onto the next. This propensity to treat nature as a free resource is fundamental to cheap food, but is also at the root of the devastation that is effected by modern food production.

Common roots

While these ethical issues are very different, they have complex origins. We can identify some common roots, including:

1 The price of food

The price of food, and the way value is added throughout the food processing chain, is perhaps one of the most complex and significant ethical aspects of the modern food industry. It embraces issues about willingness to pay, ability to pay, transparency about the components of food and also about how money flows through the international food system. For all of us, it is the price of food that dictates access to food of an appropriate nutritional quality and at the time that it is needed. To facilitate healthy choices, we need to be provided with food choices that are not only cheap but also wholesome and healthy. For the environment, the price of food should dictate the extent to which negative impacts can (or at least could) be addressed or even avoided and biodiversity protected. For farmers, the price they receive for food needs to allow the move from subsistence to a cash economy or to access technology that will make the farm sustainable (financially, environmentally, and socially) in the long term.

For many thousands of small farmers, the mechanisms for pricing food have changed little since the Sumerians first traded food in the second century BC. For them, the price of food is the value they can acquire from the local market. This value may be financial, but could equally be an exchange of products. Food producers at this scale have little choice or influence over the value they derive for their crops.

Within the global food system, however, the price we pay for our food is often divorced from the production of that food. This is because of the system of subsidies, the way value is added to that food throughout the supply chain and the way food is traded on the stock market.

In most capitalist societies, so called 'free trade' prevails, unhindered by tariffs, quotas, or other restrictions. It is free trade (and the difference in, for example, labour costs between one country and another) that lies at the very base of our access to cheap food. Free trade is, however, deceptive. Theoretically, trade in food works within the rules established by GATT, now enshrined by the World Trade Organisation. In reality, the playing field for food trade is far from level and subsidies and protectionism are common. For example, the United States offers significant subsidies to its dairy farmers. These have been price-protected since the Agricultural Act of 1949. Scheduled to end in 1999, the programme was extended until 2001, then extended via a 2002 Farm Act and further through a 2007 Act for five additional years. The US is not alone. The system of protection and subsidy exists in most countries to a greater or lesser extent. Where systems of subsidy favour large over small-scale farming or extend beyond national boundaries, they can cause significant damage to indigenous farming systems.

Food prices are also influenced by the global stock market. Food is one of the four most commonly traded commodities in the world (see Figure 4). Food trading on the stock market is not new, nor necessarily bad. However, some commentators note that food trading on the futures market (allowed only after a petition from Goldman Sachs in the 1980s) may be at the base of the volatility in food prices post 2007 (Ghosh, J., 2011). In times of growing population it is likely that this volatility will increase as traders use the futures market to gamble on rising food prices and short stock availability. And volatile food trading prices will further affect the ability of those who live in food insecure communities and households to feed themselves.

The value chain in the food industry is another factor in the food price issue. Major food manufacturers (of whom we have seen there are few), are able to trade in a global market place. They can buy cheap raw ingredients, remove high value elements of these ingredients for a secondary process, add cheaper elements (such as palm sugar), ensure all food processing is done in areas where labour is cheap and sell products in markets where they attract a premium.

The combined impact of this system of trade protection and liberalism is a food system that is predicated against small farmers and local food production. Fair Trade systems have played a role in addressing one challenging aspect of this system, but this does not address the underlying structural cause.

Table 3: Commodities most commonly traded on the global stock market

1. Crude oil
2. *Coffee*
3. Natural gas
4. Gold
5. Brent oil
6. Silver
7. *Sugar*
8. *Corn*
9. *Wheat*
10. Cotton

http://www.stockmarketdigital.com/top_ten/top-10-business/top-10-most-traded-commodities-in-the-world

2 Externalities of food production

In the words of Tim Lang, the perpetuation of cheap food 'ignores the new fundamentals coming into play: climate change, water shortage, land pressures, a rocketing population, energy uncertainties, the loss of soil fertility and biodiversity and urbanisation on an unprecedented scale. Today there are next to no food stocks, either globally or nationally. The 30,000 items arrive in supermarkets through just-in-time delivery systems, laser bar codes, computerised logistics and satellites, all held together by tough contracts and international food purchasing lines.' (Lang, 2013)

These new fundamentals include the fact that current food production systems do not take into account the environmental costs of modern agriculture. No balance sheet exists to account for the millions of acres of land that fall out of use every year because they have been damaged by over watering. No account is taken of the carbon sequestration capacity of the thousands of acres of forest that are felled each year to make way for coffee, palm oil or soya plantations. These externalities are either paid by the governments in the countries in which they are based or remain unaccounted for (with the anticipation that future generations will pick up the tab). As we have seen with the honey bee, in some instances, the significance of these services is all too often under valued and when amelioration is required the tab is frequently picked up by governments and tax payers, rather than the organisations that may have caused the damage in the first instance.

3 The dominance of a small number of very large companies

The domination of the food industry by a small number of very large companies is compounded by vertical integration: a tiny number of companies directly or through joint ventures have a significant level of control over food from the production of seeds through to the distribution and sales of food products. In some instances, these companies are also becoming land owners, thus controlling food throughout the food chain.

Most of these companies are household names and some have very good corporate responsibility (CR or CSR) programmes. Regardless of the CSR programmes, each of these corporations is more powerful than the governments that seek to control them. Their decisions will influence what is – or is not – available in the food chain, the access that farmers have to technologies, the implications of these technologies, what is in the food that is available and the price that is paid for access to seeds and technologies, the human rights policies that dictate the working practices and the extent to which the environment is protected or degraded.

These companies have often been portrayed as 'the villains' of the international food system. And the implications of the operations of many have been far from benign. The new found quest for ethical behaviour is, however, causing several to review their practices, in some instances with interesting results. In fact many campaign groups are now making a Faustian bargain with these companies, because they recognise that they have the potential to address the structural ills of the food industry that lie beyond the reach of the average consumer.

4 Lack of food literacy

All too often, the ills of the modern food system are blamed on consumers who lack food literacy and who make poor food choices. While simple and convenient, this is far from the truth. Food has always been complex and those who are less wealthy typically have access to food that is less pure than the marketing messages would have us believe. Some additives in food play a positive role (for example, the addition of iron or other vitamins/minerals). Others are less positive. In most cases, their use is deliberate (Friends of the Earth, for example, estimate that palm oil is used in one in ten foods in UK supermarkets). As we have seen in the horse meat incident in Europe, in other instances they are not. Complex supply chains have coincided with our desire for cheap food to produce a food system that is opaque. Under such circumstances, it is little surprise that many consumers do not understand the real implications of their food choices (even when they do have choice). In those instances where choice is constrained, for example, because of urban planning processes that allow for a very high concentration of fast food outlets in a neighbourhood, obesity is a likely consequence. Even for those consumers who have good food literacy, there is all too often little information from which to make truly informed choices.

Customer choice (or in the terms used by policymakers 'personalisation') is often presented as one of the key mechanisms to reduce the impacts of food on health and the environment. Customers, however, can only choose from the options that they can afford and that are made available to them. They can only choose the 'ethical', fair and sustainable options if products that meet these criteria are provided, information from which to differentiate between products is clearly communicated, and these products are available at a cost that is affordable for most consumers. Within the current food system, customer choice is unlikely to be the harbinger of change that many herald it to be.

A strange irony …

It is a strange irony that the only organisations that have the scale to make 'ethical' food choices available for the masses, rather than the elite few, are the very food production, processing, retail and service businesses that are accused of unethical practice. These are the businesses that control the global food system. As long as customers remain confused about ethical issues around food – and the prices of so called ethical food remain high – they are unlikely to exercise their choice in any meaningful way. The growing awareness among food companies that the current systems of food production and processing cannot continue because of the range of pressures explored earlier in this chapter, means that change is likely to come.

To date pressure for change has rested with aid agencies, governmental organisations and certification systems. These have singularly failed to deliver the change required – instead they have produced a subset of the food industry known as ethical food that is available to those who can afford it and care sufficiently about the issues.

As the world faces the need to feed the seven billion people now and nine billion by 2050 the responses of the past will not be sufficient to provide a safe and secure food system. There is an emerging view that there is enough food to feed the global population. What is required is more equitable means of production and distribution. Governments have failed to secure systems to deliver this and the winds of change are blowing from an unexpected direction. Some of the international companies that dominate the international food system seem to be taking the issue of food ethics to their core and major organisations such as Unilever have made very public commitments about their intent. An intent to be the best in their business, and to ensure that they address issues of human rights, environmental protection and health, as a part of a long term commitment to ethical practice. As to whether they are really committed or will succeed – only time will tell. One thing is certain, these organisations are among the few who have the power and the global reach to address the root causes of so many of the ethical issues that permeate our food system.

Bibliography

Black R.E., Morris S.S., Bryce J. (2003) 'Where and why are 10 million children dying every year?' *The Lancet*, Vol 361 Issue 9376 2226-34.

Black, R.E., Allen, L.H., Bhutta, Z.A., Caulfield, L.E., De Onis, M., Ezzati, M., Mathers, C., Rivera, J. (2008) 'Maternal and child undernutrition: global and regional exposures and health consequences', *The Lancet*, Vol. 371, Issue 9608, 243-260.

Cafiero, C. and Gennari, P. (2011) 'The FAO indicator of the prevalence of undernourishment', Food and Agriculture Organization

Carroll, A. (1991) 'The Pyramid of Social Responsibility'. *Business Horizons*, July - August, 39 - 49.

Chen, S., and Ravallion, M. (2004) 'How have the world's poorest fared since the early 1980s?' World Bank Policy Research Working Paper 3341, Washington: World Bank.

Cook, J.T. and Frank, D.A. (2008) 'Food security, poverty and human development in the United States' *Annals of New York Academy of Sciences*, (1136), 193 - 209.

Euromonitor, 2013 Food Industry: Trends, Analysis and Statistics. Euromonitor

Food and Agriculture Organization (2002) 'Reducing Poverty and Hunger, the Critical Role of Financing for Food, Agriculture, and Rural Development'.

Food and Agriculture Organization (2006) 'State of World Food Insecurity 2006'.

Food and Agriculture Organization (2010) 'The State of Food Insecurity in the World 2010'.

Food and Agriculture Organization (2011) 'The State of Food Insecurity in the World 2011'.

FCRN & WWF (2010) How low can we go - *An assessment of greenhouse gas emissions from the UK food system and the scope for reduction by 2050.* Food Climate Research Network

Ghosh J., (2011) 'Considerations on the relationship between commodities, futures, markets and food prices', World Development Movement.

Haidt, J. (2006) *The Happiness Hypothesis: putting ancient wisdom and philosophy to the test of modern science.* New York: Arrow Books.

Hawkins,R and Bohdanowicz P, (2011) *Responsible Hospitality: Theory and Practice,* Oxford: Goodfellow Publishers

Headey, D. (2011) 'Was the Global Food Crisis Really a Crisis? Simulations versus Self-Reporting', IFPRI Discussion Paper 01087.

Institute of Mechanical Engineers. (2013) 'Global Food - Waste not want not', London: IMeche.

International Food Policy Research Institute (2010) '2010 Global Hunger Index'.

Izzo, P. (2011, July 07). *blogs.* Retrieved July 7, 2011, from wsj.com: blogs.wsj.com/economics/2011/07/07/the-connection-between-obesity-and-poverty

Kleanthouse, A. (2010) 'Eating Earth', Food, Drink and Innovation Network.

Lang, T. (2013) A Farming Revolution is Needed, *The Telegraph,* 8 June

Masset, E. (2011) 'A review of hunger indices and methods to monitor country commitment to fighting hunger' *Food Policy,* **36**, 102-108.

Mintel (2006) 'Attitudes towards ethical food', London: Mintel.

National Health and Nutrition Examination Study, 2011, http://www.cdc.gov/nchs/nhanes.htm

Patel, R. (2010). *Stuffed and Starved. The hidden battle for the world food system.* New York: Portobello Books Ltd.

Pelletier D.L., Frongillo E.A., Schroeder D., Habicht J.P. (1995) 'The effects of malnutrition on child mortality in developing countries'. *Bulletin of the World Health Organization* **73**: 443–48.

Simms, A. (2008). *Nine Meals from Anarchy - Oil dependence, climate change and the transition to resilience,* London: New Economics Foundation.

SUN movement, 2012, Scaling up nutrition - SUN Movement Progress Report, SUN Movement Secretariat

United Nations High Commissioner on Refugees (2007) 'Statistical Yearbook 2006 – Main findings'.

United Nations High Commission on Refugees (2008) 'Global Report 2008 – The Year in Review'.

World Health Organisation (2009) Unhealthy diets and physical inactivity. NMH Fact Sheet, WHO, Geneva.

Food of the Scattered People

Jessica B. Harris

Jessica Harris is the author of twelve cookbooks documenting the foods and foodways of the African diaspora. She has written extensively about the culture of Africa in the Americas, lectured widely, and made numerous television appearances. Jessica is an English professor at Queens College, CUNY, and consults at Dillard University in New Orleans, where she founded the Institute for the Study of Culinary Cultures. She is a founding member of the Southern Foodways Alliance, and a member of the IACP and Les Dames d'Escoffier.

From time immemorial, the world's peoples have been in movement. Groups have been scattered, resulting in communities in regions and parts of the world with which they have no historic connection. In the 21st century, with more access to travel and the relaxing of immigration laws, the movement continues. Increasingly, those leaving their traditional homelands for other destinations are said to be in diaspora. This is the reason that *tikka masala* is now considered the national dish of the United Kingdom; that *chop suey* is found throughout the United States, but not in the same style as in China; and that variants of West African fritters are found throughout the New World.

While the word 'diaspora' is now ubiquitous, and is used in relation to the patterns of movement of almost any people on an enforced or voluntary basis, its origins are more focused. It is derived from the Greek *dia*, meaning 'across', and *speirein*, meaning 'scattered'. As noted by Kenny (2013), its earliest use is commonly held to be in relation to the migration of Jews, as referred to in the books of Genesis and Exodus from the Hebrew Bible. The Jewish people were led '...from Babylonia (in present-day Iraq) to Canaan, which they named *Eretz Israel*. Famine soon drove Abraham's descendents out of Canaan to Eqypt...' (p. 3). Applied to ancient Jewish history, the term has come to mean imposed exile and suffering, and subsequent efforts to return.

Despite its meaning now embracing many more groups, it is still most commonly applied to those who have been moved on an involuntary basis, as a result of negative forces such as slavery, famine or war. The assumption is that those who have not chosen to be dispersed have a stronger emotional attachment with and sense of longing for their place of origin, and that their need to find cultural legitimacy may be greater than of those who have moved of their own free will. The study of diaspora often centres on how cultural assets are used, consciously or otherwise, to help individuals or groups maintain a sense of identity.

Chaliand and Rageau (1995) recognise that a strict definition of diaspora allows the inclusion of very few groups commonly said to be in diaspora, and therefore add to the definition, 'the role played by collective memory, which transmits both the historical facts that precipitated the dispersion and a cultural heritage (broadly understood) – the latter often being religious.' (p. xv).

In this discussion, the aspect of diaspora studies on which we will focus is the role of food and foodways in helping scattered communities maintain a sense connection with their places of origin. We will also explore the means by which culinary traditions are used, consciously or otherwise, to influence the culture of the 'host' destination of those who have moved from their homelands. The complexities involved in maintaining a culinary culture in alien lands are legion. Nevertheless, three of the world's diasporas have had a massive and transformational effect on the way the Western World eats: those of China, the Indian subcontinent, and the African Continent (especially its western coast). This chapter will look at selected examples from the Indian and Chinese diasporas and then offer a more in-depth study of the food of the African diaspora.

The Indian and Chinese diasporas

Tan (2012) estimates that the ethnic Chinese and the Chinese diaspora world-wide number more than 40 million. There are almost three and a half million in both Singapore and in the United States and over a million and a half in Canada. The Caribbean has various enclaves of Chinese population, notably in Trinidad, in Jamaica, and in Cuba. The United Kingdom numbers 347,000, but possesses one of the fastest growth rates for its Chinese population. Although referred to as the 'overseas Chinese', they may come from more than 56 different ethnic groups and speak various languages. Some are the result of early emigration, others travelled because of famines and wars, still others were enslaved or indentured, and in more recent years, migration has been voluntary for either economic reasons or as a result of political uncertainties.

Peoples from the Indian subcontinent have also long been travellers. Early on, maritime communities including the Gujaratis, Mappilas, Paravas, Chulias, and Chetiars established trade routes, and sailors journeyed as far west as Constantinople and Alexandria, and as far south as Zanzibar and Madagascar in the 12th century AD. The Indian diaspora, though, is generally dated to the 19th century and the labour shortages in the Sugar Islands of the Indian Ocean and the Caribbean following the emancipation of enslaved Africans. A system of indentured Indian emigration was devised that popu-lated the islands and spread Indians and their culture around the globe in what is known as 'The Old Diaspora' (Lal: 44-47).

In discussing the scattering of peoples from the Indian subcontinent, it is important to begin with a definition. The term 'Indian' will be used to describe the peoples of the subcontinent. Lal (2013) explains why this term is preferred. Before 1947, the definition was straightforward; everyone was Indian, whether Muslim, Hindu, Tamil or Sikh. Post-1947, the word has a politically restricted meaning, referring to 'Indian nationality'. Immigration figures and other data dating before 1947, therefore, would not have been divided among Indians, Bangladeshi, and Pakistani, but rather would encompass Indian people from across the entire sub-continent.

In the space of less than one century, more than 2 million Indians were in diaspora. In the eastern hemisphere, some 453,000 souls headed to Mauritius between 1834 and 1900, and 250,000 to Malaya between 1844 and 1910. In the Caribbean region 240,000 headed to British Guiana between 1838 and 1916, 36,000 went to Jamaica between 1845 and 1913, and 143,939 were destined for Trinidad. On the African continent 39,282 went to Eastern Africa between 1896 and 1921 and in slightly over 50 years between 1860 and 1911, 152,184 went to Natal in South Africa (Lal: 46).

Chinese and Indians alike carried memories of their food and their foodways with them. For both the Chinese and the Indians, the voyages across the *kalapan* (the dark seas) as the Indians called them were harrowing at best, and offered the first glimpses of the culinary changes that many would be forced to make. Cooked rations were distributed on most ships with little if any recognition of dietary restrictions or culinary preferences. For Indians, the caste system further complicated the trials of indenture, as caste rules forbid Brahmins from eating foods prepared by non-Brahmins. The Chinese suffered similar indignities. For them, rations were scant and often starvation was to be endured as much as the voyage itself. For both groups, culinary choices varied enormously depending on their ultimate destinations. But wherever they landed, Chinese and Indian alike transformed their food and had a major impact on the food and foodways of the places in which they arrived.

Almost three and a half million overseas Chinese form the ethnic majority in Singapore and they have had a major impact on the food of that nation. The Chinese of Singapore prepare much the same food as their ancestors did in the southern Chinese provinces from which they came. Proximity with chilli-loving Indians and Malay has added previously unknown degrees of heat to the Singaporean cuisine. Diaspora has resulted in another type of food in Singapore as well - *nonya* food, or the food of the Straits Chinese. Nonya food is a fusion of traditional Chinese cuisine and the cooking of the Malay that makes ample use of coconut milk and chillis as well as of more traditional ingredients. The food of the Straits Chinese is eaten throughout Malaysia and parts of Southeast Asia.

In the Western Hemisphere, in Peru, in Lima's Chinatown and around the city, Chinese restaurants called *chifas* serve that country's Chinese food, making use of Pacific seafood and local ingredients. In the Caribbean, Chinese-Jamaican families run many of the grocery stores and Chinese ingredients like star anise are readily available and used by all. In the Dominican Republic invention has created Peking Chicken using the more readily available bird instead of the traditional duck. Soy sauce is a regular ingredient in the food of that island as it is in Trinidad, where there is a relatively large Chinese population. Traditional dishes are served as well, but always with a bit more heat than might be usual in the homeland.

In the United States, some of the earliest Chinese food was that from the province of Canton. Tastes were adapted to those of the United States and dishes like chop suey and chow mein came into being, demonstrating the ingenuity of people in diaspora. In later years as migration expanded from other regions of China, the food of Szechuan and Hunan became more popular and recently the fish dishes of Fukkein have begun to enter the culinary repertoire of Chinese restaurants in large cities. In New York City in the 1970s and 1980s, alongside restaurants serving Chinese food from various provinces and American Chinese food, there were a number of restaurants boasting *Comidas Chinas y Criollas* (Chinese and Creole meals). They were run by Chinese who had migrated to Cuba and following the revolution fled to the United States: another example of how food in diaspora moves.

Memoirs like *Sour Sweet* by Timothy Mo and *The Rice Room* by Ben Fong-Torres, among numerous others, give an idea of the exigencies of Chinese immigrant life and provide fodder for any student of the Chinese diaspora. *Chop Suey: A Cultural History of Chinese Food in the United States* by Andrew Coe, *China to Chinatown: Chinese Food in the West* by J.A.G. Roberts, and *Spicing Up Britain: The Multicultural History of British Food* by Panikos Panayi, offer popular and scholarly overviews.

The Indian diaspora is the world's second largest and is estimated at 30 million people. In the early years of diaspora, many journeyed to Southeast Asia or to areas with similar climates to the ones left behind, where they were favoured with a wide choice of familiar produce and therefore able to maintain in various degrees of authenticity their traditional foodways. In Singapore's Little India, it has long been possible to snack on dishes like *idli* and *dosa* and Southern Indian vegetarian foods, which often arrive served on traditional banana leaf chargers.

There had been trade between the Indian subcontinent and the East African coast for centuries. Indian ways found parallels with Arab ones and those of the Swahili coastal culture that thrived in Mombasa and Malindi. In the mid to end of the 19th century, as Indians in diaspora journeyed further afield, some arrived in East Africa in search of their fortune, to build the railroad or to work in colonial service. 'The arrival of Indian emigres was fashioned into a parable of divine reward. Their gods had gifted them with a piece of earthly paradise in recognition of noble deeds in previous lives.' (Alibhai-Brown: 2009, 42). Others were victims of the trafficking in humans – the trade of enslaved Indians into East Africa. For those who survived, thrived, and built communities, the idyll lasted and they became East African Asians. They curried East African bananas and prepared snacks of deep fried cassava. Then, on August 4, 1972 Idi Amin ordered the expulsion of 60,000 of the country's Asians. The decree was later amended to include virtually all 80,000, many of whom had lived there for generations. Uganda's Indians were again in diaspora. Many journeyed to other East African countries, but they also journeyed to England, Canada, Australia, and the United States. They took with them very little, but they retained the taste for the dishes that they had created using African ingredients and Indian culinary techniques.

In South Africa, the Indian experience was less harrowing. Madhur Jaffrey, in *The Ultimate Curry Bible*, discusses how in colonial Durban, despite strict rules of *apartheid*, Africans purchased curry illegally from small Gujarati-owned shops that they called *bania chow*. The name stuck and the originally meatless curry served in hollowed out bread became a national treat under the corrupted name of bunny chow. In South Africa, though, Indian cooking techniques are maintained as much as possible and it is for that reason that young Indian brides received instruction to maintain traditions.

Indians arrived in the Caribbean region in the mid nineteenth century. There, in Trinidad, during the 1860s the standard ration for a worker was rice, ground corn, true yam, vegetables, salted herring and codfish, and coconut oil. There was also the availability of ingredients like flour and lentils and imported spices at local markets. (Lal: 109) Over the years and with the end of indenture a wider variety of Indian foodstuffs gradually came into the market.

In the Caribbean, indentured Indians lived proximate lives with the emancipated Africans that they had come to replace; this meant that there was culinary transference. A communality of cooking practices such as frying in deep oil and a taste for the well-seasoned, set the stage. The result is a contemporary Trinidadian cuisine where there are dishes like *roti* that are typically Indian as well as more creolized ones like Tobago's crab and dumplings, in which curried crab is served over an oval, bread-like, African-inspired dumpling. In Trinidad, as elsewhere, classic Indian foods are relatively unchanged from their origins. Indeed, they may be preserved in time variants of dishes that have evolved in different ways on the mother subcontinent. Interestingly these Trinidadian variants of Indian foods now meet up with those of their region of origin as a result of the further movement as West Indians migrated to England post World War II. By the 1970s, with continuing migration from East Africa and other parts of the former colonial empire, varying culinary cultures of the Indian diaspora met up with Indians from the subcontinent itself offering a wide diversity of Indian and Indian-inspired dishes.

Throughout the Caribbean region, curry powders are used, especially Madras Curry powder (Jamaica and Trinidad) and *poudre de colombo* in Martinique and Guadeloupe (the powder takes its name from the former capital of Sri Lanka from whence some of them hailed). Classic Caribbean dishes such as Jamaica's curry goat and Martinique's *colombo de porc,* all bear witness to the subcontinent's culinary influence on the region. No Indian-inspired dish has more captivated the region than the Trinidadian curry-filled crepe that is the preferred fast food of the eastern Caribbean. It is called by the Hindi name for the crepe - *roti.*

Cookbooks like Ramin Ganeshram's *Sweet Hands: Island Cooking from Trinidad & Tobago,* and *Singapore Food* by Wendy Hutton, give a sampling of the diversity of the recipes of the Indian diaspora. Memoirs like *Motiba's Tattoos* by Mira Kamdar, and *The Settler's Cookbook: A Memoir of Love, Migration, and Food* by Yasim Alibhai-Brown, give personal voice to the recipes and deepen the sense of what it means to be in diaspora, while *Spicing Up Britain: The Multicultural History of British* Food by Panikos Panayi, explains the multicultural background of the food of Great Britain.

The African diaspora

The case of the African diaspora differs vastly from those of the Chinese or the Indians; the African dispersion involved many more souls and took place over a lengthier period. Over centuries, Africans in diaspora and their descendants, who numbered upward of 140 million, have formed major segments of the population in virtually all of the countries of the Western Hemisphere with Brazil leading with 96,587,036 people of African descent or mixed race and the United States comes second with 42,020,743 (CIA Factbook). The result of this African diaspora is a transformation of the food of the Western Hemisphere. The reason is that the conditions of enslavement meant that for more than three centuries, enslaved Africans and their descendants were in charge of kitchens throughout the hemisphere. They were also involved in agricultural pursuits and with animal husbandry in the countries to which they journeyed, making for even greater influence. However, unlike the diaspora of the Chinese and the Indians ,there are virtually no culinary histories and few cookbooks that document the African hand in what have become the national cuisines of many New World nations. Although some dishes maintain an African flavour that is flagrant, that in some cases can even be traced to points of origin on the African continent.

Statistics from *The Atlas of the Transatlantic Slave Trade* by David Eltis and David Richardson reveal the extent of the scattering. The information on the origins of slave ships and the destinations of captives is especially useful as the culinary connections become evident.

Consider that from 1668 to 1829 of the 145,000 enslaved shipped out of the port of Saint Louis de Senegal by French vessels, 41,000 went to Saint Domingue, 36,000 went to the Eastern Caribbean including 5,000 to Dominica, 7,800 to Martinique, and 5,100 to Guadeloupe. In the continental United States 10,000 went to Charleston and 5,700 to the Gulf Coast, probably entering through New Orleans or Mobile.

Between 1727 and 1863, 582,000 Africans were shipped out of the Dahomean port of Ouidah. Of them, 175,000 went to Hispanola, 43,000 to Martinique, 11,000 to Guadeloupe and 242,000 to Salvador da Bahia, Brazil. 96,000 went to Pernambuco, 2,600 to the Gulf Coast and 37,000 were shipped to the Cuban ports of Havana and Matanzas. Of the 139,000 souls shipped from Porto Novo, also in Dahomey, 72,000 were destined for Haiti and 39,000 for Salvador da Bahia, Brazil. Of those 318,000 unfortunate Africans shipped out of Cape Coast Castle in today's Ghana, 98,000 were shipped to Jamaica, and 114,000 to the Eastern Caribbean islands, including 50,000 to Barbados.

To be sure, the ports were not necessarily the points of origin of the enslaved who were shipped, but it is highly probable that in each case there were enough from a particular ethnic group to ensure a cultural critical mass. Many in the West tend to think of the African continent monolithically when dealing with culinary culture. However, while generalities can be drawn, the food of the African continent is as regionally distinctive as that of Europe.

Senegambia and the Bight of Benin, and Angola and Cameroon further to the south, are known for their leafy green soupy stews that are called *sauce feuilles* (leaf sauce) *sauce gombos* (okra sauce) and *soupikania* (*kania* means okra in Senegal's Wolof). Those regions sent numerous captives to Saint Domingue, Salvador da Bahia, Brazil, Martinique, Guadeloupe, and The Gulf Coast and Charleston in the continental United States. It is not surprising then that a trail of green soups and stew-like dishes abound in these areas.

The trail of the dishes begins with Brazil's *caruru*, an okra-based stew prepared annually in Salvador da Bahia, Brazil, on the feast day of the Saints Cosme and Damian who are syncretised with the Yoruba Ibeji or twin spirits that also hark back to the Gulf of Benin where a similar dish is known as *amala*. The name changes only slightly from *caruru* in Brazil to *callaloo* or *kalalu* in the southern Caribbean, especially in Trinidad, Martinique, and Guadeloupe, where it is a prepared from a variety of greens including in Trinidad the leaf of the taro plant that is also known there as *callaloo*. The term is disputed and may be either Kimbundu or an African adaptation of a Tupi-Guarani word, but the dish is undeniably Afro Brazilian and Afro-Caribbean. In Antigua and in more northern areas of the Caribbean region, a similar soupy stew is known as pepperpot. [Note – in the southern Caribbean and in Guyana, pepperpot is a different dish entirely. It is a multiple meat stew prepared with cassareep, a cassava-based condiment].

Moving from the Caribbean into the continental United States, the West African soupy-stew becomes known as gumbo, a term that is probably based in the term in the Bantu languages for the vegetable okra: *quingombo* and *ochingombo*. The cooking of southern Louisiana, especially the Creole cooking of New Orleans has a range of gumbos including those thickened with okra, known as okra gumbos, and those thickened with a sprinkling of powdered Native American sassafras known as *file*. The okra gumbos are descendants of the soupy stews of western Africa. There are also okra gumbos in Charleston, South Carolina, but they are prepared without the flour and oil roux that is typical of those in southern Louisiana.

Diaspora is never just about starting points and ending points, but also about continuum. The northern Caribbean's pepperpot next shows up in the mid-Atlantic city of Philadelphia, Pennsylvania, where in the 19th century it was hawked on the streets by women of West Indian origin under the name Philadelphia gumbo.

As came green soupy stews, so came rice and composed rice dishes. Studies suggest that Lowcountry rice planters expressed a preference for slaves from rice-growing regions in Western Africa (Midlo-Hall: 1992, 91-93). They valued Africans from the rice-growing areas of Liberia, Sierra Leone, Guinea, and southern Senegambia. These rice-growing regions have long had a considerable repertoire of rice recipes that are at the origin of some of South Carolina's favourite dishes. Records also indicate that in Charleston, while rice was a commodity and therefore not to be consumed with frivolity, slaves were often given rations of broken rice, a discarded part of the crop, at particular times of the year. Broken rice would seem to be a poor ration. However, it might actually have been preferred as it still is in parts of Senegambia, where it is reputed to better hold the sauce. In addition, a complex system was used in the cultivation of rice that allowed free time for the enslaved who had completed their tasks, which many used to tend their own provision grounds. Some even had their own small plots of rice along with the vegetables that would have gone into the rich one pot meals of their West African homes: Guinea squash (eggplant), tomatoes, okra, and field peas of several types. Provision grounds supported more balanced diets among the enslaved. They also provided them with a limited means of controlling their culinary (and occasionally social) destinies, as many of them traded their provisions with their masters in exchange for goods and privileges. This also had the effect of adding African ingredients to the masters' diets and to those of other slaves.

Many of the items grown in slave gardens turn up in the tomato-coloured rice dish known as *Charleston's Red Rice*. In ingredients and preparation it is very similar to the tomato-based rice that is the underpinning of Senegal's national dish, *thiebou dienn,* a red rice and fish dish. A similar dish appears in the 1933 *Savannah Cook Book* by Harriet Ross Colquitt under the name *Mulatto Rice*. The *Joloff* rice of the English-speaking areas of West Africa makes reference to the Senegalese dish *thiebou dienn* in its name (Joloff is a reference to Senegal's Wolof empire), and also in its tomato-induced reddish orange colour, which also shows its connection to Charleston's red rice. Joloff rice may also include minced onion and bell pepper, which are found in some versions of Charleston's red rice. A similar dish of rice reddened with tomatoes, vegetables, and meat – often chicken and/or sausage is known as *jambalaya* in southern Louisiana.

The Senegalese black-eyed pea pilaf called *thiebou niébé* also bears a startling resemblance to Hoppin' John, with the exception that it uses lamb instead of the pork. In Charleston it is prepared with field peas, while in other parts of the American South it is prepared with black-eyed peas. Red Rice, Hoppin'

John, Jambalaya, and other derivative rice dishes turned up on the tables of the Big Houses of the American South and have become classics of the region.

Perhaps the African-inspired dish that has the most compelling history is the fritter. While gumbos and rice dishes were traditionally served in homes, fritters were street foods, consumed on the streets where they were prepared and sold by women of colour. The food of street vendors, most with a direct link to West African tradition, allowed enslaved women and men a modicum of self respect, and many went on to become hallmarks of their country's good cooking. They came straight out of the West African tradition. In regions of the continent's West Coast, market women have long not only controlled the purse, but have also wielded considerable political power. In earlier times, they were the region's economic foundation. It is certain that their forceful style of vending arrived in Brazil, The Caribbean, and the American South, where the majority of street vendors were of African descent. The newly emancipated brought with them a wit, a verve, and an aggression to marketing their wares that was all their own.

Street vendors were so typical of southern cities that they became arche-types: the praline seller, the *cala* vendor, and others. They were drawn by visiting artists and featured in articles in the newspapers of the day. Artist Leon Frémaux was one of the first to capture the images of the peddlers. Made as early as the mid 1850s, his drawings depict those who would become the city's standbys. In one, he depicts the *cala* seller with her fritter batter and her bowl precariously perched atop her tignon, or head tie. She carries a small brazier and a cloth covered basket of the final product that Frémaux opines are 'coarse and greasy'. In the method of vending, the fritter sold by Fremaux's cala seller is exactly like the *acaraje* sold by her cousin in diaspora in North-eastern Brazil.

The *cala* sold in New Orleans and the acaraje sold on the street in North-eastern Brazil are culinary relatives, and both are descendants of the classic West African fritters known as *akara*. It is claimed by the Ghanaians that the fritter gave its name to their capital, Accra. It seems however to be truly owned by the Yoruba of south-western Nigeria. There, the *akara* is prepared from white beans that are skinned, pounded into dough, and fried in bubbling red palm oil. Nigerian poet laureate Wole Soyinka vividly describes their preparation in an episode in his memoir *Ake: The Years of Childhood*. His description of the preparation of the food could be transferred across the Atlantic to Salvador da Bahia, Brazil, where street vendors serve a fritter prepared from the cowpea known as *feijao fradinho* - a small white-eyed pea. In Bahia, the fritter is still fried in red palm oil, there called *dende*. It even keeps its Yoruba name and is called *acaraje*, a corruption of the Yoruba *akara* meaning 'fritter', and *ije* for 'food'.

The fritter moves up into the Caribbean region where it keeps its West African name, but the spelling and ingredients change. It becomes an *acrat* or accra and is prepared most often from salted codfish or saltfish. The codfish fritter is a hallmark of Caribbean snacks and is sold both in restaurants and as street snacks. They go by various names including *fish cakes* in Barbados, *bacalaitos* in Puerto Rico, and *stamp and go* in Jamaica. It is in the Caribbean that the fritter takes a curious turn and once again contains beans. It happens in Curacao, in the cookbook of the sisterhood of Temple Mikve Israel-Emanuel, the oldest active Jewish congregation in the Americas, that dates back to 1651. There it is possible to find a bean fritter prepared like the Brazilian *acaraje*, but with the name of another West African fritter, the *kala*. The fact that a bean fritter with links to Brazil turns up in the cookbook of a Jewish temple in Curacao is not surprising as the temple is Sephardic, and indeed was founded by Jews who journeyed to Curacao from North-eastern Brazil. The fact that the *kala* exists under the same name in Bong country, Liberia, is startling and speaks to fusion within the diaspora.

The *kala* also appears in New Orleans (spelled *cala*), not as the bean fritter of Curacao, but as the original rice fritter. However, as reported by Robert Tallant and Edward Dreyer in *Gumbo Yaya*, a WPA project that documents much of New Orleans culture, the fritters known as *cala* were available in two forms – rice-based, and with black-eyed peas!

Finally, rice fritters are also found in South Carolina's Lowcountry where they were given as treats to children. This is possibly a cultural holdover from the food that was given as alms by West African Muslims and called *sarakala*, perhaps a hint at the origin of the word *cala* or *kala*. In her book *Servants of Allah: African Muslims Enslaved in the Americas*, Sylviane A Diouf, a Senegalese writer on the culture and history of Africans in the American diaspora, details the importance of the Islamic community among the enslaved in the Lowcountry. This Islamic presence in the Lowcountry is the result of the large number of enslaved from the Senegambia and the Guinea Coast, some of the early areas of Western Africa to be Islamised.

The third pillar of Islam is *zakah – to* give alms – often in the form of money or food. Diouf's cultural perspective allows her to make a connection between the rice cakes that were prepared in the Lowcountry at specific intervals and served as a treat for children, and those of Western Africa. She also affirms that the cooking method of the traditional West African rice cake remains the same as that recorded in South Carolina's Lowcountry.

The circuitous journey of the *akra/cala* is only one demonstration of the intricate complexities of food in the African diaspora. The orality of the cultures of the enslaved coupled with the traditional improvisational nature of cooking within the African diaspora means that there are few recipe books neatly tied with fraying ribbon containing a family's culinary heritage. Instead, the recipes are gleaned from snippets of memory and flashes of intuition bound only by the constraints of academic methodology. Unlike for the Chinese and Indians, there are few overviews of the food of the African, diaspora even within specific national boundaries. The scattering took place over centuries and the conditions of enslavement have resulted in the food becoming part of the culinary heritage of the adopted country. In studying the food of the African diaspora sources are disparate. Various national cookbooks are invaluable, but it is wise not to limit the study to cookbooks. Because diaspora is about maintaining a sense of place left or lost, memoirs, novels, journals, and travellers accounts are some of the best sources. Ralph Ellison's evocative passage about a displaced African American southerner smelling sweet potatoes cooking in the streets of the north, following the early 20th century Great Migration, tells more about the importance of that tuber in African American cooking than any recipe. Works by Jorge Amado evoke Afro-Brazilian food more than all of the recipes in Dona Benta. Even more than cookbooks, these accounts, along with culinary memoirs, offer insights and personal reminiscences that put the food in context and speak to the tastes of the diaspora, and to continuous adaptations.

However, if the diaspora is about loss and nostalgia, it is also about discovery and evolution. It is about the human will to survive and about the search for better places. Whether in diaspora because of the slave trade, a contract of indenture, or of their own volition, people in diaspora leave their point of origin with the tastes of home on their tongues, and arrive in new destinations where they must discover how to transform them, keeping alive the savour of the past with which to season the future.

References

Alibhai-Brown, Y. (2009) *The Settler's Cookbook: A Memoir of Love, Migration, and Food*, London: Portobello Books.

Allison, R. (1952) *Invisible Man*, New York: Penguin

Chaliand, G. and Rageau J.P. (1995) *Penguin Atlas of Diasporas*, London: Penguin.

CIA – The World Factbook.CIA.gov.

Coe, A. (2009) *Chop Suey: A Cultural History of Chines Food in the United States*, Oxford: Oxford University Press

Colquitt, H.R. (1933) *The Savannah Cook Book*, New York: J.J. Little and Ives

Diouf, S.A. (1998) *Servants of Allah: African Muslims Enslaved in the Americas*, New York: New York University Press

Eltis, D. and Richardson, D. (2010) *Atlas of the Transatlantic Slave Trade*, New Haven: Yale University Press

Fong-Torres, B. (1994) *The Rice Room*, New York: Penguin

Ganeshram, R. (2010) *Sweet Hands: Island Cooking from Trinidad & Tobago*, New York: Hippocrene.

Harris, J (1991) *Sky Juice and Flying Fish: Traditional Caribbean Cooking*, New York: Fireside

Harris, J (1998) *The Africa Cookbook: Tastes of a Continent*, New York: Simon & Schuster.

Harris, J. (2011) *High on the Hog: A Culinary Journey from Africa to America,* New York: Bloomsbury.

Hutton, W. (1979) *Singapore Food,* Sydney: URE Smith.

Jaffrey, M. (2003) *The Ultimate Curry Bible,* London: Ebury

Kamdar, M. (2000) *Motiba's Tattoos,* New York: Public Affairs

Lal, B. (2013) *Encyclopedia of the Indian People,* Honolulu: Hawaii University Press

Midlo-Hall, A. (1002) *Africans in Colonial Louisiana,* New York: Public Affairs

Mo, T. (1982) *Sour Sweet,* Ann Arbor: University of Michigan Press

Morgan, P. (1998) *Slave Counterpoint: Black Culture in the Eighteenth Century Chesapeake and Lowcountry,* University of North Carolina Press

Overseas Chinese (2008) *New World Encyclopedia.* Retrieved June 24, 2012 from http://www.newworldencyclopedia.org/index.php?title-Overseas_Chinese&oldid=766818.

Panayi, P. (2008) *Spicing Up Britain: The Multicultural History of British Food,* London: Reaktion.

Roberts, J.A.G. (2002) *China to Chinatown: Chinese Food in the West,* London: Reaktion.

Soyinka, W. (1989) *Ake: The Years of Childhood,* New York: Vintage

Tallant, R. and Saxon, L. (1987) *Gumbo Ya-Ya: Folk Takles of Louisiana,* Gretna: Pelican

Tan, C.B. (2012) *The Routledge Handbook of the Chinese Diaspora,* Abingdon: Routledge.

Embedding Food and Drink Cultures: The case of Burgundy

Claude Chapuis and Benoît Lecat

Claude Chapuis is a lecturer in the Department of Languages and Culture of the Burgundy School of Business, specialising in English, French culture, negotiation, wine and history. He has written extensively, with a special focus on wines, viticulture and Burgundy.

Benoît Lecat is a lecturer in the Department of Marketing at the Burgundy School of Business. His research has focussed on pricing and promotion in the wine sector, and the marketing of luxury goods.

'Real Burgundy is neither old Burgundy covered with forests nor young Burgundy laying its sweet carpet of meadows. It is the eternal Burgundy of vines; Burgundy in winter with its bare, shriveled stocks; Burgundy in spring with its festoons of tender little leaves; Burgundy in summer with its purple grapes full of juice; Burgundy in the fall with its lush crimson and gold leaves lit up by the October sun which is ever faithful to the vintage rendezvous.' (Poupon, P., 1970)

Certain countries and regions are known to have strong and embedded food and drink cultures. Such cultures shape reputation, stimulate pride, define collective identity and drive local and national economies. They can also generate tourism, drawing large numbers of visitors to sample renowned produce.

Emergence of food and wine culture in Burgundy

Historical analysis reveals the emergence of Burgundy as a world-renowned centre of wine production and gastronomy, based not only on the quality of its produce, but also on instrumental business tactics employed by key individuals. The analysis starts with the rising interest in food and wine in the late 18th century. An exploration of the automobile industry and the wine roads, and also of events such as *la foire gastronomique de Dijon*, will reveal the development of gastronomic tradition, as well as contemporary trends.

Burgundians are proud of their region. They like to praise the beauty of the landscape that they have contributed to shaping: vine stocks which are impeccably aligned along straight rows, stone walls separating the plots and stone huts at the edge of the plots.

Burgundy also boasts one of the richest architectural and gastronomic heritages in France. It produces some of the world's best wines and yet, for a long time, the fame of its vineyards was not enough to attract tourists. The wine villages and the golden slopes of the Côte d'Or didn't inspire painters and artists. With the exception of painter Charles-François d'Aubigny's masterpiece: *Vintage in Burgundy* (1863) and Mr Gentet's lithographs which illustrate Doctor Lavalle's famous book of wine published in 1855, the iconographic representation of Burgundy's vineyards was very poor until the beginning of the 20th century. What is true is that before the phylloxera crisis (1878–1895) vines grew in a disorderly, unkempt, anarchic way.

Historical documents show that for a long time, travellers showed indifference to the landscapes even though they were happy to meet the growers.

In 1778, Malesherbes, the courageous barrister who defended King Louis XVI, who also enjoyed wine a great deal, visited Burgundy. In his diary, he mentioned the 'vines of these grands crus of our best wines.' But Malesherbes didn't describe the landscape.

From March 4th to March 10th, 1787, Thomas Jefferson, then the US ambassador in France, visited Burgundy. Jefferson identified on a map the names of La Baraque (Marsannay), Chambertin, Vougeau, Veaune, Romanie, Nuys, Beaune, Pommard, Voulenaye, Meursault and Montrachet. He noted that Chambertin and Montrachet, the most prestigious wines, were located at the edges of the Côte, and described the nature of the soils and their colour – all as preparation for planting his own vines at his home in Monticello, Virginia.

On 2nd August 1789, English agronomist Arthur Young traveled from Dijon to Beaune by cabriolet. He stopped at Clos de Vougeot and noticed that contrary to the other vineyards, there were no trees in the Cistercians' estate. He was not impressed by the 650-year heritage of the Clos and jotted down that it was not like the beautiful vineyards of Champagne but was situated at the foot of a rocky hill. He ironically pointed out that the monks paid a lot of attention to the 'matters of spirits'.

Exiled from Paris by Napoleon in April 1806, Madame de Staël entertained her friends in her château of Vincelles, near Auxerre, but provincial life bored her to death. The hills covered with vines that she saw from her window stirred no emotion in her. She only saw a horizon of posts. Like Madame de Staël, historian Jules Michelet, who travelled in winter, found that Burgundy was sad with its 'death-grey posts' and its hills with an often barren top. In his book *On reading,* Marcel Proust (1907) spoke of the pleasure he took when he walked in the cobbled streets of Beaune, but he didn't mention vineyards.

In *Memoirs of a Tourist,* Stendhal (1838) used the word 'tourist' for the first time in the title of a book. He didn't invent the term, but popularised it. Contrary to many romantic authors, he was in search of neither new surroundings nor exoticism in Burgundy. A wine lover, he was more interested in people than in landscapes. He was even disappointed by the scenery: 'If it were not for its wonderful wines, I would find nothing uglier in the world than this famous

Côte d'Or. Côte d'Or is just a small, very dry, ugly little mountain; but one makes out the vineyards with their small posts, and all the time one finds an immortal name: Chambertin, Clos de Vougeot, Romanée, Saint Georges, Nuits. With the help of so much glory, one finally gets used to Côte d'Or.'

For a long time, the beauty of vines was not acknowledged. Tourists just passed through Burgundy on their way to the Riviera. In the guidebooks published by the *Touring Club*, the few places of interests mentioned were Vézelay, Dijon, Beaune and Autun. In 1912, as mentioned by Laferté (2006), the tourist information office of Burgundy advised visitors not to visit the vineyards: 'You may go from Gevrey to Nuits via the National Road and you'd be going past the most famous crus of France... But for tourists in love with natural beauty, this route is uninteresting.'

Development of the current wine road

In 1934, the wine road of Burgundy was inaugurated. It was the first in France. Until then, only roads leading to castles, churches, abbeys, museums or even restaurants were mentioned in guidebooks but Alsace, which opened its own wine road in 1953, was to set an example. Very early, the Alsace wine road was recognised as the major tourist route of the region and it put the vineyards at the heart of the beautiful landscape and cultural heritage. It went across the villages from North to South, rolling at the foot of the Vosges, passing in front of the ruins of medieval castles, dainty houses decorated with flowers, romanesque churches and Renaissance fountains. Tourists were warmly welcomed to taste wine in 'winstubs' and visit cellars. In the meantime, Burgundy was still mostly associated with the now mythical Route Nationale 6 lined with famous restaurants in Joigny, Avallon, Saulieu, Arnay-le-Duc, Chagny, Tournus and Mâco. These celebrated places had in fact been coaching inns before being turned into gastronomic restaurants.

During the depression of the 1930's, a handful of Burgundy producers recognised the potential of positive public relations. In 1934, the Brotherhood of the *Chevaliers du Tastevin* was founded by two wine merchants from Nuits Saint Georges. Its chapters were soon very much sought after: artists, writers, scientists, movie stars, politicians and even royals swarmed to Clos de Vougeot after World War II. These famous guests were knighted *Chevaliers du Tastevin* (knights of the wine-tasting cup) in a ceremony reminiscent of Rabelais's writings and Molière's plays. They, in turn, became ardent propagandists of Burgundy wine. This successful attempt was imitated and today, many villages throughout Burgundy have their own brotherhoods. To mention just a few: the *Piliers Chablisiens* in Chablis, the *Cousinerie de Bourgogne* in Savigny-les-Beaune, the *Chanteflûte de Mercurey*, the *Grumeurs de Santenay*, and the *Vignerons de Saint Vincent* at Mâcon.

Viticulture was still not regarded as a tourist asset in the 1930s. The wine magazine *La Revue des Vins de France,* founded in 1927, advocated estate wines against the blended wines offered by merchants. A few growers entertained regular customers, visitors and tourists who were passing through. They conveyed the image of humble, warm, cheerful country people sticking to the good old methods, the famous 'local, loyal and steady uses' and were happy to share their wine with amateurs. But there were no concerted efforts between the producers of a given village or between growers and tourist offices. As a matter of fact, winegrowers who, most of the time, worked alone in their vineyards, were characterized by their individualism.

At that time, wine growers were still living in poverty. The decree of 30th July 1935, controlling the appellations d'origine, eventually put an end to their difficulties. Each appellation is specified by its area of production, the authorized cultivars, the pruning, the training of the vine, the yield and the minimum and maximum degrees of alcohol. Of course, the large number of appellations creates a complex environment. Regional appellations (55% of the total production) apply to wines coming from anywhere in the Burgundy area, such as *Bourgogne aligoté, Bourgogne Hautes Côtes de Nuits, crémant de Bourgogne*. Village appellation (35% of the production) apply to wines produced from grapes coming from within the defined area of some villages (eg. Chablis, Pommard,). First growth appellations (*premiers crus* – 13.5% of the production) come from some plots,'climats', which are considered as the best and which are subject to a specific delimitation (eg. *Beaune premier cru*

Les Grèves). Grands crus (great growths), which brought fame and fortune to Burgundy, account for barely 1.5% of its total production. Their names alone are an adequate description: *Chambertin, Musigny, Romanée-Conti, Corton, Clos-de-Vougeot* and *Montrachet* are among the 33 Grands Crus of Burgundy.

Wine tourism developed in the New World and also in Germany, Spain and Italy. In France, any operation aimed at attracting visitors and wine buffs was held in suspicion. 'Good wine doesn't need advertising!' was the watchword for a majority of growers. In most cases, there was no name on the winegrower's front door. France has just recently jumped on the bandwagon and wine tourism is now becoming a major flagship product alongside cultural tourism in the regional economy, but it is still not extensively developed, and tourists remain daunted by the complexity of wine appellations.

There are now four wine roads in the region. The oldest, the *Route des Grands Crus*, which crosses the vineyards of the Côte de Nuits and the Côte de Beaune, was created in 1934. Paul Murray (1984) an Australian journalist wrote, 'driving along this road is like reading the wine list in a topnotch restaurant.' It is sometimes referred to as the *Champs-Elysées* of Burgundy. The *Association de la Route Touristique des Grand Crus de Bourgogne* was created on the initiative of the Chambers of Commerce of Dijon and Beaune in partnership with the regional government and the local villages. Original wine colour road signs, bearing a logo representing a grape, guide tourists through the 47 villages along the road and some hills and landmarks are lit at night.

More roads have been opened of late, and tourists now have the opportunity to drive along 1000 km of wine roads in Burgundy. In 1934, three different routes linked Northern and Southern Burgundy: (1) the *route des grands crus*, the 'historical road', (2) the *route des grands vins*, (3) the *route des vins Mâconnais-Beaujolais*. Besides, the *route du crémant* (Burgundy sparkling wine road) was opened in 2007. Three roads, around Auxerre, Chablis and Tonnerre enable tourists to drive across the Yonne vineyards. However, the site which attracts the largest number of tourists in Northern Burgundy is undoubtedly the *Basilica de Vézelay* (800,000 visitors per year). The popularity of Vézelay led Marc Meneau, the famous chef of *l'Espérance,* to replant vines which had vanished at the time of the phylloxera crisis. There is also the road of the hills of Pouilly-Sancerre, West of the region.

In its new awareness of the economic interest of wine roads, Burgundy has joined Alsace and Champagne for a promotional campaign targeted at American tourists. The wine roads of Alsace, Burgundy and Champagne have defined a 'triptyque' named ABC in order to 'sell' a wine route associating their vineyards. For instance, American holders of the *ABC of France Privilege Card* are entitled to a discount of up to 20% on their visits to historical buildings, restaurants, museums, cellars and some shops along 'the most beautiful wine roads of the world' as Lignon-Darmaillac (2009) pointed out.

Nevertheless, these wine roads all still fail to attract large numbers of tourists. Each road has its own history and there may be too many of them. In spite of the efforts which have been made, a unifying principle is still lacking.

Development of events

Burgundy is also a region in which symbolically significant events help to maintain and extend the reputation of its wines. The first *Saint Vincent Tournante,* the celebration of the wine growers' patron saint, took place in Chambolle-Musigny in 1938. The annual wine auction of *Hospice de Beaune,* initiated in 1851, remains a major event in the Burgundian calander. And the day after the sale, the *Paulée* of Meursault takes place in the château of the village. *Paulée* is the end of vintage meal, traditionally offered by estate owners to thank their grape pickers for their work. The *Paulée* of Meursault, initiated in 1924 by Comte Lafon, gathers together Meursault estate owners and 600 guests who taste their wines. The three events: the banquet at Clos-de-Vougeot on Saturday, the wine auction and popular celebrations in Beaune on Sunday and the *Paulée* of Meursault on Monday, are referred to as the *trois glorieuses* (three glorious days).

The *Saint Vincent Tournante* is still organized in partnership with the *Chevaliers du Tastevin.* It is held in a different village every year and it requires months, if not years of preparation. As a result, it attracts thousands of visitors.

The village is decorated with paper flowers, exhibitions and displays on the theme of wine take place in various public and private buildings and wine is poured lavishly. The *trois glorieuses* are still celebrated in November in Clos-de-Vougeot, Beaune and Meursault, but now the wine auction of the hospices of Beaune is organized by Christie's, which aspires to expand the international renown of the longest-established and most famous charity wine auction in the world. Every other year, importers, journalists, wine writers and various influencers are invited for a week in spring (*Les Grands Jours de Bourgogne*) to taste the wines of the different sub-regions of Burgundy. As for the *Paulée de New York,* it is a yearly fund-raising dinner for charity based on the *Paulée de Meursault.*

Dijon and the birth of a gastronomic tradition

When they hear the word Burgundy, many people think of wine and food. One of the reasons given for Burgundy's gastronomic reputation is the excellence of its products. While it may be an exaggeration to suggest that Burgundian gastronomy is a recent invention, it was only after World War I that it became renowned. The rich land of the region enabled farmers to produce quality products: notable areas include Charolais (beef), the Yonne plains (fruit, especially cherries) the Nivernais (dairy products), the Morvan range (pork meat), the Bresse plains (poultry), and the Côte d'Or (wheat and wine). And Louis Daubenton (1716 – 1800) is credited with the introduction and improvement of the merino sheep breed in the Châtillonnais (Northern Burgundy) in 1776. But farmers, though they produced quality, if not luxury products, remained poor.

An elaborate, refined cooking based on wine sauces developed. As Burgundy is at a crossroads, it managed to take advantage of all possible new opportunities. For instance, people from the Bresse adopted the Inca corn imported by their Spanish masters to feed their hens, Morvan people raised pigs in their forests, and wine growers collected snails and picked dandelions and lamb's lettuce on their way back from work. Wily gourmets borrowed recipes from other provinces, notably Auvergne, and gave them Burgundian citizenship by adding wine sauces. Such was the case of *coq au vin*. Bordeaux writer Philippe Sollers scandalized Burgundians when he lambasted their wines, saying that they were 'wines for sauces!' In Burgundy, even more than in the other French regions, wine cannot be considered independently from food. Here, people seldom drink wine alone, as they do in Germany. Gastronomy does not simply consist in preparing dishes and planning the order in which they should be served, but also in choosing the wines which will accompany them – wine enhancing food and vice versa. In Burgundy, the match between wine and food is considered an art and it is said that wines shouldn't be chosen to accompany food, but rather food should be chosen to accompany wines.

When visitors come to Dijon, they often visit the Dukes' kitchens. Indeed, the dukes, especially those from the Valois dynasty, lavishly entertained their guests. When Burgundy became French, the rich didn't serve dishes from the province on their table. Pierre-François de la Varenne, who was the Marquis d'Uxelles's cook, wrote famous cookbooks but none of them contains recipes of Burgundy dishes. Cooking started becoming 'Burgundian' in the 19th century, after the French Revolution, when the bourgeois classes hired cooks, mostly women, who brought with them their family's traditions and recipes. By the end of the century, cooks were very proud of their roots. Gustave Garlin, the author of many cookbooks boasted that he was born in Tonnerre and the famous Alfred Contour (1891) called his book of recipes *Le cuisinier bourguignon*.

For a long time, there was no tourism policy in France, just private initiatives. The *Club Alpin Français,* which was founded in 1874, was a closed society of aristocratic members interested in good cooking. The *Touring Club de France,* which was founded in 1890, was less hierarchical, more open and welcoming. In 1893, the arrival of the car industry was marked by the birth of the *Automobile Club.* These associations aimed to promote access to natural sites and monuments, mostly focused on the wealthy.

Despite the shadow that continued to be cast by more charismatic parts of the country – Brittany, Provence, Auvergne, Alsace and the Alps, the first edition of the Michelin Guidebook, published in 1905, had a positive impact. At this time a craze for regionalism developed as a reaction to an increasingly urbanized society and as a backlash against standardization. This was to benefit Burgundy, where the quality of wine, the impact of its distinctive *terroir*, and its growing reputation appealed to those in search of 'authentic' tastes.

At the beginning of the 20ᵗʰ century, tourists stopping in Burgundy started favouring comfortable little hotels and inns held by the owners with home-style cooking. 'We want to eat steaks, not Louis XIV armchairs,' wrote a critic quoted by Gilles Laferté (2006). Luxury didn't guarantee quality and appeared to be inauthentic. Gourmets relished dishes cooked with simple ingredients. Only upstart 'nouveaux riches' appreciated cuisine based on caviar, truffles and foie gras, which required a great deal of money. True gastronomy appeared to be the art of preparing ordinary food, albeit with a touch of genius. This also played to Burgundy's strengths as a region from which many of the most influential French chefs of this period originated. Even if they moved on to other parts of the country, their connection with Burgundy was maintained. For example, the Mère Poulard, who has achieved fame for her omlettes at her eponymous restaurant in Mont Saint Michel, was born in Nevers; the Troisgros family was from Mâlain; and Fernand Point was born in Louhans.

Numerous clubs and associations revolving around gastronomy were founded. The *Club of 100,* which was born in 1912, included journalists, lawyers, car manufacturers and dealers, hotel owners and politicians. All were interested in developing tourism, especially automobile tourism and gastronomy. The rise in the use of cars stimulated demand for comfortable hotels and good restaurants.

After World War 1, a regionalist vision developed and gastronomy was more actively promoted. Gaston Gérard, a barrister and professor of law and advertising at Burgundy School of Business, understood the importance of tourism in Burgundy's economy. His ambition was 'to revive the cooking and gastronomic traditions of the province of Burgundy, illustrated by its famous wines and the equally famous cuisine of its dukes', Laferté, (2006). He considered that tourism was an economic asset, a tool of economic growth which could benefit France. He was elected mayor of his hometown in 1919.

Likewise, Louis Forest, president of the *Club of 100* said, 'tourism is a national industry.' By making tourism and gastronomy more dynamic, Gaston Gérard aimed to help hotels, restaurants, their suppliers (farmers) and local shops. He also hoped tourism would contribute to re-rooting the population of the provinces, deserted because of the movement into towns caused by industrialisation.

In 1867, the food industry accounted for 13% of employment in Dijon. In 1911, this figure rose to 28.7% and Dijon was one of France's leaders in the food sector. In 1886, the Richard brothers purchased the Pernot biscuit factory and led an innovative production and commercialisation policy. 800 people were employed in 1900, rising to 1000 between the two World Wars. Likewise, Armand Bizouard founded what was to become the Amora mustard company in 1919. The food sector was also represented by such flagships as the gingerbread brands Mulot et Petitjean, and Philbée, cassis companies like Lhéritier-Guyot, Lejay-Lagoutte and Boudier, and the Lanvin chocolate company. All of them found markets in France and abroad. Some directors of these companies were elected members of the Chamber of Commerce of Dijon. Lucien Richard (Pernot biscuits), who presided over the company from 1913 to 1930, was also a member of the *Academie de Dijon* and several tourist associations. Together with Mayor Gérard, he created the gastronomic fair in order 'to revive the old rank of capital once held by Dijon.' The idea of the fair was not readily accepted by the food industrialists and traders of Dijon. In his book, *Dijon, ma bonne ville*, (1928) Gaston Gérard recalls that he had summoned thirty notables of the town to his office. Seventeen of them showed up and listened to his project, expressing a lot of scepticism, giving him mocking smiles suggesting, 'don't count on me!' When he asked them what they thought of his project, they remained silent. The young mayor was about to declare the meeting closed when the President of the Chamber of Commerce spoke. He simply said the idea was interesting and getting it under way would benefit the town.

The fair was planned on a shoestring. It took place in November 1921, a point in the year when there is not that much to do in the vineyards. The growers participated, especially those from the nearby Côte de Nuits. The PLM railway company offered a pavilion in which food products were displayed and the Vilmorin company organized an unforgettable flower show. The first gastronomic fair of Dijon was declared a rousing success. The town, which had given a subsidy of one franc to the event, made a profit of 73,000 Francs!

In the 1920s, Gaston Gérard staged around 600 events focused on Burgundy, its wine and gastronomy, in 32 countries. 'Gastronomy,' he said, 'will free us from sloth, spinelessness, filth and the unbearable horror of international cooking.' The young mayor, who so far had the image of a small town politician, was the first in France to actively promote gastronomy. In the words of Gilles Laferté (2006) 'the gastronomic fair of Dijon can be considered as an ex nihilo invention of regional cooking based on local products but suitable for bourgeois palates.' Members of the Club of 100 regularly attended and in 1925, 600,000 visitors came to the two-week event, which takes place every year at the beginning of November, to this day.

In the 1920s, dishes took on a more resolutely regional identity and in restaurants people ate eels from Seurre, crayfish from Ozerain, Morvan ham, Bresse chicken, Burgundy snails or coq au Chambertin. The names of the Dukes of Burgundy, which were given to some dishes, added an aristocratic flavour to the food, as was the case of *pâté truffé Charles le Téméraire* offered at *Les Trois Faisans*. The appellations d'origine contrôlée system was on its way, the first laws about the origin of farming products had been enacted in 1919 and people felt that more precise territorial identification would ensure better quality food. From then on, Dijon achieved the image of a gastronomic capital and a tourist centre much more than that of an industrial town, in spite of the presence of heavy industry, in the form of the Terrot motor cycle company.

His local achievements were a springboard for Gaston Gérard's political career. He was appointed High Commissioner in charge of tourism in 1930, the first ever in France. He achieved a little part of immortality with his recipe of *poulet Gaston Gérard*. In 1930, his wife served it for the first time to

Curnonsky, 'the prince of gourmets.' It consisted of chicken cooked in a white wine, gruyère cheese, mustard and cream sauce and accompanied by white Burgundy wine.

In 1929, shortly after her wedding, Marie-Louise Fisher, a newly married young American woman who was to become one of the world's most celebrated writers on food, arrived in Dijon where she spent three years. The 'Colette of the Napa Valley,' as Leo Lerman called her, reported her discoveries in her book *Long ago in France,* reissued in 1991. The passages that she wrote about Dijon and Burgundy describe the atmosphere of the region between the two World Wars and the high regard in which cooking was held. She admired her landlady, Mrs Ollagnier who 'had a passion for making something out of nothing.' Mrs Ollagnier was a wonderful cook and yet she worked in unlikely conditions, 'Her kitchen was a dark cabinet, perhaps nine feet square, its walls banked with copper pots and pans, with a pump for water outside the door. And from that little hole, which would make an American shudder with disgust, Madame Ollagnier turned out daily two of the finest meals I have yet eaten.'

Gaston Gérard's successors honoured the tradition started by their predecessor. Canon Kir, who was mayor from 1945 to 1968 used to offer *blanc cass* (2/3 aligoté wine 1/3 cassis) as was the rule in Burgundy when entertaining guests. Aligoté wine, produced in big quantities before the AOC system, was so acidic that it was almost undrinkable. It was even nicknamed 'wine of three' because it was said that it took three people to drink it, one to hold the glass and two to maintain the drinker on his chair! Blending this tart product with sweet blackcurrant made sense. Kir, being a popular character in Dijon and bearing an easy-to-pronounce name was delighted to christen *blanc cass* by giving it his name. Today, aligoté is much better than it used to be and it is almost sacrilegious to blend it with blackcurrant, but traditions die hard in Burgundy and serving kir to guests is still a must!

The law instituting the appellations d'origine contrôlée system, passed in 1935, didn't just apply to wine. It was extended to other products, notably cheese. The characteristics of cheeses (type of milk, location of meadows, ingredients and fat content) were determined according to strict specifications. Thus, *cîteaux, chaource,* époisses, and more recently, *mâconnais* and *charolais* cheeses obtained their 'birth certificates'. A certification of compliance of the food product with strict specifications guarantees its quality. Such regulations apply to Burgundy's beef, lamb, pork, poultry, rabbit, wheat, and cooked snails. As for mustard, *Dijon mustard,* which contributed to the fame of the town, is a brand, not an appellation. It can be made anywhere in the world as long as the Dijon recipe is applied. 80% of the mustard seeds used in the production of the mustard made in Dijon come from Canada and mustard has almost deserted Burgundy's fields. However, a re-introduction programme is now under way. The La Moutarderie Fallot company in Beaune produces mustard with seeds sourced exclusively from the region. Burgundy's seed producers have applied for an IGP (protected geographical indication) and, in all likelihood, one day, a *moutarde de Bourgogne* appellation will be created. This should help to further legitimise one of the products most closely associated with Burgundy.

Rules and norms

Mention has been made of the distinctiveness of Burgundian wine and food and the ways in which this impacts upon perceived 'authenticity', credibility and popularity. Legitimisation has been supported by the emergence of formal 'rules' that govern methods of production and the nature of consumption. Born of factors such as agricultural conditions, climate, legislation, social and professional networks and governance, oenological and gastronomic conventions have been established, are embedded, and remain largely unchallenged. Beyond their functional influence they serve to reinforce the identity of Burgundy and of its people.

With respect to food, to this day the most obvious of these conventions relates to the products that that are known to be typical of the region. The products are grown or reared locally and are sold in the village and town markets, and the dishes appear consistently on restaurant menus. Based on

Poulain (2011), Meffre and Covin (2009), Carpentier (2009), Downie (2010) and Morin (2004), Table 1 provides a brief inventory of dishes of Burgundian origin.

Table 1: Products and dishes of Burgundian origin

Cheese	Brillat-Savarin
	Chaource
	Cîteaux
	Epoisses
	Soumaintrain
Salads	Cabbage
	Dandelion
	Mâche (lamb's lettuce)
	Mushroom
	Wild onion
Beef	Charollais
	Bœuf Bourguignon
	Pot-au-feu (beef broth)
	Daube (beef braised in wine)
Chicken	Pulet de Bresse
	Coq au vin
	Poulet de Gaston Gérard
	Rable de lièvre (hare salad0
	Civet de lapin (rabbit stew with red wine)
Pork	Andouille (offal sausage)
	Boudin (blood sausage)
	Saucisson (pork sausage)
	Jambaon persillé
	Potée Bourgiugnonne (pork sausage stew)
Fish	Pôchouse Bourguignon (fresh water fish stew)
Additional specialities	Escargot (snails)
	Gougères (puffed cheese choux)
	Mustard
	Pain d'épices (ginger bread)
	Vegetables: beans, cabbage, peas, potatoes
Cooking with wine	Chabrot
	Trempée
	Meurettes (poached eggs in red wine and onion sauce)

While wine and food pairing may be considered by some to be a matter of personal taste, in Burgundy this is a realm in which culinary conventions are well-established. While elsewhere in France one might make food choices, and then decide which wines to serve, in Burgundy tradition decrees that a region-alist approach is taken where possible. For purists, wines are chosen, which dictate the dishes that are served. The appropriately named Bourguignon, in *L'accord parfait* (1997), identifies Burgundian wines and matching dishes, and provides extensive justification for his conclusions. Table 2 gives a summary of his proposed pairings.

Table 2 – Burgundian wine and food pairing

Wine family	Food pairing
Vosne-Romanée	Grilled beef cutlet
	Pheasant
	Roast duck
	Woodcock
	Young roast partridge
Volnay	Aged gruyere cheese
	Braised oxtail with mustard
	Flank of beef with chips
	Meurettes
	Roast duck with gilled thigh
Morgon	Beef's ruffle
	Coq au vin
	Plate of assorted meats
	Sainte Ménehould pig's trotter
	Young rabbit terrine
Meursault	Foie gras terrine
	Black radishes
Mâcon	Black radishes
	Cheese soufflé
	Pike dumplings
	Shellfish
	White veal stew
Chablis	Oysters
	Prawn fritters with mushrooms
	Summer Beaufort cheese

Conclusions

We hope that this chapter has shown that historical analysis reveals why the wine and food of Burgundy have come to characterise the region more than any of its other cultural assets. While there may be no universally applicable criteria by which the strength of gastronomic cultures can be determined, in this case we see that a combination of factors have played their part.

Image is shaped by the mark of history: since the time of the Dukes of Burgundy the region has been associated with wine production. Changes to the transport infrastructure, including the development of 'wine routes', encouraged drivers to divert off the main roads heading south, and in doing so stimulated wine tourism. Influential individuals have played a key role in establishing Burgundy as a pre-eminent gastronomic destination. Figures such as Gaston Gérard mobilised the business community to recognise the role that wine and food could play in economic development. There has also been a recognition that the symbolic value and reputational power of culture can be manufactured through the creation of events, elaborate rituals and exclusive societies. To be inducted as a *Chevaliers de Tastevin* carries immense prestige, and for wine lovers worldwide the draw of *les trois glorieuses* is irresistible. Both represent the concerted and collective efforts of Burgundians to maintain their heritage and to enhance the allure of their region.

And what of the future? Well, as our yearning for authentic cultural experiences grows and our fascination with distinctive regional tastes intensifies, the place of Burgundy as one of the world's great wine and culinary destinations looks secure.

References

Abramson, J. (2006) *Food culture in France, Series: Food culture around the world*, Westport, Connecticut: Greenwood Press,

Bazin, J.F. (1996) *Le vin de Bourgogne*, Hachette.

Bonin, S. (2005) L'Elysée à table: un siècle de menus présidentiels, *Magazine 3 étoiles*, Numéro 5, Mars-Mai.

Bourguignon, P. (1997) *L'accord parfait*, Editions du Chêne.

Broadbent, M. (2007) *Pocket Vintage Wine Companion*, London: Pavillion Books.

Carpentier, G. (2009) *Cuisine bourguignonne: 107 recettes d'hier et d'aujourd'hui*, Editions Ouest-France.

Chapuis, C. (2006) *Vineyard Trails. What you haven't yet been told about Burgundy wines*, Editions de Bourgogne.

Chapuis, C. & Lecat, B. (2011) Wine climates in Burgundy and holy names: will the consumer be influenced by religion?, Conference on "Religion as brands, the marketization of religion and spirituality", Lausanne, Switzerland, October 13-15.

Coates, C. (2008) *The Wines of Burgundy*, Berkeley: University of California Press.

Cole, M. C., Vopndrasek, R. and Liew, C. C. T. (eds) (1994) *Food and Wine the Westin Way*, Michigan: Brendan International Publications.

Contour, A. (1891) *Le Cuisinier bourguignon*, Beaune: Imprimerie Lambert.

Culinary Institute of America (2002) *The New Professional Chef,*_7th Edition, NY: John Wiley and Sons.

Culinaria Spain (1999) Cologne: Konemann Verlagsgesellschaft mbH.

de Grand-Maison, A. (2000) *Le guide des vins et des mets d'accompagnement*, les éditions Québecor.

Delpal, J-L. (2007) *Les mets et les vins*, Editions Artémis.

Dion, R. (2010) *Histoire de la vigne et du vin en France des origines au XIX° siècle*, PUF, Paris 1959, New edition in 2010.

Downies, D. (2010) *Food-Wine-Burgundy*, The Terroir Guides collection, New York: The Little Bookroom editions.

Duijker, H. (1983) *The Great Wines of Burgundy*, London: Mitchell Beazley .

Fielden, C. (2010) *Exploring the World of Wines and Spirits*, London: WSET.

Fisher, M.-L. (1991) *Long ago in France [The years in Dijon] A destination book*, Prentice Hall Press. (reprint)

Fried, E. (1986) *Burgundy, the Country, the Vines, the People,* New York: Harper Collins.

Garrier, G. (2006) *Histoire sociale et Culturelle du Vin,* Hachette, in extenso.

Gérard, G. (1959) *Dijon, ma bonne ville.* (Re-issue with a preface by Pierre Taittinger) Éditions des états-généraux de la gastronomie française. Dijon: Imprimerie Jobard.

Goldstein, E. and Goldstein, J., Pool J. (2006) *Perfect Pairings,* University of California Press.

Guicheteau, G. (1994) *Mets et Vins,* Petits Pratiques Hachette.

Guide Michelin France (1935) editions Michelin

Guide Michelin France (2011) editions Michelin

Hailman ,J.R. (2006) *Thomas Jefferson on Wine.* Jackson: University Press of Mississipi.

Hanson, A. (2003) *Burgundy,* Classic Wine Library, London: Mitchell Beazley.

Harrington, R. (2007) *Wine and Food Pairing – A Sensory Experience,* Oxford: John Wiley and Sons.

Johnson, H. (1989) *The Story of Wine,* London: Mitchell Beazley Publishers.

Johnson, H. (2006) *Hugh Johnson's Pocket Wine Book,* 30th edition, London: Mitchell Beazley.

Kolpan, S. Smith, B. & Weiss, M. (2010) *Exploring Wine,* NY: Van Nostrand Reinhold, New York.

Laferté, G. (2006) *La Bourgogne et ses vins. Images d'origine contrôlée,* Paris: Belin.

Lavalle, J. (1855) *Histoire et Statistique de la Vigne et des Grands Vins de la Côte d'Or,* Ivry, France: Phénix Editions, (réédition 2000).

Lignon-Darmaillac, S. (2009) *L'oenotourisme en France, Nouvelle valorisation des vignobles.* Editions Féret.

Lucand, C. (2011) *Les négociants en vins de Bourgogne: de la fin du XIXe siècle à nos jours,* Bordeaux: Féret.

Meadows, A. (2010) *The pearl of the Côte: The Great Wines of Vosne-Romanée,* Winnetka (USA): Burghond Books.

Meffre, A-C., Covin, C. (2009) *Escapades Gourmandes en Bourgogne,* Paris: Editions ereme.

Meiselman, H. (2000) *Dimensions of the Meal: the science, culture, business, and art of eating.* Aspen Publishers Inc.

Morelot, D. (1831) *La vigne et le vin en Côte d'Or*, 1831. Reprint éditions Cléa in 2008.

Morin, S. (2004) *Les recettes du pays de Baubigny: 100 recettes bourguignonnes d'hier et d'aujourd'hui*, Asssociation les fines bouches.

Morris, J. (2010) *Inside Burgundy: The Vineyards, the Wine & the People*, London: Berry Bros & Rudd Press.

Parker, R. (2008) *Parker's Wine Buyer's Guide*, 7th edition, New York: Simon & Schuster.

Parker, R. (1990) *Burgundy*, New York: Simon & Schuster.

Pitiot, S. & Servant, J-C. (2008) *The wines of Burgundy*, Collection Pierre Poupon.

Poulain, C. (2011) *Potage, Tortue, buisson d'écrevisses et bombe glacée…*, *Histoire(s) de menus*, Paris: Agnès Viénot Editions.

Poulain, J.-P. (2011) *Sociologies de l'Alimentation*, Paris: PUF.

Poupon, P. (1970) *Toute la Bourgogne, portrait d'une province*. Paris: PUF.

Proust, M. (1907) *Sur la lecture*. Actes-Sud, reprinted in 1988.

Remington, N., Taylor, C. (2010) *The Great Domaines of Burgundy: a Guide to the Finest"* 3rd edition, London: Kyle Cathie Ltd.

Remington, N. (2010) *Grand Cru: the Great Wines of Burgundy through the Perspective of its Finest Vineyards*, London: Kyle Cathie Ltd.

Rosengarten, D. & Wesson, J. (1989) *Red Wine with Fish: The New Art of Matching Wine with Food*, New York: Simon and Schuster.

Senderens, A. (2000) *Le vin et la table*, Livre de Poche, N° 16551.

Simon, J, (1996) *Wine with Food*, New York: Simon and Schuster.

Sloimovici, A. (1992) *Ethnocuisine de Bourgogne*, Jeanne Laffitte.

Stendhal (1838) *Mémoires d'un touriste*, Paris. Slatkine reprints. 1986.

Sutcliffe, S. (2006) *Wines of Burgundy*, London: Mitchell Beazley.

Vinfox 2010 (2009) *The Comprehensive Wine Buyers' Guide*, Zürich: Vinfox Verlag.

Wine Spectator Ultimate Guide to Buying Wine (2004) 8th edition, Philadelphia: Running Press Book Publishers.

Young, A. (1909) *Travels in France during the years 1787, 1788 & 1789,* London: George Bell & Sons.

Yoxhall, H.W. (1968) *The wines of Burgundy,*London: Pitman.

Truffles and Radishes:
Food and Wine at the Opera

Fred Plotkin

Fred Plotkin is one of America's foremost experts on opera and has distinguished himself in many fields as a writer, speaker, consultant and as a compelling teacher. He is an expert on everything Italian, the person other so-called Italy experts turn to for definitive information.

"It's raining truffles, radishes and fennels," says Sir John Falstaff, the richly humane and deeply funny title character of Giuseppe Verdi's final master-piece. While there are many ways that food, wine and other libations have been used in opera, somehow this line best captures both the grandeur and common touch that opera and gastronomy possess. For every rare and fragrant truffle, there are plenty of common but no less essential radishes and fennels, all of which have their metaphorical place in opera and real place in cookery.

Giuseppe Verdi (1813-1901) was probably the most important Italian creative artist since the Renaissance. Not only was he the foremost composer of Italian opera and, for many, the greatest opera composer of all, but he was a knowledgeable gastronome and farmer as well. His most famous operas include tragedies and dramas such as *Rigoletto, Il Trovatore, La Traviata, Aïda* and *Otello*, but it was in his last work, the human comedy *Falstaff*, that he achieved his fullest expression of a philosophy that believes 'All the world is a joke and man is born a clown.'

Verdi used a libretto (text) fashioned by Arrigo Boito, who built the story around the character of Sir John Falstaff from Shakespeare's *Henry IV: Part One* and *The Merry Wives of Windsor*. In addition to his work as a composer, Verdi was one of the leaders of the Risorgimento, the movement for unification that helped form the nation of Italy in the 1860s. He overcame censorship, the deaths of two wives and both of his children, and all kinds of challenges and disappointments that would have undone most people. And yet, thanks to Boito and the character of Sir John, Verdi was able to find humour and insight at the end of his life that put all of this in perspective. Falstaff is a character who loves his food and drink as much as he loves ideas and of the pursuit of pleasure.

The composer was born in the tiny hamlet of Roncole, not far from Busseto, in the province of Parma. This part of Italy, in the region known as Emilia-Romagna, is a culinary paradise even in a nation that arguably has the best food in the world. Parmigiano-Reggiano cheese, prosciutto di Parma, aceto balsamico tradizionale (the real balsamic vinegar), and magnificent fresh pasta made with golden eggs, are but the most famous food products of the area. Even though he grew up in a rural setting, Verdi's situation was unusual. His parents ran a small restaurant with lodgings on the post road from Milan to Bologna. They produced their own food, made pasta by hand, and served local specialities that would, today, be considered *alta cucina* in the best Italian restaurants of New York or London. The quality of cooking at the Verdi family's trattoria was such that mail carriers made a point of stopping there for the night to have an exquisite meal and a good night's rest for themselves and their horses. As they came to know the highly intelligent boy who lived there, the mailmen brought books of literature, history, theatre and music that few children living so far from the citadels of education and culture would have ever read. Verdi's education and sense of the world came through these books, which he devoured as voraciously as the mail carriers consumed his mother's *tortelli di erbette*.

Verdi was fortunate that Antonio Barezzi, the father of the first woman he married, took an interest in supporting his musical ambitions and had the means to do so. Barezzi was one of the most important traders of food products in the Busseto area, not only exporting locally-made products but bringing in excellent liquors and all manner of spices and condiments. Verdi came to know these flavours and developed a discerning palate as sensitive as his discerning ear. He was not in any way a 'foodie', as modern terminology would describe it, but an *intenditore*, which suggests a good judge or connoisseur.

Although Verdi's marriage to Virginia Barezzi lasted only four years, ending with her early death in 1840, he remained close to Antonio Barezzi until the latter's death in 1867. Antonio was like a surrogate father to Verdi, providing not only financial and emotional support but all manner of good food and drink. Even after achieving great fame throughout Europe and massive wealth from the performance royalties of his operas in theatres everywhere, Verdi never turned his back on his local roots. In fact, after the extraordinary successes of *Rigoletto*, *Il Trovatore*, *La Traviata*, which were produced between 1851 and 1853, Verdi bought an important parcel of land at Sant'Agata, not far from Busseto, where he lived with his second wife, the retired opera singer Giuseppina Strepponi. The couple established a working farm around the villa they built. Wheat was grown, cows were milked and cheese made, and pigs were raised to then become all manner of *prosciutti e salumi* (hams and cured meats). When Verdi encountered a particularly recalcitrant theatre manager or prima donna, he would hand-write his secret recipe for *spalla di San Secondo* and attach it to a freshly-butchered, carefully-wrapped pork shoulder and have it delivered to Milan, Venice or wherever the difficult person was. Inevitably, this gesture enabled Verdi to get his way.

When Verdi was invited, in 1862, to St. Petersburg to write and produce *La Forza del Destino*, he determined that it was necessary to bring along the proper provisions to eat in a way that pleased him while in the Russian imperial capital. It fell to Strepponi to make the arrangements. She hired two railway cars in Parma. One was set up for the Verdis and their possessions. The other was loaded with hams, cheese, pasta, olive oil, vegetables packed in oil or vinegar, fruit preserves, flour, spices, salt, and other needs. At the same time, a railway wagon was arranged in France that contained red wines from Burgundy and Bordeaux, various white wines and generous amounts of Champagne. The cars from Parma and France were transported to Berlin and were joined there before completing the journey to St. Petersburg. Such arrangements might seem excessive and extravagant, but there is an underlying logic. Food gives pleasure and a sense of place as well as sustenance. While that railway car from Italy might seem to contain luxury items, in fact it represented the customary larder of most families in and around Parma, then as well as now. Other artists and musicians might be more interested in sampling the local fare in the places they visit, but the food Verdi brought to Russia represented a security and predictability that would be reassuring in an environment in which so much else would be unfamiliar.

This phenomenon still exists. When Luciano Pavarotti went to perform in China in 1986, a time when that nation was only just opening up to the world, his plane was filled with provisions for his Chinese sojourn. The great Italian tenor was from Modena in Emilia-Romagna (the same region of Parma), and grew up on similar foods to those that Verdi ate. Italian food and opera, and the people who excel at producing them, are ambassadors of the best that nation can send to the world, as was Pavarotti.

Throughout history, there have been opera composers who ate well, or knowledgeably, or excessively, or idiosyncratically. Georg Frideric Händel (1685-1757) was a German who lived most of his life in London and was, for all intents and purposes, Britain's first great composer of operas. He lived in a house on Brook Street, where he wrote his music and gave lessons as well as concerts. He also managed theatres and dealt with high-strung prima donnas. We know that he had little romantic life of any kind and his outlet and consolations came in copious dining. On many occasions he would reserve a table for three, order food for three persons and be asked by the waiter, "wouldn't you like to wait for your guests?" to which came the curt reply, "there will not *be* any guests."

Wolfgang Amadeus Mozart (1756-1791), in his short life, created some of the greatest operas. They are masterpieces musically, dramatically and spiritually. Even if most composers are touched by genius, Mozart got an extra helping of it and also had a special grace. Many of his works, including *Die Entführung aus dem Serail, Le Nozze di Figaro, Don Giovanni* and *Così fan tutte*, include scenes of consumption of food and drink. Mozart enjoyed his food but was not as discerning as one might expect from a man whose music is the epitome of elegance and refinement. Given his druthers, he would likely have indulged primarily in the superb cakes and sweets for which his native Austria was so famous.

Ludwig van Beethoven (1770-1827) wrote only one opera, *Fidelio,* but it is a brilliant work in its depiction of a noble woman, Leonore, who disguises herself as a young man and finds work in a prison where her husband, Florestan, is held in a dungeon for revolutionary activities. In fact, Florestan is a political prisoner on the side of good and has been jailed by a corrupt regime. He has lived on only bread and water for two years (although the burly tenors who sometimes play him stretch credulity) and is on the brink of death from starvation when Leonore courageously produces a gun and liberates him. Beethoven himself was one of the least food-oriented of composers. In part because he was deaf, dining with others was of little interest to him. He never developed much of a palate and felt such an urgency to keep composing that eating represented an unwelcome interruption. He was a famously fast and sloppy eater, often startling people who knew him as a genius but observed him eating with the manners of a starving animal.

Richard Wagner (1813-1883) was, along with Verdi, one of the two titans of 19th Century opera. His works, which he considered music dramas, are often long and are suffused with sublime music that was composed to words he wrote himself. Wagner's operas are often mythic and his characters grapple with huge existential issues. Even in such marathons, they are not the biggest eaters. The gods in his tetralogy, *Der Ring des Nibelungen,* seem to subsist on magic apples. Wagner studied all sorts of philosophy and religion, including Buddhism, and was for quite a while a vegetarian, although he returned to hearty meat eating toward the end of his life, despite suffering from heart disease.

A key figure in the food and opera equation is Gioachino Rossini (1792-1868). If Verdi was a true gourmet, Rossini was more of a gourmand. It is fair to say that he was much more truffles than radishes or fennel. In fact, his signature salad dressing included olive oil, lemon juice, salt, pepper and minced truffle. He wrote, 'To eat, to love, to sing, to digest – these are, in truth, the four acts of the comic opera we call life. Whoever lets it pass without having enjoyed them is a total fool.'

Rossini was born in Pesaro, on the Adriatic, but studied in Bologna (in Emilia-Romagna) and quickly learned to love the cuisine of that region. He could be discerning about food products - one bite of dried pasta could tell him if it was produced in Naples or Genoa. But his love of excess made him the stereotype of the overindulged opera man. Rossini doted on foie gras, beef, cream sauces, truffles and other rich foods. Anytime one sees a recipe named for Rossini, these ingredients inevitably are included. Rossini is most known for comic operas such as *Il Barbiere di Siviglia* (The Barber of Seville) and *L'Italiana in Algeri* (The Italian Girl in Algiers), but he also wrote magnificent dramas and tragedies. One of these, *Tancredi*, includes an aria called 'Di tanti palpiti'. Rossini referred to this as 'the rice aria' saying that it took him as long to compose it as it did for him to prepare a risotto. He was a very fine cook and social lion who gave dinner parties at his home in Paris, where he moved in his mid-thirties because he could find better medical there for the syphilis he contracted at the age of fourteen.

Our received notion of Rossini, and of opera in general, is of the luxurious excess that is part of both opera and gastronomy. But this hardly represents the totality of the experience. Opera combines sublime and prosaic elements. The art form was born in Florence in 1597 when a group of academics called the Camerata Fiorentina decided that it was possible to take all of the arts that had existed since antiquity – painting, singing, instrumental playing, poetry, theatre, dance – and combine them to create a new art form called *opera lirica* (lyrical work). In fact, this experiment was a failure because the men of the Camerata did not know how to combine these diverse art forms. This is not unlike cookery. You can have gorgeous ingredients but, if you do not fully understand their properties and limitations, you will not know how to combine them. You can have a ripe banana, a filet of fresh salmon and a wedge of Stilton cheese and know that, while they might be wonderful on their own, there is not much you can do with them when combined.

Opera lirica only took off when Claudio Monteverdi (1567-1643), from Cremona, arrived in Florence, learned of the activities of the Camerata, and came up with a revolutionary concept that now seems so obvious: To tell a dramatic story on stage in words and music, the music composed must not only exalt the *sound* of the words but also express the *meaning* of the words. For example, if the word *amore* is set to music, this music must convey what kind of love is being expressed. Is it romantic or erotic love? Is it the love between parents and children or perhaps between friends? Is it love for a monarch or a deity? The genius of Monteverdi and subsequent opera composers came in knowing how to unleash the magical alchemy in which the combination of words and music creates something greater than what these elements could be on their own. Add visual arts, acting, dance and a vast range of musical instruments in the orchestra to provide all sorts of colours and textures, and you get opera, something so much greater and more enchanting than any of these components on their own.

Similar magic can happen in food and wine when superb ingredients are placed in the hands of a wise and sensitive cook who understands how to exalt the best properties of these ingredients. This means that we must emphasize a respect for the primary materials (the ingredients) as singers learn to respect the words and music created by librettists and composers. This is more important, and successful, than trying to make a personal statement that attempts to show off the interpreter (be it a chef or a singer). If you realize that the banana, salmon and Stilton do not work well together, you use your imagination and sense memory to come up with combinations that show these ingredients at their best. Or, sometimes, the best thing is to allow these ingredients to shine on their own, just like an unaccompanied human voice. Humility, thoroughness, and mastery of craft are as rare in cookery as they are in the performing arts. It takes constant work, dedication, and a willingness to fail spectacularly so as to learn how to do things better. For every person who completely devotes him or herself to mastering the complicated intricacies of performing opera or of creating a recipe, a dish, a cookery book or a restaurant, there are many more people who try to figure out how to cut corners, which inevitably means a diminution of quality. There are no shortcuts on the road to achievement.

One of the miracles of opera is that singers make the beautiful and powerful sounds they do *without* amplification. This might seem inconceivable, but it is true. A singer spends decades developing and maintaining what is known as a technique. This involves remarkable discipline in addition to the natural gifts of a beautiful voice and the requisite physical attributes (stamina, intelligence, a well-trained body that supports the breath) to achieve this. The singer must get his or her sound across the footlights and be heard over an orchestra of up to one hundred instruments at full cry as well as a chorus that booms from the stage.

The stereotype of the 'fat lady' opera singer is just that. Opera singers come in all sizes, shapes and nationalities. The art form might have been born in Italy, but it spread to France, Austria, Germany, England, Russia and then subsequently to many other nations. The principal languages of opera are Italian, German, French, English, Russian and Czech, although operas exist in many other languages as well. A century or more ago, a corpulent singer, male or female, would often be referred to as 'prosperous'. The implication was that the weight indicated that the singers enjoyed ruddy good health and had the stamina required for the intense and beautiful performances that were expected of them. Heavy singers were more the norm then, but that model is out-dated.

Some opera companies, without officially declaring a prejudice, now cast pretty people who are just adequate singers rather than those rare persons with gorgeous voices who are also great singers (possessing a glorious voice does not necessarily mean that a person knows how to sing). This preference for pretty faces and nice bodies is based on the offensive notion that it is not believable that two average-looking people could fall in love. But when you have the very best singers sing love music, it is entirely believable because the music and their singing make it so. If you listen to Joan Sutherland and Luciano Pavarotti as Lucia and Edgardo, sing a love duet from Donizetti's *Lucia di Lammermoor*, you will fully understand.

We should put aside, once and for always, the notion that people who are heavy are unlovable and do not have sex appeal. Such prejudice is a product of our modern society that promotes bodies that are either wraith-thin or musclebound hard. Whether we like it or not, the majority of people in most developed nations are overweight, and yet their love lives and sex lives are no less active than the more idealized exemplars of physical fitness and beauty.

No matter what their size and shape, opera singers have very distinct and personal regimens for eating and drinking. An opera can be three or four hours (and some are as long as six hours). This asks singers to pace themselves so they have the strength and voice to go the distance without flagging. Most singers eat and drink moderately before performances, and some do not consume anything at all. One of the reasons for this is they feel that having food in their stomachs would make it more difficult to manage their technique, which involves creating support from the diaphragm. Another reason, obvious and intimate though it might be, is that certain opera costumes are rather difficult to get in and out of quickly and if there is a 'call from Nature' that needs to be responded to, that cannot be done expeditiously. Singing under hot lights in a long opera while wearing a heavy costume (some can weigh up to 15 kilos/33 pounds) makes great physical demands. Singers often lose weight during performances through perspiration and the expenditure of energy.

To keep their mouths and throats moist during performances, opera singers might consume water or perhaps tea, although tea contains tannins that could fall on the vocal cords and affect singing. Most opera singers seldom consume wine in any setting because of the tannins that are a natural element in wine, especially reds.

There are, of course, many exceptions to the sparing consumption of food and drink before and during performances. The protean dramatic soprano,

Birgit Nilsson (1918-2005), often kept a bottle of beer in the wings of the stage to drink down and then joyously burp before returning to the rigors of singing Wagnerian heroines such as Brünnhilde, Puccini's icy princess Turandot, or crazy girls such as Elektra in operas by Richard Strauss. After performances, Nilsson restored the calories she expended during her exertions by feasting on Scandinavian specialties such as meatballs or fresh seafood.

The era of opera singers eating heartily, before and after performances, was in the late 19th to mid-20th centuries. Because that time coincided with the growth of photography, our received imagery of the heavy singer in large costumes – the proverbial 'fat lady'– became entrenched as a stereotype. In almost every role, it was the voice and the vocal acting (through superb singing) that persuasively created a character on the stage. There are a few exceptions, though. The iconic role of Violetta in Verdi's *La Traviata* is a young courtesan, admired for her looks and charm. This being tragic opera, she is also dying of tuberculosis yet manages to sing beautifully for a couple of hours before expiring. Nowadays, Violetta is one of the few roles that, by rights, should be the province of singers who look the part, including being thin. But that was not always the case. Both Nellie Melba (1861-1931) and Luisa Tetrazzini (1871-1941) were acclaimed Violettas despite the fact that they had more than the requisite *physique du rôle*.

More than any other singer, Frances Alda (1879-1952), subscribed to the notion that eating would give her the energy to sing. She believed that added weight would give her additional vocal power in addition to stamina. Born in New Zealand and raised in Australia, this soprano seemed to have never met a dish she did not like. She would eat a full breakfast before practising her scales. Then lunch would include shellfish and perhaps a stew made of chicken. On days when she was scheduled to perform, she invariably ate *steak Tartare*, chopped raw beef with onions, oil, raw egg, capers and other condiments. She believed that the dish provided her with the fuel necessary to sustain a performance. She was indeed a powerful and compelling singer.

Many opera singers were not gourmands and often preferred to eat the same foods all the time because they were familiar and thus did not present challenges to the palate or the digestive tract. The Italian soprano Renata Tebaldi (1922-2004) grew up near Parma, raised by a single mother with limited financial means. What money was available was used for singing lessons. As a child Tebaldi ate a pan-cooked chicken breast with rosemary most days and that was the dish she consumed before almost every performance even when she was a major star.

The great Neapolitan tenor Enrico Caruso (1873-1921) grew up poor and his association with food was more about security than extravagance. The one meat product his family could afford when he was a boy were the occasional chicken livers that would flavour tomatoes for the sauce that dressed the spaghetti or macaroni for the daily meal. As an adult, Caruso's meal before he sang was pasta with a sauce of tomatoes and a much more abundant amount of chicken livers. These were a form of nostalgia but he also felt they gave him energy for singing. In the same vein, Caruso consumed large amounts of spinach. If his breath smelled of these foods, co-stars seemed not to mind because his voice and singing were so sublime.

The American soprano Beverly Sills (1929-2007) had a routine of always eating a steak in the mid-afternoon on performance days. When asked about this, she said that steak gave her pleasure and so did singing and she associated one with the other in a life that had as many challenges as it did satisfactions.

The examples cited above are, in some way, exceptions. Most singers eat very little before performances. Those who wait until after often eat what is available. It might be well past midnight and they are tired, so they consume dishes that are quickly prepared, often in restaurants. These foods might be rich and more savoury than nutritious. If singers then go to bed on full stomachs, they often gain weight. If the singers are appearing in cities away from home, they do not always have access to kitchens. Therefore, they must avail themselves of what they can secure. And, of course, just because someone can sing well does not mean that person is knowledgeable about cookery. Other singers overeat because of nerves or loneliness. All of these are reasons why some opera singers have a tendency to become overweight.

Contemporary singers make more of an effort to eat food that will keep them slim, although it is not a given that they are eating nutritiously. They worry that they will lose a role due to the current emphasis on looks rather than how well someone sings. Nonetheless, being careful about what they eat and when they eat it poses a challenge as it would for anyone who works long hours, travels, and does not have complete control of how their food is prepared.

It should also be pointed out that many opera singers in the 19th and 20th centuries were as outsized in their love lives as in their other appetites. Food, music and sex have been conjoined since antiquity, what with orgies and banquets that aroused all the senses. High-strung divas and divos, with their nerves (the pressure of accurately hitting high notes can prove stressful) and the frequent absence of spouses, communed with Eros as much as they did with Orpheus, the god of music. The marital bond was a mere technicality, in part because the passions of operatic music and stories fanned libidinous flames and in part because spouses were often back home, wherever that was.

Feodor Chaliapin (1873-1938), the powerful Russian bass who was one of the most compelling actors in opera, was as engaged at the table and the bedroom as he was on the stage. Being a fine actor and a very vain man, Chaliapin felt that his body had to be appealing and serve him well on the stage. With his bass voice, he often played villains, malevolent kings, devils or old men. It frustrated him that his characters seldom wound up with the girl, at least in the operas he performed in. They wound up with the tenor, no matter how tubby, because that man had the gorgeous voice and the most romantic music. Chaliapin's need to avoid rich foods to keep his form was quite frustrating for him and his discipline was variable. He was known, when a guest in someone's home, to demand a great deal of fancy food, although his favourite indulgence, when in Britain, was an extravagant English breakfast. He also loved chocolate, fanatically, until Boris, his pet monkey, died when he consumed all the chocolate bonbons and truffles that had been sent to the bass from an admirer. Sex, for Chaliapin, was an appealing pastime for all of the obvious reasons but also because it represented an expenditure of calories.

Women always made themselves available to him and it was his custom to wear three large rings on his hand when his wife was expected, thus signalling to all the others to stay away. This brings to mind the character of Mozart's Don Giovanni, who sniffs at the prospect of fidelity by saying "whoever is faithful to one woman is unfaithful to all the others." When asked by a journalist what he considered essential in an ideal woman, the bass replied that she not be too thin, she must have long hair to keep one warm in the winter, and she must be a fine cook.

Luisa Tetrazzini, who refused to diet ("it would make my face sag"), was a cheerful and generous woman, a wonderful singer and cook who had a very busy love life. In addition to her husband she would often spot an attractive man and invite him back to her suite for a meal and a night of love, sometimes with her husband (who was a conductor) present and sometimes not. When she performed in different cities she insisted on having a kitchen as part of her accommodations. In London she stayed in suite 412 at the Savoy Hotel. She was from Tuscany and her standard meal (just one of many consumed each day) was a big bowl of tagliarini pasta and a bottle of Chianti, whose tannins seemed to have no negative effect on her voice. What she did avoid were spices and fried foods, which she believed were bad for the vocal cords. It is very likely that the soprano had a hand in creating a dish known as Turkey Tetrazzini, a combination of pasta, pieces of turkey, mushrooms, milk, butter, flour, Parmigiano-Reggiano and chicken broth. There are so many versions and corruptions of the recipe, but it seems that Tetrazzini created this dish in San Francisco, where she often sang and enjoyed a huge audience. In 1910, she gave an outdoor concert there to more than 100,000 people, and without the benefit of microphones.

There are many dishes, whether created by chefs, musicians or anonymous cooks, which connote singers, operas or composers. Very famous is *pasta alla Norma*, made with aubergine (eggplant), tomatoes and ricotta salata. It is the favourite dish in Catania, Sicily, the birthplace of Vincenzo Bellini (1801-1835), whose masterpiece is the opera called *Norma*. For many, *Norma* has the most beautiful music of any opera.

Once upon a time, top chefs vied to create recipes to honour singers who were appearing at the local opera house. The most famous was Auguste Escoffier (1846-1935), who cooked at the Ritz Hotel in Paris and the Savoy and Carleton Hotels in London. Escoffier was a legendary chef not only because of his gifts in the kitchen but because he understood that being a mere technician was not enough. Like opera singers and most creative artists, Escoffier believed in being attuned to life, taking everything in so as to have in memory ideas and references for when they might be required. He said, 'As far as cuisine is concerned, one must read everything, see everything, hear everything, try everything, observe everything, in order to retain, in the end, just a little bit.' Think of it as you would in making a stock: all of the bones, meat, fennel, radishes, root vegetables and a dash of truffle combine and simmer to produce a broth that is complex and essential. Escoffier's classic book is the *Guide Culinaire*, which is required reading for anyone who wants to learn the fundamentals of the art of cooking when France claimed preeminence in that field. It is also essential for people learning opera, in that Escoffier created dishes in honour of composers, including Bellini, Bizet (who wrote *Carmen*), Donizetti, Gounod (who wrote *Faust*), Massenet, Rossini and Verdi, and many opera characters, including Aïda, Carmen, Otello and Tosca. He also made dishes inspired by singers such as Emma Calvé, Victor Maurel, Sibyl Sanderson and Adelina Patti (1843-1919), who was the inspiration for *poularde à la diva*, a half-boned chicken stuffed with rice, foie gras and truffles. The singer most closely associated with Escoffier was the Australian soprano Nellie Melba, whose surname was adapted from Melbourne, the city of her birth. For Melba, Escoffier named the dessert *peach Melba* (flambéed peaches, vanilla ice cream and a topping of puréed fresh raspberries) and many other dishes. Melba struggled with her weight for years and, it should not surprise you, her weight won. A doctor she consulted suggested she could slim down by subsisting primarily on dry toast. Escoffier had recently created a way of slicing bread thin and toasting it twice so that it would be crisp. He presented it to the diva and thus was born Melba toast. They likely did not enable her to lose much weight - for such a bland food they can be curiously addictive and, ultimately, not very pleasing. One wants to put rich food on top of them.

Food and drink make appearances in the plots and stories of numerous operas, although they seldom have the centrality a gastronome might wish for. The simple reason for this is that opera singers cannot eat and sing at the same time and they do not want any bits of food to catch in their teeth or throats, coat their tongues or prickle the linings of their cheeks. As often as not, singers mime eating and, if they must eat something, it is often a piece of soft apple that has been peeled and then cut into the shape of the food it represents. Other foods for the stage are made of banana that is carved or sliced to resemble the item that is called for in the libretto. Large foods, such as a joint of beef or a roasted turkey, are made of plastic and painted to resemble the real thing. If a singer must eat a piece of this, the facsimile food (made of apple, banana or something else) will be cut and coloured and placed next to the plastic model. Property men or woman, those persons who produce 'props' that are used onstage, are most creative at making food facsimiles that can be easily consumed without complicating the act of singing. Dark berry jams are surrogates for caviar in fancy party scenes. Strawberry preserve is a stand-in for some red foods. Half of a poached apricot (typically made from dried fruit) atop blancmange suggests a cooked egg.

The food served at the wedding of the Japanese teenager Cio-Cio-San (Puccini's Madama Butterfly) to the American Navy man, Benjamin Franklin Pinkerton, is described by the groom as 'flies in aspic and beetles and bumble-bee jelly', none of which is served onstage. In fact, it is extremely rare to see any food served in productions of *Madama Butterfly* apart from the occasional cup of tea.

There is more latitude in depicting beverages onstage. Red wines are suggested with coloured water or diluted grape or cranberry juice. White wines might actually be a glass of diluted apple juice or lukewarm tea. Ginger ale or other sodas become a surrogate for Champagne. When beer is supposed to be consumed in an opera, such as in the tavern scene in Offenbach's *Les Contes d'Hoffmann* (The Tales of Hoffmann), metal steins are passed about and performers pretend to quaff with pleasure.

An opera that is inextricably linked with wine is Gaetano Donizetti's bittersweet *L'Elisir d'Amore* (The Elixir of Love). This is the story of the poor, illiterate Nemorino, who pines for Adina, a well-schooled young woman who, unlike most, knows how to read. She also owns land on which food is grown. Her achievements stand in contrast to the rustic Nemorino but he, being a tenor, has some of the best music. A charlatan arrives in town promising to have an elixir that cures everything. In fact, it is inexpensive Bordeaux which, when consumed in enough quantities, can make even the most unlikely people fall in love. And so it happens in this beautiful opera, which is rare in that it has a happy ending.

In Pietro Mascagni's perfect one-act tragedy, *Cavalleria Rusticana*, wine figures in important ways. Set in a small Sicilian town, it is the story of Santuzza and Turiddu, the man who impregnated her and then rejected her. He goes on to seduce another woman, who is married. According to the social codes of that time and place, he must be killed. His mother, Mamma Lucia, owns a small tavern and serves food and strong local wine. At the end of the opera, when his fate is inevitable, he sings, "Mamma, quel vino é generoso" about how powerful his last glass of wine is that he has consumed to prepare for his inevitable demise. It is a highly dramatic scene.

In Mozart's peerless opera, *Don Giovanni*, with a libretto by Lorenzo da Ponte, the title character murders the father of Donna Anna just after seducing her. The Don then goes on a maniacal pursuit of women to take to bed, often using his servant Leporello to set the table for these seductions. In the famous Champagne aria, the Don tells Leporello to spare no expense in throwing a party full of village girls for him to pick from. This opera, which many experts consider the very best of all (if there can be only one 'best' opera), combines realism and the supernatural, rollicking cynical humour with high tragedy, plus generous helpings of food, drink and sex. And the music is phenomenal. What more could one ask for? At the end of the opera, the Don has invited the 'Stone Guest', the sculpture from atop the tomb of Donna Anna's father that comes to life just long enough to come to dinner and then exact his revenge on Giovanni. Even if someone has no experience with opera, this scene is unforgettably mind-blowing.

It is important, always, to remember that good, healthful, tasty food is a life-sustaining gift that is not readily available to more than a billion people in the world each day. Hunger to them is a painfully enduring fact of life. There is an opera, perhaps an unexpected one, in which hunger is central to the story of the two title characters. *Hänsel und Gretel,* by Engelbert Humperdinck (1854-1921) – the composer, not the British pop singer – is the story of two children with little to eat at home who venture into the forest and are led to dangerous places in their search for food. When looked at through the prism of hunger, *Hänsel und Gretel* is powerfully affecting, rather than being the oddly cute tale of a resourceful brother and sister who free themselves from the grasp of a witch who wants to cook and eat them. Food metaphors and representations appear throughout the opera and the team of stage director and designers who undertake a new production often go over the top in this regard. But other productions respect and are informed by the words and music of this great opera, which should be used as a teaching tool for children on the subjects of opera as well as hunger.

In George and Ira Gershwin's *Porgy and Bess,* the characters are desperately poor but some of them might purchase honey, strawberries or devilled crab from itinerant vendors singing gorgeous music as they offer their wares. This is one of the most sensual evocations of food in all of opera.

Giacomo Puccini's *La Bohéme* is one of the most popular operas of all. It is remembered by most operagoers as the story of two young people, Rodolfo and Mimì, who meet and fall instantly in love in 1830s Paris. Rodolfo is a writer who lives in an unheated garrett with three male friends, one a painter, another a musician, the third a philosopher. This group of Bohemians, which also includes a lively young woman named Musetta, strategize to find enough to eat. In the last act the fellows try to make light of the fact that there is nothing to eat and matters get worse when Mimì, near death, arrives. She expires as the others watch, helpless to do anything. The music is so beautiful that the tragic nature of the story often escapes modern opera audiences, most of whom do not worry about finding enough to eat. And yet, hunger is a human drama that should never be far from our thoughts.

The traditions of food, wine and opera are not limited to those who write these works or perform in them. Audiences the world over enjoy meals and libations before, during and after performances. The truly knowledgeable, both in terms of those who want to enjoy their operas and their food, know that the smartest thing is to eat just enough before the performance so that being hungry will not be an issue, to then have a small bite during an interval (intermission) and then another small bite, perhaps something sweet, after the performance. In other words, eat as an opera singer might. Those operagoers who do not know better might eat a large meal and pair it with cocktails and wine, perhaps after a day of work, and then promptly fall asleep and miss the performance. This verges on tragedy and is a big disappointment for someone who has looked forward to hearing great singers fill an auditorium with glorious music. A feast before the opera is sure to ruin the opera for you.

Many opera houses sell good, tasty food that appeals to the palate without overwhelming the digestive system. The Bavarian State Opera in Munich has delicious items such as cherry juice and little sandwiches filled with crab or ham and cheese. At the Royal Opera in Stockholm, one can purchase (often by prearrangement for the interval) a platter with herring and smoked salmon. Almost the entire audience at Amsterdam's Musiktheater will spend just a few euros at the interval for a bowl of soup or a small sandwich and a cup of coffee. The elegant bar next to Milan's La Scala prepares exquisite, saffron-scented *risotto alla milanese* which is ladled into small bowls and consumed standing up before the opera and at the first interval. The Lyric Opera of Chicago has two restaurants that serve small meals before and after performances. The food is not haute cuisine but is tasty and pleasing. Other opera houses have restaurants that propose grand dining but the cooking usually falls short of what one would find in restaurants that are entirely about eating. These opera house dining places must, of necessity, give primacy to getting customers out of the restaurant and to their seats on time. In almost every opera house, latecomers are not seated as this would disturb audience members already in their seats. This priority does not necessarily suit chefs who care about cooking on a schedule that is convenient for them.

In an ideal world, operagoers would eat just enough before a performance to stave off hunger and then have a delicious small meal after. Yet, in modern times, as people work longer hours, the post-opera supper has become less common. Some cities are more geared to this practice. In Vienna, the tradition of tasty eating after an opera is called *souper*. Several restaurants near the Vienna State Opera remain open for operagoers to have a small Wiener schnitzel or a bowl of goulash and a glass of good local wine while analyzing the performance they just attended. There are two very popular wurst kiosks across the street from the Opera where hardcore Viennese opera fans engage in spirited arguments about the relative merits of different performers while biting into a juicy *Käsekrainer* and drinking a beer.

In Paris, the post-opera custom might be a platter of coquillages (mixed crustaceans) on ice or simply six or a dozen oysters and a glass of Muscadet. In New York, those who go out after a performance at the Metropolitan Opera often have thin crust pizza or a platter with cooked vegetables and seafood or perhaps fresh mozzarella and sliced prosciutto. In some cities, including New York and Vienna, it is not uncommon for operagoers to have their post-performance meal in a restaurant seated at the next table from the singer who, onstage, just met a tragic death. It is one of the miracles of opera that these performers are not only resurrected when they take their curtain calls but discover they are ravenously hungry and seek a meal to restore themselves after their exertions.

Not everyone who loves opera can hope to be a performer – the gifts and good luck required come to very few of us. Most anyone can learn the fundamentals of cookery but, like opera, it takes hard work, sensitivity, sacrifice and a love of tradition to excel at it. Those who write or perform in opera for the public, like those who endeavour to cook for the public, understand that these pursuits are a combination of art with a generous expression of love.

In Puccini's *Tosca*, the title character sings an aria in the second act in which she says "Vissi d'arte, vissi d'amore" (I lived for art, I lived for love), which could be the motto for people of all types who seek to create things that give beauty, pleasure and sustenance. Tosca's adversary is Baron Scarpia, who has imprisoned her lover, Mario. She comes to seek Mario's freedom, interrupting the Baron's dinner. In perhaps the most famous conjunction of food and opera, he leaves the table and tells her that Mario will be freed if she will have sex with him. He offers Spanish wine to calm her nerves. At first, she consents but finds the prospect so repellent that, when she sees a carving knife next to his meal on the table, she grabs it and kills him. Ultimately, *Tosca* is about passion, that mysterious and fundamental ingredient that enriches the experiences and work of anyone who lives life to the fullest, which is what opera is about, what food and drink are about, and which, sad to say, is always in short supply in our modern world.

If you find your passion, then every aspect of what you do, whether it is more truffle or more radish, will result in *un'opera lirica* – a lyrical work.

Selling culture:
The Growth of Wine Tourism

Damien Wilson

Damien Wilson runs the MSC in Wine Business at the Burgundy School of Business. He is a prolific researcher and writer and engages with consumers via radio and television with as much ease as he teaches students face-to-face or online. Marrying a new-world perspective of the wine industry with an old-world taste for product excellence, Dr Wilson drew from his academic education and solid professional background in wine marketing to create the MSc in Wine Business in 2009. The programme has gone from strength to strength and enjoys worldwide recognition.

We've learned that tourists look for a short-term change in their lives; a sense of excitement in the unfamiliar, and to live life of 'the other' albeit briefly (Ooi & Laing, 2010; Smith et al., 2010; Getz & Cheyne, 1997). Tourists actively search for experiences that enrich their lives.

'Tourists bring money and jobs to [a] local economy' (Xie, 2011, p. 162); but this new-found commercial appeal, while it might deliver economic development, is a two-edged sword. As any local economy grows, the spending power of tourists inflates prices, affecting the capacity of local communities to maintain their lives in their traditional manner. The charm of an authentic experience of life in another culture quickly begins to wane once tourist services overtake local culture. In essence, the commodification of culture can damage the lived experience of indigenous people.

The challenge for an increasing number of wine regions is to balance the need for economic growth through tourism with the requirement to maintain the very traditions that stimulate tourist demand. In this chapter I explore the need for authenticity in the wine tourism experience, using three case studies to highlight different approaches. They illustrate that wine is part of the appeal of local culture, but that alone it is insufficient to generate significant levels of tourist activity. The provision of additional services is an essential prerequisite for making tourism a profitable pursuit for the wine businesses. Additionally, although the provision of services may directly affect the perceived authenticity of wine producing regions, a balanced approach can result in the maintenance of cultural authenticity alongside economic growth.

Traditionally, the simple process of tending to grapes and making wine, largely for local consumption, was motive enough for the vigneron. Increasingly, the explicit communication of cultural integrity and authenticity, however they might be defined, has become central to sustainability and growth. And a certain form of tourism, built upon the distinctive cultural characteristics of particular locations, lends itself to many wine producing regions.

Cultural authenticity in wine tourism

While some still challenge the existence of wine tourism as an identifiable category (Wangbickler, 2012), commentary on the topic has grown considerably in recent years. Central to studies, such as those conducted in Australia (O'Neil and Charters, 2000), is the concept of authenticity – what does it mean, how is it maintained, and what are the benefits of it to consumers and producers?

The proposal that wine regions need to communicate their authenticity in their offer to tourists has been explored, in the context of France, by Frochot (2003), who reveals evidence from numerous surveys on the importance of gastronomy, including wine, as a motive for tourist activity. Despite the central role of gastronomy in French culture, it seems to be relatively inconsequential in the minds of tourists. However, linked to the concept of *authenticity*, encompassing *history*, *tradition* and *nature*, it takes on greater importance and meaning. It is also crucial to the marketing of specific regions: 'most of the messages portrayed ... have an indirect meaning of authenticity and traditions [for] these French regions. [These confer] ... the wish by regions to ascertain their cultural uniqueness but also the authenticity of their assets to attract potential visitors.' (Frochot, 2003: 91)

Expressing food and wine tourism as culture

The concept of wine and food tourism has changed markedly over the years, from travelling for the simple pleasures associated with consumption, to encompass a more formal educational dimension (Cohen & Avieli, 2004; Frochot, 2003). Through research undertaken with representatives of wineries and regional tourist boards in the United States, New Zealand, Australia, France and Portugal, Frochot (2003) highlights common tactics used to attract wine tourists, and in doing so reveals the manner in which wine tourism has developed. For example, dedicated visitor centres for wine tourists, which provide information on regional history and products, and well-signed wine routes, are now commonplace.

Despite the increasing sophistication of the tourist infra-structure, challenges remain. While tourists often have rose-tinted perceptions of culturally 'authentic' wine experiences, wine-makers often bemoan the disruptive impact of visitors and do not successfully adapt their approach to meet the demands of a new audience. This fuels frustration amongst tourists, who encounter a distinction between their expectations and reality. In a sense, the efforts of wine-makers to maintain true authenticity, rather than a distilled or contrived interpretation, prove problematic.

Observations on food tourism can enhance our understanding of the potential of wine tourism. 'Food means more than eating. Food relates to issues of identity, culture, production, consumption and, increasingly, issues of sustainability' (Hall & R. Mitchell, 2000: 29).

In reference to the symbolic value of food, it can only be considered part of local gastronomy (i.e., be accepted as such) if it is adopted, as characteristic, by the inhabitants of a region/country (Bourdieu, 1979 in Frochot, 2003). The dislike of certain Asian countries for cheese, the British repulsion for snails or the dislike of the French for haggis, confirm that food is culturally conditioned. 'Men do not eat what they like, they eat what they are used to' (Bourdieu, 1979, 345 in Frochot, 2003).

Further, food defines cultural identity for inhabitants of particular regions and becomes a unifying trait (Bourdieu, 1979; Ryan, 1997). This also implies that food can be a strong identifying theme in tourism promotion: 'Food is therefore intimately tied up with the production and consumption of the cultural meaning of place and space' (Hall & R. Mitchell, 2000: 35). This remains the case in France, 'where the identity of its regions is tightly linked to the local production of specific food products, wines and regional cuisine.' (Frochot, 2003: 81) For foreign visitors to France, knowledge of local recipes and embedded food habits can be used to affirm status among peers. Food acts as a form of cultural communication, and the way in which it is eaten and shared creates strong social bonds (Poulain, 1996; Ryan, 1997 in Frochot, 2003). Thus by eating local food and sharing it with local inhabitants in a genuine setting, the tourist becomes an actor within that culture instead of a simple spectator (Frochot, 2003). '…one can clearly see that most of the existing motivations pertaining to tourism consumption can be experienced through a culinary experience' (Frochot, 2003: 82). Food tourism is positioned as providing opportunities for tourists to relax in typical restaurants and cafes; to experience the excitement of trying new food and new dining scenarios; to escape the pressures of everyday life; to acquire social and cultural capital; and to engage in educational activities.

Frochot (2003) argues that food tourism can be used to reinforce destinations' cultural distinctiveness, and to shape their identity in the tourist market. 'In the Riviera, the image of chefs, palaces and restaurants is associated to that of *luxury*, […] while in Burgundy it is more closely linked to its true rural and traditional dimension and of course to its long term reputation of a land for gastronomes.' (Frochot, 2003: 93)

It should also be noted that while food and drink might play a central role in shaping the tourist experience, they are not themselves sufficient to meet the diverse needs of tourists. As Carlsen (2004: 7) notes, 'the notion that a discrete wine tourism market exists within domestic and international tourism markets needs to be questioned.' Williams (2001), in a study in Canada, also noted the increasing use in wine tourism brochures of other leisure and recreational pursuits. Equally, the development of wine trails that integrate visits to heritage monuments and tourist sites testify to this secondary role (Frochot, 2000). In other words, 'food and wine represent a strong unifying theme for a tourism product but probably not its core appeal' (Frochot, 2003: 80).

Applied wine tourism – three contemporary cases

As the wine sector is being adapted, and presented as an authentic component of regional culture, its role in tourism is growing. Analysis of wine tourism strategies of these regions reveals how wine is integrated within broader tourist experiences and how it is used to stimulate visitor numbers.

Discussions with wine sector representatives in France, Italy, Australia, South Africa, Chile and the United States invariably turn to tourism as a potential revenue stream. Even a region as isolated, and topographically non-descript as Coonawarra in Australia has unique geology, historical architecture, a racecourse, local caves and a welcoming local culture, to go with its world-class wines.

With attractions such as this historic, unused railway station (Figure 1), clearly wines aren't the only source of appeal. However, with Coonawarra also being a four-hour drive away from both of the nearest state capitals, Melbourne and Adelaide, attracting tourists there would be significantly more challenging than to a picturesque, and comparatively more accessible region. Tourists don't just pass by the region, wine tourists plan to stay there as part of their holiday experience (O'Mahoney et al., 2005; Bruwer et al., 2002). As wine increasingly becomes a lifestyle beverage and more acceptable and desired by a wider spectrum of consumers, there is a greater need to understand wine consumer values, consumption patterns and profiles. This research recognises that lifestyle is inextricably linked to values and the processes by which people seek to achieve their values through various modes of expression, including the consumption of wine.

Figure 1: Coonawarra railway station. Image courtesy of the Coonawarra Vignerons Association

Consider the difference in application of wine tourism for a region like Cinque-Terra in Italy, which has stunning natural beauty, is serviced regularly by trains and incorporates a well-travelled tourist path. The fact that wine has been made in the region for centuries, on steeply terraced slopes, is simply an additional appeal for tourists. Thus, for regions with innate appeal, accessibility and strong associations with wine, the delivery of a diverse tourism product is less challenging.

Figure 2: Dusk photo of Cinque Terre provided courtesy of Antonella Petitti

Case one: Burgundy

'Wine tourists and visitors to wine regions can be viewed as actual or potential consumers of a lifestyle beverage, who visit wine regions in order to have wine-related experiences' (Alant & Bruwer, 2004: 27). An exploratory wine tourism research study in the Coonawarra and McLaren Vale wine regions in South Australia measured the motivations for engaging in wine tourism and specific behaviours. The results of the study are exposited by means of a suggested conceptual motivational framework for wine tourism. The framework is a simple constant consisting of three main dimensions: the Visitor, Wine Region and Visit Dynamic (viewed in terms of first-time or repeat visitation).

It is impossible for any visitor to France to escape the fact that the country is defined by its gastronomic heritage. When in 1962, General de Gaulle highlighted the challenge of presiding over a country with more than 246 cheeses, he may not have been aware of how valuable his words would prove to be in attracting visitors. The diversity of wine regions is equally appealing.

France is the most popular tourist destination in the world (UNWTO, 2012) and wine is one of its most defining products. This would seem to provide the perfect platform for the development of successful wine tourism. However, this cannot be achieved without a supportive infra-structure. The case of Burgundy, one of France's most popular wine regions, has been used as a case in point.

Burgundy is a region that is well-known within France for its gastronomy and rich local history. The best wines of Burgundy are some of the most expensive in the world, and many of its vineyards are clearly marked and easily accessible.

Burgundy also has historically important towns – Dijon and Beaune – an abundance of bicycle and walking trails, rivers and lakes for recreational activities and numerous national parks. The region is accessible by high-speed train in less than two hours from Paris, and tourists can easily cross the region via the motorway, or the picturesque wine roads. There are many châteaux, of interest to those fascinated by Burgundian bourgeois history. So Burgundy has wine, beautiful scenery and an extensive array of attractions for tourists. It should be an ideal region in which wine tourism can prosper.

Discussing the appeal of wine tourism in Burgundy with representatives of the tourism office and regional associations, as well as a small number of wine producers, suggests that there is still a lot to do in regard to developing wine tourism. The tourist who drives south from Dijon could be left in no doubt about the commercial focus of Burgundy. From the outskirts of Dijon, in Marsannay-Les-Côte, and all the way south via RN74 to the picturesque town of Mâcon, the road is almost universally flanked by vineyards.

Although there's little question of the desirability of a region like Burgundy as a destination for the wine enthusiast, when asked about the challenges the region faces in being able to commercialise wine tourism, interviewees high-light: 'a lack of [effective] road signage'. Signs are in place to remind tourists that they are travelling along the 'Route des Grands Crus', but unless they understand what this means, or what those Grands Crus are, such notification is not helpful.

Adding to tourists' confusion, signage between towns, indicating distances from one to another, is rare. Once particular villages have been located, finding specific vineyards can be challenging. Rather than being identified by brand names, as in the New World, vineyards are known by family names.

Even for the tourist who is familiar with the producers' names, booking visits and understanding established conventions can prove impossible. Most wine producers open only by appointment. They can vet their potential visitors to assess their potential value to the business, and permit or restrict access on this basis. Whilst this may help to cut the costs of wastage, and ensure there are no 'unnecessary' interruptions, it is hardly conducive to establishing a loyal customer base. Remaining closed to passing tourists means that wineries must rely on agents and existing clients to encourage new business. For those that proclaim to be open for visitors, open appears to mean "please come to our premises. If someone happens to be available to receive you then they will", as opposed to being open and welcoming, come what may.

One of the major disappointments expressed by respondents, who had been unannounced visitors to a winery, was the lack of a warm welcome. Even when there is a staff member available, they are almost exclusively working in another capacity. The requirement to attend to customers appears to be a distraction from more important tasks – a 'necessary evil', as opposed to a profitable part of business. Further, employees indicated that training in service skills and attention to customer needs are frequently identified in job descriptions, but are never tested, nor are they considered to be mandatory requirements of employment.

In French culture, the customer must remember that the vigneron is an artisan. Therefore, his wines must be respected and appreciated, like all good works of art. Until a customer illustrates such understanding, the vigneron feels little. Consequently, there will be a very limited range of wines for new and undeserving customers to try. Only those customers who have an existing relationship with the business deserve the best service and access to the full range of wines. As one English respondent commented:

"We knew where we wanted to go. We had the address plugged into our sat-nav, but when we arrived at the destination, it was a private [and unrelated] residence. After heading to the tourism office, they provided us with the same address, only to show us on the local map that the correct street name was a hyphenated version of what we already had. To make matters worse, when we finally arrived, the winery wouldn't see us because we didn't have an appointment. When we told them that our brochure said one was unnecessary, they responded by saying the new brochure says otherwise. We travelled more than 600 miles to visit this place because we liked their wine, only to find out they didn't care! We could have gone to Spain for the sunshine instead!"

Case Two: Napa Valley

The experience for tourists in the Napa Valley is somewhat different. Travelling from San Francisco along Highway 1 provides easy access to the USA's most famous wine region. Joining Highway 29, which runs through the valley, regular signs indicate individual wineries and provide reliable directions to appealing locations. In Napa itself, friendly and well-informed staff in a centrally located tourist office are able to offer useful advice. The only challenge is negotiating the traffic – a reflection of the region's popularity.

On arrival at every winery there are either welcoming staff, or clear signs indicating what visitors need to do to attract the attention of staff. If the winery charges for a wine tasting it is clearly communicated.

"What struck me the most about V Sattui is that I had never heard of the winery before coming here [the Napa Valley]. I'm not super educated about this region (yet) but I still feel like I recognize a lot of the big names from wine lists and retail shelves. So why didn't I know V Sattui? Check out that photo [...] and look closely. Do you see it? The sign? 'V Sattui wines are sold ONLY at the winery'." (O'Connell, 2012).

This is an example of a winery that used tourism as its only means of distribution. All wines from V Sattui are sold directly from the winery. As O'Connell (2012) explains, the winery has developed 'tourism to the point where it replaces wine's traditional path to market'. The V Sattui winery has put in place an array of appealing and consistent features that cater specifically to the wine tourist. Not only is there ample parking, but also the provision barbecue facilities and a shop selling local foods.

Figure 3: Promotional image of Domaine des Beaumont, Morey-Saint-Denis, France. Image courtesy of Vincent Beaumont, Domaine des Beaumont.

Figure 4: Promotional image of tasting room of V Sattui winery, Napa, USA. ...ge courtesy of Ryan O'Connell, Domaine O'Vineyards.

Promotional images used by two regions to stimulate wine tourism provide a clear indication of the very different approaches that are adopted. The image of a winery at Domaine des Beaumont, in Burgundy, is regarded as sufficient to attract tourists, given that it is located in the well-known and highly regarded Appellation of Morey-Saint-Denis, in the Côte de Nuits.

The owners of the winery request visits by appointment only. For the enthusiast who fails to prepare in advance, Domaine des Beaumont's wines are also available at a tasting room in the centre of town, along with other local wines. A sign on the entrance gate communicates this to visitors

The image in Figure 4 was taken by winemaker Ryan O'Connell, author of *Love that Languedoc*, on a fact-finding mission to the Napa Valley. During his visit to V Sattui in the Napa Valley, he recognised that in addition to selling wine, they had much else for sale that appealed to tourists, including cheeses, olive oil and clothing. V Sattui also promotes its accessibility via a Twitter account, encouraging social interaction with followers, and supporting real-time promotion. What's more, V Sattui produces more than 500,000 bottles of wine a year, and these are only available through the winery. Such volume of sales requires a lot of tourists!

Case Three: Coonawarra Destination

Between the extremes of product-focused and visitor-focused wine tourism, certain regions face particular challenges. Not big enough to attract tourists, or not known well enough to attract wine enthusiasts, the development of wine tourism requires distinctive and innovative approaches. A focus on the local market can prove successful. With over 80% of tourists to a wine region travelling for no more than two hours, the possibility of exploiting local interest to provide a market for wine tourism experiences is greater than that for the international market (O'Mahoney et al., 2005).

But what if the local population is in the hundreds, rather than the millions? For such regions wanting to develop wine tourism, the prospect of attracting regular visitors and day-trippers is low (Bruwer and Johnson, 2010; O'Mahoney et al., 2005). The logical alternative is to design a wine tourism offer that engages the tourist in local culture, and encourages them to stay for an extended period.

Coonawarra has always been an agricultural centre. It began as an orange grove in the mid-19th Century, but has been a wine-producing region since the early part of the 20th Century. It is well serviced by the small town of Penola and is roughly equidistant between two major Australian cities. Accordingly, Coonawarra is primarily on a tourist drive as opposed to being a region that is itself frequented by travellers.

The Coonawarra Vignerons Association (CVA) has encouraged the creation of tourism facilities and stages a series of events that appeal to the segments of the market that drink wines from the region. Of the six annual events, one sees Coonawarra vignerons travel to the major centres around the country to 'bring Coonawarra to the consumers'. The annual race day attracts more than 3000 people to the local township. Given that the township's usual population is closer to 500, this is quite significant. Although the revenue from the event is crucial, of more value is the goodwill generated, the loyalty established and on-going sales. Visitors comment on the joy of the occasion and 'how a rural township on the fringes of the country can for one day can feel like you're living in the centre of the Universe'.

Figure 4: A day at the races. Image courtesy of the Coonawarra Vignerons Association

Planning for these events begins a year in advance. Accommodation and the provision of facilities for visitors is the greatest challenge. However, most wineries elect to provide accommodation for visitors, and many local residents offer rooms in their homes to meet demand. Such experiences, built around immersion in a community dedicated to wine production, are seldom possible for tourists.

Service culture: A conflict with authentic wine culture?

As noted earlier, one of the key elements that distinguish successful tourism is the provision of services. While the regional associations in Burgundy are doing what they can to stimulate wine tourism, accessibility, levels of customer service and the breadth of products on offer are insufficient to satisfy tourists' needs.

Vignerons argue that their refusal to implement better signage and improved facilities reflects their desire to maintain the authenticity of local culture, as these features would be added for tourists, not locals (Rusher, 2003; Urry, 1990). Residents 'know' where wineries are, and the provision of public communications affects both the ambiance of the region and the impression of authenticity. Traditionalists may fear the commodification of wine, and pour scorn on the Napa Valley for representing an insincere approach.

The counter argument from the sales and tourism literature is more compelling: tourists want to take memories with them of their experience (Page, 1995). Further, earlier research in purchasing behaviour illustrated that variety-seeking consumers actively purchase competing brands (Lattin and McAlister, 1985). Most tourists that visit a wine region intend to visit at least two, and up to six different wineries a day (O'Mahoney et al., 2005). With the tourist already planning to visit a number of different competitors, there is every expectation that the tourist requires more than wine during a day-trip, or short-stay in the region. Accordingly, providing facilities and products that enhance tourist stays is good marketing practice. Encouraging the improved encoding and potential retrieval of the tourism experience encourages repeat sales (Whittlesea, 2002; Bettman, 1979).

The growth in wine tourism: An evocation of culture

'This […] is a shifting of emphasis away from authenticity of a [niche] culture, an issue widely discussed by tourism researchers, to the processes of authenticating [the] culture. It focuses on what authentication is, how it works, who is involved and what are the problems in the process. It aims to examine who authenticates [niche] tourism rather than to assess adherence to some absolute and arbitrary standard of authenticity of tourism products and experiences.' (Xie, 2011: xiii) The question must then be posed: 'how can wine regions develop their offer to appeal to the needs of tourists?' The factors that must be taken into account include visitor types, the facilities provided, the community's capacity to deliver, pricing strategies, brand awareness, and cellar door media coverage (Carlsen, 2004).

The search for authenticity in the tourist's gaze can be illustrated through a contemporary interpretation of a traditional phenomenon. 'Using the example of Mickey Mouse's 'home culture' as evidenced in Hong Kong's Disneyland park shows how an authentic cultural icon from a foreign culture can be adapted to cater more effectively to a foreign culture, and in so doing be better received, and regarded as an authentic example of an home cultural representation' (Xie, 2011: 34).

An analogy to the experience in the wine sector is to look at what's happened to wine tourism in non-European countries. As in the case above, in which Mickey Mouse is a representation of authentic American culture and 'McDonaldization' is the product of postmodernism; to be implemented effectively, the principles of wine tourism require a highly credible wine product, with the application of services being seen as a New World iteration from old-world traditions. Therefore attempts to apply traditional authenticity onto a new-world wine region are, by definition, futile.

On the flip side, we see the wine sector encouraging wine tourists to seek 'experiential authenticity' in new regions where the original wines are no longer meaningful. The authenticity now sought of the modern wine experience centres on being believable for the tourist rather than being original (Xie, 2011).

Consequently, we find that the tourist is attracted to the authenticity of wine's adopted image in the new culture. Irrespective of how long the tourist remains in contact with the foreign culture, the importance of authenticity in the wine experience is to stimulate memories of 'real' wine regions. The development of facilities that cater to tourists, as opposed to the local culture, is one way that the tourist measures the 'reality' of their experience. Accordingly, the more distinct the local culture is from a 'tourist culture' the more difficult it becomes to implement 'real' cultural experiences for the tourist.

The challenge for any wine region is that most have never been designed for the attention of tourists. Vineyards and wineries are almost exclusively located in regions assigned to agriculture. By definition, such regions are designed for farmers, in which agricultural practices dominate. Tourists have seldom been a consideration for any farmer, at any time in history (Correla et al., 2004; Frochot, 2002). Grape-growing is an authentic part of rural culture, irrespective of the era. Tourism is not.

However, the past thirty years have borne witness to a change in this oft-neglected element of agro-business (Preston, 2008). While grape growers traditionally produced wine for their families, with surplus being sold to the local cooperative, the importance of wine tourism to a region is increasingly being recognised in the creation of specialized local and regional organisations (Correla et al., 2004). These regional identities become the public image of local cultures, promoted by tourist agencies to stimulate visitor numbers (Preston, 2008).

Wine tourism is often seen as the primary path to regional development (Jaffe & Pasternak, 2004). By providing services in addition to the basic product, a simple commodity can achieve greatly enhanced value. As explained in Marzo-Navarro and Pedraja-Iglesias (Marzo-Navarro & Pedraja-

Iglesias, 2012), services and the destination are the primary incentives for tourists wanting to visit a wine region. The wine producer must ensure that there is sufficient interest in the wine. Such a task is facilitated by the region's cultural attachment to wine.

Conclusion

The importance of wine as a tourism product for the wine enthusiast cannot be understated. However, to assume that all wine drinkers could be classified as wine enthusiasts would be incorrect. It has been found that an understanding of the consumer's level of interest in a product or service can help identify motivations and price sensitivities (Zaichkowsky, 1985; Mitchell, 1979). As wine may be considered important to a number of such enthusiasts; tradition, purity, arts and crafts and other interests may be more popular for those tourists without such a core interest in wine. Accordingly, a wine region's capacity to evaluate tourists' level of involvement with its products and services will go a long way to developing appealing tourism experiences (Novelli, 2005; O'Mahoney et al., 2005).

Even though wine may be an integral part of a region's attraction, it is invariably considered as part of the holistic tourism experience. Wine regions with intrinsic natural beauty, like Cinque Terre and the Rheingau, will attract tourists who may happen to have an interest in wine. Providing helpful and easy access to wineries and having complementary relationships with local service providers are essential for sustaining revenue streams. Regions that aren't blessed with natural attractions need to focus more heavily on the tourist. The creation of culturally relevant events can be used effectively to help generate tourism.

Our knowledge of the needs of the wine tourist is not well developed. Wangbickler (2012) explained that it is premature to develop specific marketing strategies for wine tourists, when those in the wine sector can't even agree on what constitutes wine tourism. If authenticity was the key motivator, then wine tourism should be the domain of the more traditional wine producing countries like France and Italy, rather than regions like the Napa Valley. Yet the case studies showed that France lacks effective infrastructure to cater to tourists, whilst the Napa Valley has developed in accordance with tourists needs.

What remains to be explained is how a new-world wine producer can rely uniquely on wine tourist revenue while European wine producers, with better reputations as wine-producing regions and higher tourist numbers, struggle to accommodate tourists. Although there is ample appeal for tourists to visit European regions, the inability of such regions to support tourism is a cause for concern. Service failure is highlighted as an explanation, but the impact of heightened expectations of tourists visiting European wine regions in comparison to the expectations of tourists in new-world regions also requires attention.

Perceived authenticity may appeal to tourists in wine regions, but it is the service they receive that determines whether they value experiences or not. Regions attracting tourists that have the infrastructure to deliver appropriate services have the potential to develop their reputation and success (Boniface, 2003).

References

Alant, K. & Bruwer, J. (2004) Wine tourism behaviour in the context of a motivational framework for wine regions and cellar doors, *Journal of Wine Research*, **15**(1), 27–37.

Beer, S., Edwards, J., Fernandes, C. and Sampaio, F. (2002) Regional food cultures: integral to the rural tourism product, in Hjalager, A.-M. and Richards, G. (Ed.), *Tourism and Gastronomy*. London and New York: Routledge, pp. 207-223

Bettman, J. R. (1979) Memory factors in consumer choice, *Reviews research & theory on human memory*, **43**, 37–53.

Boniface, P. (2003) The wine dimension, in *Tasting Tourism: Travelling for Food and Drink*, Hampshire, England, UK; Burlington, USA: Ashgate, pp. 131-140

Bruwer, J. and Johnson, R. (2010) Place-based marketing and regional branding strategy perspectives in the California wine industry, *Journal of Consumer Marketing*, **27**(1), 5–16.

Bruwer, J., Li, E. and Reid, M. (2002) Segmentation of the Australian wine market using a wine-related lifestyle approach, *Journal of Wine Research*, **13**(3), 217–242.

Carlsen, J. (2004) A review of global wine tourism research, *Journal of Wine Research*, **15**(1), 5–13.

Cohen, E. and Avieli, N. (2004) Food in tourism: attraction and impediment, *Annals of Tourism Research*, **31**, 755–778.

Correla, L., Passos Ascenção, M. J. and Charters, S. (2004), Wine routes in Portugal: A case study of the Bairrada Wine Route, *Journal of Wine Research*, **15**(1), 15–25.

Eurostat. (2012) National accounts – GDP – statistics explained, *National Accounts - GDP*. April 3rd, 2012 http://epp.eurostat.ec.europa.eu/statistics_explained/index.php/National_accounts_%E2%80%93_GDP

Frochot, I. (2002) Wine tourism in France: A paradox?, in Hall, C. M., Sharples, L., Cambourne, B., and Macionis, N. (Éd.), *Wine Tourism Around the World: Development, Management and Markets*, Oxford, UK: Butterworth Heinemann, pp 67-80

Frochot, I. (2003) An analysis of regional positioning and its associated food images in French tourism regional brochures, *Journal of Travel & Tourism Marketing*, **14**(3/4), 77–96.

Getz, D. & Cheyne, J. (1997) Special event motivations and behaviour, in Ryan, C. (ed.), *The Tourist Experience: A New Introduction*, London: Cassell Publications pp 136-154

Hall, C. M. & Mitchell, R. (2000) We are what we eat: food, tourism and globalization, *Tourism, Culture and Communication*, 29–37.

Hu, Y. & Ritchie, J. R. B. (1993) Measuring destination attractiveness: a contextual approach, *Journal of Travel Research*, **32**(2), 25–34.

Jaffe, E. & Pasternak, H. (2004) Developing wine trails as a tourist attraction in Israel, *International Journal of Tourism Research*, **6**(4), 237–249.

Jenkins, O. H. (1999) Understanding and measuring tourist destination images, *International Journal of Tourism Research*, **1**(1), 1–15.

Lattin, J. M. amd McAlister, L. (1985) 'Using a variety-seeking model to identify substitute and complementary relationships among competing products', *Journal of Marketing Research*, **22**, 330–39.

Marzo-Navarro, M. and Pedraja-Iglesias, M. (2012). Critical factors of wine tourism: incentives and barriers from the potential tourist's perspective, *International Journal of Contemporary Hospitality Management*, **24**(2), 312-34.

Mitchell, A. A. (1979) Involvement: a potentially important mediator of consumer behavior, *Advances in Consumer Research*, **6**, 191–196.

Novelli, M. (2005) *Niche Tourism: Contemporary issues, trends and cases*, Burlington: Elsevier Butterworth-Heinemann.

O'Connell, R. (2012) Wine tourism on Highway 29 in Napa Valley, 14th March 2012, http://kidnapa.posterous.com/wine-tourism-on-highway-29-in-napa-valley

O'Mahoney, Hall, J., Lockshin, L., Jago, L. K. and Brown, G. (2005) Understanding the impact of wine tourism on future purchasing behaviour : wine tourism experiences and future behaviour, Internal-pdf://O'Mahoney et al 2005-3277552128/O'Mahoney et al 2005.pdf

O'Neill, M. & Charters, S. (2000) Service quality at the cellar door: implications for Western Australia's developing wine tourism industry, *Managing Service Quality*, **10**(2), 112–122.

Ooi, N. & Laing, J. H. (2010) Backpacker tourism: sustainable and purposeful? Investigating the overlap between backpacker tourism and volunteer tourism motivations, *Journal of Sustainable Tourism*, **18**(2), 191–206.

Orth, U. R., Stöckl, A., Veale, R., Brouard, J., Cavicchi, A., Faraoni, M., et al. (2011) Using attribution theory to explain tourists' attachments to place-based brands, *Journal of Business Research*, (0), http://www.sciencedirect.com/science/article/pii/S0148296311003717

Page, S. J. (1995) *Urban Tourism*, New York: Routledge.

Preston, D. (2008) Viticulture and winemaking in contemporary rural change: experience from Southern France and Eastern Australia, *Journal of Wine Research*, **19**(3), 159–173.

Rusher, K. (2003) The Bluff Oyster Festival and regional economic development: festival as culture commodified, in Sharples, L., Mitchell, R., Macionis, N., and Cambourne, B. (Éd.), *Food tourism around the world: Development, Management and Markets*, Oxford: Butterworth Heinemann, pp 192-205

Skinner, A. M. (2002) Napa Valley, California: A model of wine region development, in Hall, C. M., Sharples, L., Cambourne, B., andMacionis, N. (Éd.), *Wine Tourism Around the World: Development, Management and Markets*, Oxford: Butterworth Heinemann, pp 283-296

Smith, S., Costello, C. & Muenchen, R. A. (2010) Influence of push and pull motivations on satisfaction and behavioral intentions within a culinary tourism event, *Journal of Quality Assurance in Hospitality & Tourism*, **11**(1), 17–35.

UNWTO. (2012) *Tourism Highlights*, United Nations World Tourism Organisation

Urry, J. (1990) The consumption of tourism, *Sociology*, **24**(1), 23–35.

Urry, J. (1992) The Tourist Gaze revisited, *American Behavioral Scientist*, **36**(2), 172.

Wangbickler, M. (2012) Wine tourism does not exist, in Perrugia, Italy. March 21st, 2012 http://balzac.com/wp/wp-content/uploads/2012/01/Wine-tourism-Does-Not-Exist_convert.pdf

Whittlesea, B. W. A. (2002) Two routes to remembering (and another to remembering not), *Journal of Experimental Psychology: General*, **131**, 325–348.

Xie, P. F. (2011) *Authenticating Ethnic Tourism*, Channel View Publications

Zaichkowsky, J. L. (1985) Measuring the involvement construct, *Journal of Consumer Research*, **12**, 341–52

Food & Drink

Case Studies

Exploring China:
a personal perspective

Ken Hom,
with Donald Sloan

Ken learnt to cook from the age of eleven when he started working in his uncle's Chinese restaurant in Chicago after school and at weekends. In order to help pay his university fees he gave cooking lessons which proved so popular that he was recommended to the Culinary Academy. In 1984, when the BBC was looking for a Chinese chef to produce a new series he was recommended by Madhur Jaffrey who had seen him giving lessons in California. Ken Hom's Chinese Cookery was the start of his UK TV career. Ken is now regarded as the world's leading authority on Chinese cookery.

While I genuinely welcome the public's apparently insatiable appetite for food-related television shows, I am not sure that the continuous diet of light entertainment and culinary competitions does much to extend our collective knowledge. I've had a long-standing ambition to write and present a series that achieves something different – that reveals the complex cultures of China through the universal language of food. With *Exploring China: a Culinary Adventure*, broadcast by the BBC in 2012, I hope that's what Ching He-Huang and I managed to achieve.

Having not been on a substantial trip to China since 1989, this was the perfect time to return. The real China still exists, thank goodness, even although westernisation and relentless progress are nibbling away at traditional ways of life – of cooking food, of eating together, of family life and community ties. We travelled from the wild frontiers of the north to the industrial megacities of the south, and saw the inevitable conflicts between tradition and modernity, between communism and capitalism. We also talked to 'real' people from many different regions, and their evident cultural pride gave me hope for the survival of the 'real' China.

In shaping the structure of the programmes, my starting point had to be personal. My motives for making the series were linked to my family history. I was born to Cantonese parents who had to flee China during the Cultural Revolution. While I grew up in the United States, I did so in a Chinese 'bubble' on the south side of Chicago, so I remained rooted to my cultural heritage. As a child I refused to eat American food, and was sent off to school every day with a lunch box filled with Chinese delicacies. But it was not until I was an adult that I visited China. Travelling to the Cantonese village where my mother was born awakened my desire to learn more about my family's origins and identity.

Tragically, my mother passed away in 2010. This, and my own brush with mortality through contracting prostate cancer, strengthened my desire to reconnect. Could I reconcile the China of yesterday with the country that it's rapidly becoming? Could I achieve emotional closure and find a new sense of belonging?

We recognised that *Exploring China* could not provide a definitive picture of Chinese food – with such scale and diversity this will never be possible. However, with carefully chosen stories from many different locations, we hoped to share our insights on a country that few foreigners understand, despite it containing 20% of the world's population.

Inevitably, it was in Beijing where we witnessed the legacies of both communism and the ancient Imperial dynasties alongside relentless growth and rampant consumerism. It's a city searching for a new identity – something reflected in its ever evolving cuisine. Hit hard by the arrival of communism, the intricate, varied cuisine of the Old Imperial China was swept away when the Red Guards forced restaurants to burn their recipe books and standardise their menus. But thanks to western influence and a growing desire to rediscover cultural authenticity, a new breed of chefs is reinterpreting classic dishes. It is a triumph of the culinary revolution over the Cultural Revolution.

Chef Da Dong, Beijing's unrivalled culinary superstar, is leading this approach. He has travelled extensively, building his knowledge of many of the world's great cuisines. While respectful of Chinese culinary traditions, he is not afraid to innovate, to challenge embedded norms, and to do so in a theatrical and artistic style. Da Dong prepared for us a sublime feast of salted duck livers, braised duck tongues and stir-fried duck hearts – homage to Imperial tastes, but presented in a manner that no members of the ancient court would recognise!

While I expected to witness rapid growth and associated urban development in Beijing, it was in the Sichuan city of Chengdu that I was most shocked by the changes to modern China. When I last visited, in 1988 and 1989, it was a sleepy backwater, almost untouched by external influence. I remember seeing local farmers take their produce to market on carts drawn by donkeys. The scenes today could not be more different. The government has recently invested over £300 billion dollars in its 'Go West' policy aimed at driving economic development. The population is set to grow by one million every year for the next decade, reaching a peak of 24 million by 2022. Of course, we had to explore how this rapid urbanisation is affecting the truly distinctive Szechuan cuisine, undoubtedly the hottest in all of China. Locally born food writer Jenny Gao took as on a walking tour of the ramshackle backstreets of Chengdu where we sampled local chillies and the unique Sichuan flower pepper, which is so spicy it leaves your mouth numb. In the famous Ming Ting restaurant we dined on Ma Po style pig brains – a delicacy that will probably not become a regular feature of Ching's diet! Despite this part of the city being set for demolition and redevelopment, it was encouraging that local chefs don't feel this will threaten long-established culinary traditions. Although dishes will continue to evolve, pride in authentic Sichuan cuisine will keep it alive for generations to come. Indeed the city fathers have created a new destination, known as Jinli, as a home for traditional street food, including deep-fried rabbit's head and sweet gluttonous rice balls, to ensure its survival.

As well as pork and Sichuan flower pepper, another ingredient that defines Sichuan cuisine is chilli-bean paste. We visited a factory in Pixian, close to Chengdu, where the persistently damp climate aids the fermentation of a simple mix of broad beans, red chillies and salt, to produce the sour and spicy chilli-bean sauce. Again, I was struck by the continued use of historic methods, unchanged for over 300 years – in this case the use of earthenware pots left outside in harsh conditions – rather than modern industrialised techniques.

Travelling south, to the opposite end of China's ancient trading route, we passed through breath-taking scenery to arrive in Yunnan, which borders with Vietnam, Laos and Myanmar. In the West we hear of the constant march of China as a modern and dynamic super-power, but our visit to Yunnan served to remind us that half the population still lives in rural agricultural communities with lifestyles that have remained unchanged for centuries. Here we met communities of the Dai minority, rural poor who live on less than one dollar a day, but whose culinary inventiveness ensures they follow a healthy and relatively diverse diet. Using techniques I had never experienced, local men prepared a fragrant chicken stew. In a marinade of chilli, ginger and Vietnamese mint, the chicken was wrapped in a banana leaf, inserted in a large bamboo shoot and steamed. Bamboo shoots were also used to create gluttonous rice with peanuts. It was from this versatile plant that our hosts also carved utensils and bowls in which the meal was served.

Yunnan is also the original home to China's now burgeoning tea industry. The Buleng minority has been growing, tending and harvesting Pu-erh tea for thousands of years. In recent years a booming export market has led them to transform their once subsistence agricultural land into large-scale plantations that service industrial units. Pu-erh leaves are fermented, a unique process that can take up to thirty years, which enhances their taste, texture and aroma. The young leaves and shoots also lend a slightly bitter taste to local dishes, and are known for their health giving properties.

We also visited Yunnan's largest city, Jinghong, where a vibrant (if rather brash and gaudy) cultural scene reflects the varying traditions of thirteen different ethnic groups. Rather than diminishing Jinghong's colour and diversity, a growing number of domestic tourists who crave authentic culinary experiences have helped to sustain its rich heritage.

On the second stage of our epic culinary journey across China's Western frontier we travelled three thousand miles north west of Jinghong to Kashgar, in the Xingjiang Region. Close to Afghanistan and Pakistan, this is a part of the country few outsiders ever visit. The old town is dominated by the Uighurs, a Muslim minority fighting to maintain its ancient culture and religious rituals. The Uighurs' lives could not be more at odds with those in the new town, the Han Chinese, whose skyscrapers and fast lives are built on wealth from oil and gas. In 2009 the Chinese government began a programme of demolishing the old town, adding to the Uighurs' sense abandonment and heightening tensions between the two communities.

Mohammed, our welcoming guide, was eager to show how culinary traditions are helping to maintain the Uighurs' cultural pride, despite them feeling disenfranchised. Unlike in other parts of China, the local delicacy is lamb, and nowhere is this more evident that at the Kashgar's weekly central market, where thousands gather every Sunday to buy and sell livestock. We were lucky enough to visit during Noruz, an ancient Persian festival marking the coming of spring, at which lamb is as essential as turkey is at a British Christmas dinner. In the home of Kashgar's finest chef we witnessed a centuries-old method of preparing lamb. Before slaughtering and gutting the animal according to halal principles, the chef must read from the Koran. The carcass is smothered in a flour and egg mixture and then lowered into a smoky pit for roasting. The cooked meat is served separately to men and women – this being the only time of year they dine apart. This was a humbling experience – one that reminded me how deep-rooted culinary rituals define who we are, help us maintain community and family relations, and enable us to express our difference from others.

The final leg of our journey took us to the city of Guangzhou in the province of Guangdong, also known as Canton - birthplace of my parents and my spiritual home. The welcome familiarity of Cantonese cuisine was exhilarating. Fresh, unadorned ingredients that are not over-powered by spices and seasoning. Of course I am biased, but we Cantonese are sure we have the most sophisticated palates in China.

This is the region of China that has seen the largest levels of migration to other parts of the world – around thirty million people in over 100 countries. It has therefore shaped worldwide perceptions of Chinese cuisine, though western interpretations of Cantonese staples, such as dim sum or sweet and sour pork, rarely live up to those served in Guangzhou.

My parents moved to the US in 1948 as newly-weds. Sadly, my father died at the age of thirty-three, when I was just eight months old. He never existed for me as more than an image in photographs. So on this journey I wanted to take time to re-connect with my father's family – to learn more about his life with my mother and possibly to gain a better sense of my place in the world. I travelled about forty miles out of the city to Kaiping, an area still dominated by paddy fields, to spend a couple of days with my cousins. Like so many others, for several generations members of my extended family were rice farmers. It was not until the 1990s, when China began to emerge from years of extreme austerity, that other opportunities arose. We gathered at the farm where my father grew up, now used by my cousin to grow vegetables and rear poultry to supply his successful restaurant. Together we prepared a dinner of sweet and sour goose, my cousin's signature dish, and bitter melon with black bean sauce, a favourite of mine as a child, and shared stories about our family, and in particular about my parents. I was struck by how the changes that have swept China over the last thirty years have transformed opportunities for my family. Their standard of living has increased, they are optimistic about the future and my cousins' children are looking forward to going to university.

We finished our epic Chinese adventure over dinner in Hong Kong – a fitting destination given it's where East meets West – and I reflected on what I had learned. China is unrecognisable from the country I last visited in 1989. It has emerged from the trauma of the Cultural Revolution and, for the most part, is revelling in its new found freedom. I remembered poor quality food, prepared without pride or enthusiasm, yet on this journey I found a culinary culture that is totally reinvigorated. In rural areas, those living in relative poverty welcomed us into their homes and served us delicious food reflecting their distinctive heritage. In the face of sweeping modernisation, those in ethnic minority groups are maintaining their unique culinary traditions. And in the mega-cities, which are more open to Western influence, talented chefs are embracing innovation while respecting embedded gastronomic conventions. I was profoundly moved by both the resilience of Chinese culture and cuisine and all the positive changes that have transformed the world's oldest continuous civilisation.

Marketing the Fertile Crescent:

The reinvention of the public market tradition in New Orleans

Richard McCarthy

Richard McCarthy is the co-founder of the Crescent City Farmers Market and the executive director of Slow Food USA. He was the founder of Market Umbrella and the Farmers Market Coalition. In 2012, he was named a "Hero of the New South" by Southern Living magazine.

Under Spanish rule in the late 18th Century, New Orleans began to enjoy the beginnings of what came to be among the more highly developed public market systems in the North America. The system served many purposes: to link regional farmers, fishers and hunters to urban consumers, to serve as gateway for global goods from the Port of New Orleans, like Central American bananas, to enable those on the economic margins to gain a foothold in the economy as business owners and to build social cohesion among a culturally complex colony. By the time post-World War II America promised air-conditioning, new housing, supermarkets and automobiles with the escape from the smelly, messy inner core of the city, the 32-strong public markets were already in decline.

Despite this decline, the collective memory of markets remained important footnotes for a city that, even to this day, maintains an uncomfortable relationship with the forces of American homogenization. Many wholesalers, bakers, grocery stores, and restaurants cut their retail teeth at one of the city's public markets. Throughout New Orleans, discussions at family gatherings often reflect upon the days when the French Market sold live crabs instead of sunglasses and T-shirts that read 'I got crabs in the French Quarter.'

For a city that has ridden the waves of different governing administrations and norms – from colonial French and Spanish to Federal American and Confederate eras – institutions like the public markets have provided local dwellers with the social and commercial space to forge bonds across the dividing lines of language, class, and race. Consider how liberating it must have been to conduct business in the racially mixed environment of the French Market (long deemed the 'Mother of all Markets' in the New Orleans public market lexicon) during the darkest days of Jim Crow. Perhaps even more liberating is the experience of slaves owned by Creoles who during the early days of New Orleans would sell the fruits of their labor on Sundays at Congo Square (presumably with the ultimate goal of earning enough to purchase freedom from owners).

In short, New Orleans' public market history provides today's food justice activists with an alternative history of a region whose inhabitants foraged, farmed, and traded goods and services in a public setting – despite the prevailing policies, norms and values of the governing regime of the day. Ancient in their structure, public markets are democratic, decentralized, and oftentimes unruly.

For a small group of civic activists who rallied around the common goal to reinvent this tradition in 1995, beneath the banner of the Crescent City Farmers Market (CCFM), it was this historical footprint that inspired action. For the various public markets that sprang up after Katrina (a decade after the CCFM's formation and reign as an often-replicated flagship), organizers readily pointed to the advantage of speed, with restarting town squares with tents and umbrellas in neighborhoods reeling from the effects of flooding and trauma. These post-Katrina markets were often monthly, blending the attributes of festivals with the regularity of markets. Here too, organizers pointed to the pitching of tents as if they were acts of defiance: striking against the prevailing wisdom of the political class (who pondered the wisdom of repopulating neighborhoods).

A decade of rediscovery

O n September 30, 1995, the Crescent City Farmers Market opened operations for what was billed at the time to be a Saturday market in the largely quiet and accessible Warehouse District in downtown New Orleans for a three-month demonstration period. It opened to much fanfare. Naysayers doubted that unfurled umbrellas downtown would attract regional dwellers in search of commerce and company. They were wrong. In contrast, the market seemed to be exactly what people wanted: an informal, public gathering around a shared, coveted asset: food.

The path to opening day was hardly smooth and simple. Of course, we knew that New Orleans had a reputation as a violent city dominated by urban elitists who cared little for rural folks or integrity. However, we had not quite anticipated just how difficult it would be to lure farmers to town. After many farm visits, meetings at Cooperative Extension offices, and telephone calls, we managed to assemble an impressive yet small group of founding vendors to commit to the demonstration period. The founding dozen vendors sold their vegetables, fruits, cheeses, bedding plants, baked goods, firewood, pecans, mushrooms and cut flowers. They were also recognized as pioneers for a new era in regional foods.

On opening day, restaurant chefs mingled on the edges of the parking lot happy but already complaining how they had expected a wider variety of products and in greater volume. Of course, we did not anticipate being overwhelmed by a thousand foodies in search of the next 'new thing' in town. But we were.

During that golden decade of learning – from 1995 to 2005 – we accomplished many great things. We are indeed proud of how we grew and what we learned together. Farmers joined hands with consumers and neighbors to reinvent a regional food distribution system based on mutual aid, trust, and dignity.

In hindsight, we were woefully unaware of just how slowly change comes. I remember farmer and Mississippi Association of Cooperatives Executive

Director Ben Burkett explain to the Greater New Orleans Foundation staff: "You must remember, changes in food production will not be seen, at best, quicker than 55 days but more often much more slowly." We had to calibrate our desire for instant progress to the pace of planting, tending, harvesting and marketing.

Also, we had not calculated just how few small farmers actually cultivate the land in an agricultural region whose economy is dominated by plantation economics. We overestimated this number of what US Department of Agriculture refers to as 'specialty crops'. The history of the region's agricultural economy is one of program crops, like cotton, sugar and soybeans. As a result, we struggled to find independent farmers who grow food. We struggled even harder to find ones willing to market their food directly to consumers who reside in a dangerous city.

On the demand side of the equation, we underestimated how fearful city dwellers were of the city. By the mid-1990s the fear of violent crime so dominated the public imagination that we felt compelled to bring an air of levity to our serious work by staging an endless parade of amusing special events and campaigns: *Shop and Chop with the Chef, Thanksgiving Yamboree, Bastille Day French Poodle Pageant, Aubergine Monologues, Learned Festival of Heat, Bicycle Beauty Contest*, and so on. If we were to animate public spaces with good people then we had to capture their imagination.

Post-Katrina market renaissance

After the waters demolished the coastal communities, flooded New Orleans, and sent populations scurrying all over the USA, we began to reassemble our community via an online bulletin board, via vendors and shoppers whom we deputized with the support of limited emergency funds. Like private investigators, our deputies followed trails, travelling to farmers and fishers to determine the level of need, and to measure interest and timing for restarting the markets.

From its reopening in November 2005, the Tuesday Market uptown served several intentional roles: as a practical point of commerce for the regional food system, as a mental health refuge, and as a depot for philanthropy, media and professional networking. Six months later, shoppers were demanding our return downtown, despite the fact that our 40-strong roster of vendors had melted away to only a dozen or more in March 2006.

So, following demand, we were now operating two markets per week. On the first anniversary of Katrina, August 29th 2006, the political grandstanders were keen to hang crepe and stage heavy, gloomy events. As it was a Tuesday, we felt compelled to respond with something more appropriate. We decided to stage a picnic, especially for the nearby schools that were just beginning to begin the fall semester. We erected a large tent and rented tables and chairs for a community picnic. We printed up important recipes one should have for that next evacuation; and the Treme Brass Band brought smiles and syncopated rhythms to the morning's activities. This event addressed a need all locals knew well: a call for lightness and fun — for happiness.

Monthly markets

We fielded many requests for help from neighborhood leaders seeking upbeat, dramatic and public expressions of life. After all, many neighborhoods were under siege by policymakers, urban planners, and developers who saw dollar signs. Knowing how difficult we found the post-Katrina management of markets, we rarely recommended that organizers pursue an orthodox farmers market (with solely farmers as vendors). There were simply not enough farmers to go round. Believers in all forms of public markets, we began to recommend and assist in the development of monthly public markets featuring caterers, restaurateurs, craftspeople, and fresh food. Operating monthly, the practical purchase of groceries would pale in comparison to the need to acquire social capital and to rebrand places as living. In short, the rise of monthly markets became the most visible expressions for the promise of Main Streets. We assisted the Harrison Avenue, Gentilly, New Orleans East and Freret Street markets with logistics, rules and regulations, and food handling. The City of New Orleans awarded Freret $10,000 as seed funding. Officials likely return to that investment as one of the major, early ones to restart a renovation that has been long desired. Today, Freret Street is alive with new eateries, Friday Night boxing, and storefront upgrades that impress even the most cynical observer.

White boot brigade goes global

We took three fishing families, who had no working docks, to New York City to introduce them to chefs who understood the meaning of trauma (thanks to 9-11) and who cared about quality produce. After an event that was billed as a *Shrimp Cocktail* in the test kitchens of the Food Network, we lined up scheduled sales of shrimp to top chefs, including Daniel Boulud and Floyd Cardoz (of the Danny Myer group of restaurants). We returned in June 2006 to thank the dozen or so high profile chefs and to add some sizzle to a week of menus featuring Louisiana shrimp. After paying for our rooms at the desirable Carlton Hotel on Madison Avenue with shrimp, we won a few minutes of fame on the Today Show. In short, the farmers market served as both training ground for this type of direct marketing madness and playful innovation.

Transact

The post-Katrina period also marked an increase in our organizational work as researchers. With support from the Ford Foundation, in partnership with innovative Brazilian NGO PSA (the Health and Happiness Project), and with research expertise provided by J. Robin Moon (now a Doctor of Public Health from Harvard University), we began to measure a public market's success to bring social capital, human capital, and financial capital benefits to a region's food economy. The trio of tools – *Seed*, *Need*, and *Feed* – has since become an important methodological instrument for the field of public markets.

Incentive campaigns

As a result of the findings from the social capital research, we began to conduct the kind of farmers market soul searching that has made our organization stronger. We asked the tough questions: How and why are people of color not purchasing local, fresh, and healthy products? Is geography the only reason for weak participation? Or is it the responsibility of the market organization to address a decade or more of under-serving all populations on the economic and social periphery? We introduced incentive programmes to enhance the level of participation from those in vulnerable communities and diversified the markets' product range, to better reflect the region's population as a whole.

It is difficult to describe just how vividly the world has changed since ringing the opening bell at the Crescent City Farmers Market in September 1995. Though one could almost smell the fertile field poised to cultivate a complex ecosystem of local foods, there were few who could visualize what this might look like. Herein lies the value of public markets in the reformation of regional food systems, based on values of dignity, respect and mutual aid, that gives teeth to the phrase , 'taste of place'.

Today, with endless varieties of 'farm-to-table' menus and urban agriculture projects, it is easy to forget that they are built on years of relationship building between farmers, once unfamiliar with the city and its tastes, and consumers whose sense of food security has been shaken.

Our goal in 1995 was to initiate and promote the ecology of the Greater New Orleans economy through food. This no longer seems to be a lofty vision. Though provocative in this age of *Occupy Wall Street*, our motto – *In markets, we trust* – seems ever more relevant if by markets we mean a public assembly of independent vendors selling the fruits of their labor directly to consumers. In our case, we do: every Tuesday, Thursday, and Saturday (rain or shine, year-round).

Jane Grigson

Geraldene Holt

Geraldene Holt is an internationally acclaimed food writer. After a successful career as a studio potter and teacher, Geraldene Holt began to write about food as result of selling her home-made cakes on a West Country market stall. Her work has been translated into eleven languages and her award-winning books on herbs have sold almost half a million copies. She is Chairman of the Jane Grigson Trust, an educational charity, and in 1999 she was elected Vice President of the Guild of Food Writers.

Cookery writing is "almost a form of autobiography," Jane Grigson remarked on a BBC radio programme in 1987. "It's been my way of finding out why I'm on this earth, and adding something to the sum of human happiness." However, when Jane left university in 1949, her food writing career lay almost twenty years ahead of her. She first worked in art galleries and publishers' offices. In 1953 she joined George Rainbird as a picture researcher and met the author and poet Geoffrey Grigson. A decade working as a translator led to the award of the John Florio Prize with Father Kenelm Foster for the translation of Beccaria's *Of Crimes and Punishment*.

Jane's interest in food developed when she and Geoffrey with their daughter, Sophie, began to divide their time between a farmhouse in Broad Town in Wiltshire and a cave house in Trôo in the Loir-et-Cher region of France.

Here, in the early sixties, Jane began to research a book on French *charcuterie* for an English friend, Adey Horton, who later suggested that she also take over the writing. By trawling through French textbooks on the subject in a scholarly exploration of the field and also compiling a comprehensive collection of recipes, Jane demonstrated her skill for research and her talent as a food writer. *Charcuterie and French Pork Cookery* was published in 1967, to widespread acclaim. The book is a well organised survey of a specialised field: highly informative yet with accessible recipes, an educational volume which retains its distinction more than four decades later, and described by Elizabeth David as a kitchen classic.

The following year, Elizabeth David recommended Jane as cookery writer for the new colour magazine of the *Observer* newspaper. In an early issue of the British *Guild of Food Writers' Journal,* Jane recalled her dilemma when embarking upon food journalism. She had proposed the topic of strawberries for her initial article. But "....I was plainly terrified. The thing that buoyed me up was the idea of earning more money than I had from translation. The thing that dragged me down was the knowledge that I knew nothing about cookery, beyond pork." She asked Geoffrey how she should proceed, " 'Right,' he said, 'we'll find out what the strawberry has meant to people, what they have done to it, how they have developed it and so on.' "

Alan Davidson, in his magisterial *Oxford Companion to Food*, describes Geoffrey Grigson as 'so widely read that he constituted a sort of walking encyclopaedia of English literature, and his contribution to Jane's work in the form of general inspiration and particular suggestions was considerable right up to the time of his death, only a few years before hers.' (Davidson, 1999: 354)

Jane finished her strawberry article and sent it to the Observer. She retained the carbon copy of her contribution and filed it in a ring-binder. Thus began her long and productive association with the newspaper, which continued until she died.

A selection of Jane's articles from her early years at the *Observer* was published under the title *Good Things*: "This is not a manual of cookery, but a book about enjoying food." She writes about the delights and solaces of cooking and quotes Careme: 'From behind my ovens, I ... feel the ugly edifice of routine crumbling beneath my hands.'

The Wine and Food Society then invited Jane to write *Fish Cookery* (1973). When the book first appeared, serving fish as a main course at a formal dinner was still unusual. By the time that Jane began a major revision of the book, the British attitude to fish had become more European with a far larger choice of species available at fishmongers and in supermarkets. Jane's expanded and updated edition of the book was published in 1993 under its new title, *Jane Grigson's Fish Book*.

With the publication of *English Food (1974)* it was clear that Jane Grigson had become a crusader for the oft-maligned cooking of the British Isles. Contending with what Jane later described as 'the realisation of how puritan the English, in particular, have always been about food' she set about converting the sceptics by demonstrating how many fine foods and dishes had been allowed to disappear from our national menus. After a recipe for Sorrel with Eggs, she writes: 'Latterly we in England have developed a most Athenian characteristic. We are always after some new thing. Which is fine in many ways, but in matters of food often disastrous. We are so busy running after the latest dish, that the good things we've known for centuries are forgotten as quickly as the boring ones.'

The success of Jane's campaign for the restoration of fine English cooking has not been restricted to cooks in domestic kitchens: restaurant chefs from Joyce Molyneux to Mark Hix often revive long-forgotten recipes highlighted by Jane. *English Food* was almost entirely revised by Jane shortly before her death and the new edition appeared in 1992.

Her next book was a collection of recipes for cultivated, woodland, field and dried mushrooms. *The Mushroom Feast* (1975) reflects the Grigsons' life spent on both sides of the English Channel in its harmonious blend of English and French opinions and differing preparations of edible fungi.

In 1978, Jane published her *Vegetable Book*, a large and masterly volume of information and recipes for seventy-five different vegetables from artichokes to yams. The book is a remarkable achievement, and Jane received the *Glenfiddich Writer of the Year Award* and the *Andre Simon Memorial Fund Book Award* in recognition of its compass and detail.

I t is, though, when you come to Jane's final two books – the ones she says she was happiest writing – that her preferred style and methods of working are notably apparent.

Food with the Famous (1979) is an expanded version of earlier newspaper articles. 'From a selfish point of view this has been the series I have most enjoyed writing, in eleven years at the *Observer*.' she writes. 'The excuse to re-read favourite novels, look again at favourite painters, visit places associated with them, spend hours in collections of letters and in journals, study early cookery books in the Bodleian Library and buy more than I could really afford, gave me a chance of relating cookery to life beyond the kitchen. Which is what, in the end, I think cookery should do.'

Adopting the pattern she had established in some of her earlier books, with an introductory essay to each chapter followed by a well-judged selection of relevant recipes, Jane explores the lives of ten eminent people from the past. In her sympathetic yet succinct biography of Lord Shaftesbury (1801-1885) she sets the scene for the cooking of this prosperous English 19th century household.

A year or so earlier, Jane had been given the manuscript recipe book of Lady Shaftesbury. Hand-written in copperplate, this unique volume forms part of Jane's personal library that Sophie Grigson, herself a food writer, has generously placed on permanent loan to the Jane Grigson Trust, an educational charity founded in Jane's name, whose collection of food and cookery books is held at Oxford Brookes University. Turning the faded pages of the notebook reveals the scope of the task Jane set herself – to select just twenty from one hundred and forty recipes that record some of the cooking of the Shaftesbury kitchen from 1855-1872. She explains their significance in the past, yet is also aware that the dishes chosen – such as Prince Raziwill's Potted Salmon, and Lady Granville's Iced Coffee – should still hold an appeal for her 20th century readers.

The assignment of translating an antique recipe into its modern equivalent is strewn with pitfalls. The original instructions might be bafflingly brief, ingredients and methods are often radically different, and cooking over an open fire or with a capricious cast-iron stove require skills not easily found in the present day. 'It's worth remembering this difference in the size of eggs," Jane writes in *English Food*. 'Such an old recipe may say, in what seems a grandiose manner, "Take sixteen eggs". The sixteen eggs of 1840 or whatever the year can safely be reduced to about ten or twelve modern eggs...'

While bearing this in mind, one still aims, when resuscitating a period recipe, to retain the spirit of the dish, which can be quite a challenge. For both reader and cook, *Food with the Famous* succeeds as an attractive collection of recipes and as a brilliant way to present culinary history.

Jane introduces her *Fruit Book* (1982), by describing mankind's 'special feeling towards fruit, its glory and abundance...Such feelings towards fruit have made this book more fun to write than any of the others.' With the same format as in her *Vegetable Book*, Jane introduces each fruit with a short essay, often with a passage of advice on buying or cooking the fruit, followed by a range of recipes from around the world. Her essay style is forthright yet entertaining, in similar vein to that of her eminent forebears who include Morton Shand, Edward Bunyard, Lady Jekyll and Elizabeth David. Jane Grigson's essays are, however, memorably enlivened by relevant information and quotations from a remarkably wide range of sources – poets, novelists, gardeners, earlier food writers and cookery manuals.

Writing about the cherry, Jane prefaces her essay with cultural and historical – even biblical – references, then recalls the cherries of her childhood in England, the cherries she usually buys in France, and finally quotes from two poems by the English poet and priest, Robert Herrick. Then she has a fascinating section on Kirsch, Cherry Brandy and Maraschino.

You could close the book at this moment and still feel enriched by how the author weaves her spell. Few food writers approach Jane Grigson's aptitude for illuminating a subject with such infectious delight: education at its most persuasive – caught not taught.

Nineteen recipes for cherries follow – no wonder the book stretches to a hefty five hundred pages. Alan Davidson, in his *North Atlantic Seafood* (1979), remarks on the thoroughness of Jane Grigson in providing not one but three versions of gooseberry sauce to accompany mackerel in her *Fish Cookery*. Some writers might husband one or two gooseberry sauce recipes for a later book or article but Jane is generous in giving us a chance to compare the different versions on the same page.

Discovering several recipes for gooseberry sauce demands diligent research – the part of the job Jane evidently relished. In her *Fruit Book*, Jane's talent for research comes to the fore: her nose for truffling out the hidden fact, the telling anecdote or long-lost story makes this book one of her most popular. Moreover, in the years before the invention of the internet, Jane conducted her research by consulting actual works – books, journals, letters, memoirs and diaries. It was a lengthy process but for the right person with a forensic talent it could be an engrossing quest.

Jane Grigson was a self-taught cook – as, I assume, are most of her readers: she learnt how to prepare food from consulting books or from friends and from her family. Her sister Mary was a gifted cook, and Jane's notebooks contain hand-written recipes such as Mary's Christmas Cake. Perhaps this accounts for Jane's friendly style of recipe writing which makes her such a sympathetic companion in the kitchen.

Domestic cooking varies in many ways from that practised in a restaurant. Compared with recipes written by a chef, Jane is especially alert to the unexpected or puzzling elements sometimes encountered when cooking from a published recipe. 'If the filling rises alarmingly, do not worry. It will fall when you take it out of the oven.' is a reassuring footnote to a recipe for Old Fashioned Apricot Tart. And how endearing of an author to confess that she always offers up a silent prayer when baking a soufflé.

Jane's readers were charmed by her newspaper contributions, often cutting them out each week to paste into scrapbooks. And she received a considerable correspondence, usually congratulatory, sometimes adding useful information and recipes, and very occasionally scolding her for lavishness in a particular article.

Colour photography became markedly less expensive in the 1970s, which encouraged the *Observer* and other weekend titles to launch cookery part-works. Three Observer Guides: *British Cookery, European Cookery* and *French Cookery School,* partly or wholly written by Jane, proved sufficiently popular to warrant hardback publication in due course.

Through her books and her journalism, Jane became an influential voice in the food culture of Britain. She ran an almost continuous campaign for an improvement in food quality which she rightly argued should be available to everyone irrespective of income. She protested against 'the philistine tread of big business, our chefs boiled in the bag, home cooks swaddled and smothered in plastic convenience.' (Observer, March 1988)

During the notorious salmonella-in-eggs scandal of 1988, I remember a Guild of Food Writers' meeting where Jane upbraided a politician from the Ministry of Agriculture, Fisheries and Food. She expressed her deep shock and anger that the government oversaw commercial food production that had deteriorated so deplorably that she could no longer safely serve small children or an elderly friend a softly boiled egg. The minister struggled to reply and then, doubtless sensing the animosity among the audience, became speechless. A few weeks later, I met Jane as she returned flushed and breathless but clearly triumphant from a policy meeting at the ministry. I think I detect progress, she whispered.

Jane's reputation as one of Britain's greatest food writers is well established. She died at only 62 years of age, but in a 23 year career her prolific writing has left a body of work that is essential reading for any historian of English life. Her books bring three-fold pleasure: as informative directories of food, as a treasure house of recipes, and a joy to read. Indeed, Jane succeeded beyond measure in her desire to add 'something to the sum of human happiness'.

A cookery book is a social document, a record of the food and cooking of the time. Jane was particularly interested in English food and its past. She lamented that we had lost so much due to modernisation and industrial practices when, for almost all of man's time on earth, he grew food naturally in a way that we now label as organic. Enlightened gardeners rarely waver from this traditional approach, and an increasing number of farmers and horticulturists have recently adopted these methods. In her work Jane helped pioneer this campaign for unadulterated food which now has a legion of supporters.

Jane was dedicated to placing food in its context, both in the present day and in the past, and was keen to emphasise the commonality of food and its role in our lives. She was disarmingly modest about her own kitchen skills but was entranced by the creative capacity of cooking: 'Cooking something delicious is really much more satisfactory than painting pictures or throwing pots. At least for most of us. Food has the tact to disappear, leaving room and opportunity for masterpieces to come.' (1971: 10)

While her own handiwork in the kitchen has long disappeared, Jane's written record continues to enthral. Her writing enlightens the reader and deepens our understanding of the complicated yet often deliciously simple business of eating. Jane Grigson made an inestimable contribution to English culture and left her distinctive signature upon the art of food writing.

References

Grigson, J. (1967), *Charcuterie and French Pork Cookery*, London: Michael Joseph

Grigson, J. (1971), *Good Things*, London: Michael Joseph

Grigson, J. (1973), *Fish Cookery*, London: Penguin

Grigson, J. (1974), *English Food: An anthology*, London: MacMillan

Grigson, J. (1975), *The Mushroom Feast*, London: Michael Joseph

Grigson, J. (1978), *Jane Grigson's Vegetable Book*, London: Michael Joseph

Grigson, J. (1979), *Food with the Famous*, London: Michael Joseph

Grigson, J. (1982), *Jane Grigson's Fruit Book*, London: Penguin

Food Memories

Yasmin Alibhai-Brown

Yasmin Alibhai-Brown is a Ugandan-born British journalist and author, who describes herself as a 'leftie liberal, anti-racist, feminist, Muslim, part-Pakistani, and … a very responsible person'. Currently a regular columnist for The Independent *and the* Evening Standard, *she is a well-known commentator on issues relating to immigration, diversity and multiculturalism. Yasmin is a founder member of British Muslims for Secular Democracy.*

A light cake summoned up in Proust the most profound meditations on lost time and mortality. He came to believe that 'When nothing subsists of an old past, after the death of people, after the destruction of things, alone, frailer but more enduring, more persistent, more faithful, smell and taste remain for a long time, like souls remembering, waiting, hoping upon the ruins of all the rest'. Food holds memory; it also consoles, stirs emotions, arouses and can often communicate unspoken (and unspeakable) thoughts and acts.

Way back in 1954, Alice B. Toklas, the lesbian lover of avant-garde writer Gertrude Stein, released in a cookbook the many flavours of their long life together in France. Replete with pleasure, the recipes are really about sex that couldn't speak its name so had to be covered in pastry and rich sauces. Elizabeth David's meticulous and evocative food writing, some think, was her way of dealing with a frenetic and ultimately sad love life.

For Claudia Roden and Madhur Jaffrey, food opens doors and brings familiarity with strangers and often fleshes out the bare bones of history or reveals forgotten truths. *Apricots on the Nile* by Colette Rossant, for example, is a dark and compelling culinary chronicle of a Jewish family in Cairo in the thirties. Jews no longer live in Cairo. They have gone.

Rossant inspired me to write the *Settler's Cookbook*, to tell, through food, the remarkable and largely unknown story of my people, East African Asians. Some were indentured labourers taken by the British from India to build the East African Railway; others were small shopkeepers and the rest were audacious adventurers drawn to the lush land full of mysteries and possibilities. Though whites ruled, Asians were the visible middle class. Lowly blacks served both sets of masters. Every evening in the Ugandan capital Kampala, Indian street food smells wafted through the streets and Indian music blared. We commandeered the very air. It couldn't last and didn't. In 1970 the violent dictator Idi Amin took over the country and within two years we were expelled from paradise.

On the plane to London, Hindu, Muslim ladies passed round Tupperware boxes with home-made delights – their last tastes of Uganda. They told each other to be happy, to think of the wonderful sweetmeats they would make with creamy, unadulterated English milk. One old woman had a box full of battered mashed potato snacks inside which she had hidden her diamond rings and earrings.

For reasons I can't explain, I brought with me cooking equipment, including a wooden contraption used to grate hairy, brown shelled coconuts. Two slabs of wood are cleverly put together to make a folding stool. A flat, oval, rusting, metal blade sticks out in front, like the head of a tortoise. The coconut was broken, its sweet, cloudy juice drained into a glass which always went to the favourite child in the extended family, always a boy, always overweight and a bloody nuisance. Then the kitchen servants sat astride the grater, as if on a saddle except it was so low their knees come up almost to the shoulders. With both hands they rolled the half sphere over the blade with a zigzag edge. Sometimes, they slashed their hands and harsh employers abused them for what they thought was native idiocy. Or for contaminating the white flesh with their inferior blood.

There was a Formica chapatti patlo, a round block with small legs, previously made of grainy wood to roll out various Indian breads. The new model (1970) was made by Mr Desai, a compulsive modernizer who went from house to house in a tweedy, dank smelling suit to demonstrate the easy-clean properties of this very latest 'British' material. My mother bought a FP, as they were known, then had to pay for it in pitifully small weekly sums. I use it often. One day in 1988, it helped me capture the heart of my Englishman, four months after my Ugandan Asian husband left me and our ten year old son. As I rolled chapattis, the man with blue eyes asked me to marry him.

Some pots I carried over were made by a crooning artisan who called himself Mr Harry Belafonte the Third. The singer has left his song in his handiwork. My rimmed, aluminium bowl capers merrily when you put it on a flat surface and a huge stainless wok bops on the cooker as the heat warms it. On the coldest days of winter, torpidity appears to enter these metals, the rocking slows down. On cold days I still miss my old country.

In among the pots were notebooks and in one I found a note, a recipe written by my university friend, an African named Sussanah. Idi Amin saw her one day and within days she became his mistress, with high hopes. The recipe was for 'Exeter stew', Amin's favourite. He had her killed after some months. The recipe commemorates the true horror of his reign. Africans were the ones who really suffered under Amin. We were lucky, we got away.

Food proved a more reliable passport than the real thing after we settled in Britain. Migrants offer it to the people in their adopted lands and hope that will ease the pain of adjustment on both sides. Asians laid their offerings on the ample lap of Brittania. The nervy natives were placated and later got addicted. Their stomach linings must have turned turmeric yellow. My people started up 24 hour corner shops which made many very rich. Food was survival and soon opened up the route to wealth and influence. But as times passes the old life calls out.

That was another reason for writing the memoir. Words, languages, faces, images, landscapes are drifting away. The other day an old auntie from Kampala gave me some ubani. "Here, take, you liked it so much when you were small, always chewing, even in the mosque. Took them from my purse, you naughty girl." I stared it the amber nuggets - edible gum resin - and wondered what they were. That naughty girl in the mosque exists in the memories of others, gone from mine.

What was I then and there? Is any of that left here and now?

Some of the deceased men and women I knew as a child come back to jostle for space in my head, calling from the other side, calling for their stories to be immortalised. Particular foods remind me of each individual. Old Maami Jena ate her coriander omelette every morning with two thick slices of white toast followed by rough bran dissolved in sweet tea to prevent heart attacks. She was the kindest, jolliest person I ever knew, even though her life had been hard as a widow with many wayward children. After dinner, she sucked on wedges of sharp, acidic oranges to break open the clogged arteries, she said. Her heart gave up anyway and she lies cold and alone in a cemetery in New York where her youngest son had moved onto after many years in Britain.

I dream of Roshan Aunty, a family friend. She was unusually tall for an Asian woman, had the grace of a gazelle. She made dainty, crisp samosas the size of large Toblerones, eaten in one bite. In her kitchen, wearing pearls and a pink, quilted housecoat, humming quietly, she rolled out the samosa pastry. My generation buys ready-made frozen piles from expert pensioners who supplement their incomes selling foods that take time and patience. Those old ladies and their skills will pass into the void soon.

In 1978, on bus number 207 in west London, my mother was ordered off by a conductor because she 'was stinking like a curry pot'. She replied (without budging) in halting English: 'Sir not to mind. You must come and taste it one day, my curry. You people love it, isn't it?' She *was* stinking, having gone out in the same cardi she wore when cooking. She died in 2006 and I have that cardi, still unwashed, still smelling of the food made by the unbeatable woman who made me what I am.

To my son and daughter I am from a sad place in Africa where there are big beasts, safari jeeps, spectacular views, but too much butchery and poverty for their refined western sensibilities. They feel detached from my complicated upbringing and when I insist on reminding them of it they switch off or rebuke me sharply. Perhaps they are apprehensive that to accept their multipart, cluttered heritage is to thin down their entitlement to be truly, purely, deeply British.

They are gluttons for East African Asian foods though. Favourites are fried mogo (cassava) and kuku paka, a coconut chicken dish originally from Zanzibar. When my daughter was a toddler, I made her what I had been fed as a child - 'red rice', boiled basmati mixed with tomato puree, garlic and butter which she loves to this day and my adult son makes his own version of chilli and sour cream to eat with what we call fish cutlets – the old English fishcake recipe only 'repaired and much better' as my mother used to put it. The next generation does pick up this baton at least.

While they eat I reminisce, link the dishes to times and places repeatedly, so when I am gone, my voice will echo in their heads to remind them who they really are, that they didn't arrive on ground zero the day they were born. I look at them and do realise how far we have come.

When first we settled, what we cooked expressed both desperate nostalgia and hardship. Happiness then was eating a mango (two if you earned more than barely enough working in factories, hospitals, or for British Rail) or adding an aubergine to spicy potato and making dhal less watery. I can make ten different potato dishes – all invented when I was a poor post-graduate at Oxford.

Then came the small savings which built up to bigger piles. East African Asian corner shops became sustainable; more imports were flown over faster. As families began to have small money surpluses, they dressed in their best and ventured out together to cafes selling Indian snacks. Food in the home grew varied and more luxuries were added. Our ancestors in East Africa went through this same cycle from deprivation to abundance. You never forget back then.

In Africa, although my ancestors still felt links to India and Pakistan, they always thought of themselves as fearless pioneers, people free of borders and too many restrictive traditions. Unusually, East African Asians were also agents of empire, felt the favoured children of the ruling Brits. What a shock it was to discover that when we migrated to Britain, we were regarded as 'blackies' and 'Pakis'. The city of Leicester even ran adverts in Ugandan newspapers instructing us not to move there because it already had too many dark skinned residents testing its tolerance. It only made people more determined to move there. And the finale is that the same city now celebrates its Ugandan Asians and some of the best Asian restaurants in the UK are found there. Thirty thousand jobs have been created by Ugandan food industrialists and not many now wish the city could turn plain English again, the way it was in the fifties.

So, yes, Britain learnt to accept us and we have slowly let go of Uganda, though most of us migrants will never forget what that country was and what it did for us. Mr Raman Patel, an old family friend, before he died, said to me in Gujarati: "We never wanted to leave Uganda. But we didn't try hard enough to belong there. No black man or woman ever ate at my table. That was the biggest mistake we made. If we had shared food and lives, maybe we black and brown would have had a future together. But In England we do that. So we do have a future together". I hope he is right.

Devon and its Evolving Food Culture

Mark Millon

Mark Millon was born in Mexico City, and lived in Mexico, California, British Columbia, Ohio, and New England before settling in Devon, England, in the late 70's. He and his photographer wife Kim have been writing books about the foods and wines of Europe and beyond for over 30 years.

Bordering Cornwall to the west and Dorset and Somerset to the east and north, Devon is one of England's largest counties. With Exeter as its capital, it is bounded by the English Channel to the south and the Bristol Channel some 70 miles to the north. In between is a bucolic landscape of gently rolling and verdant pastures for the grazing of dairy cattle and sheep; rich arable farmland; and the rugged, upland country of Dartmoor and Exmoor.

This is enviable agricultural country. Devon's beautiful pasturelands provide grazing for dairy cattle and the county is the source of rich dairy products such as milk, cream, Devon's famous clotted cream, as well as an increasing and outstanding range of farmhouse cheeses. On upland farms, native breeds such as Red Ruby and South Devon cattle, as well as lamb raised on Dartmoor and Exmoor, provide excellent meats. Organic vegetables and fruit are cultivated in the rich red earth of Devon. Wild foods such as game as well as mushrooms and plants foraged in woodlands add to the local diet, while an increasing range of artisan, hand-crafted foods are produced on both small, cottage scale as well as at a level that allows for national and even international distribution. A fabulous catch of fish and shellfish is landed by day boats and trawlers alike in the ports of Brixham and Exmouth. Regional foods are most ably washed down with traditional cask-conditioned ales, raspingly tannic Devon farmhouse 'scrumpy' or cider, and an increasing number of award-winning Devon wines.

Says Michael Caines, executive chef at two Michelin star country hotel Gidleigh Park on the edge of Dartmoor, "Devon has the best larder not just in the UK but in all of Europe. We can compete with and stand proud alongside the greatest food regions, including Provence, Burgundy and Tuscany."

This is a bold and challenging statement to make. Caines, who worked under Bernard Loiseau in Burgundy and Jöel Robuchon in Paris as well as Raymond Blanc in Oxfordshire, has been at Gidleigh Park since 1994. He is widely considered an intelligent chef as well as a spokesman and ambassador for his home county. At Gidleigh Park, he has gained considerable acclaim for a style of cooking that is based on classical and modern European cooking techniques utilising the finest bounty found on his own Devon doorstep.

"The French speak about *terroir* - the exceptional habitats and micro-climates that result in food and wine that is superior and uniquely different from anything else on earth. I believe that Devon too has its own outstanding *terroir* that results in foods and drinks of real personality and outstanding character and quality."

Caines is not the only one who believes in the bounty and excellence of Devon food and drink. Indeed, in recent years, the county has become something of a food destination. The Exeter Festival of South West Food and Drink, an annual food festival that since its commencement in 2003 has grown into one of the most important regional food festivals in the country, attracts some 20,000 visitors a year to the county's capital city. Its purpose is to highlight and celebrate food and drink from all of South West England, including of course Devon. There is a real pride in the quality and diversity of what is on offer, with farmers, producers, chefs, restaurateurs and retailers eager to talk to an interested and ever more discerning public.

I f Devon today is rightly considered a food destination then this has been a remarkable and apparently recent transformation. Just a few decades ago, Devon was known primarily as a seaside tourist destination, or else a county to pass through en route to Cornwall. It may long have held many attractions for visitors but, apart from the famous Devon cream tea, food was probably not amongst them. Indeed, two decades ago, was food a tourist attraction anywhere in Britain?

How and why has this transformation come about? Indeed the success of Devon in raising awareness of the excellence of its traditional food and drink raises broader questions relating to the evolutions of food cultures elsewhere in the world.

Darts Farm, located just outside of Topsham, in East Devon, is a good starting point. The business began nearly forty years ago when the late Ronald Dart created one of the first pick-your-own farm stalls in the country, a concept he had seen on his travels in the US. In the intervening decades, this simple roadside stall has evolved into first a larger farm shop and today into an award-winning, nationally regarded food emporium selling primarily the produce of hundreds of the region's best local food and drink producers, including produce from the Darts' own farm on which it is still located.

"Our father began a business that was rooted in local produce long before this became a widespread trend," explains James Dart, who oversees the food hall, working with his brothers Michael and Paul. "Today's consumers - or at least a significant number of them - really do care about where their food comes from. It matters that the asparagus in our food hall, available for only a few short months, is grown by Chris Easton just down the road and picked fresh for us each morning. It matters that meat from our own herd of Red Ruby cattle, which graze on the marshlands of the Clyst River adjacent to the food hall, is available from our butchers Gerald David & Sons".

"Supporting local farmers is important for many reasons, and not just because the food is fresher and better. It is also a way to maintain traditional ways of life, skills, and the beautiful countryside that makes Devon so special. Furthermore, it has a massive impact on the local economy. Farm shops, farmers markets and independent retailers are the lifeblood of many small producers. Part of our role is to educate consumers about the many benefits of buying local produce. Above all, our passion is for preserving Devon's food culture, keeping farmers farming sustainably, and protecting the beautiful landscape in which we live, for future generations."

James Clark, chef at Route 2 Café Bar and owner of The Travelling Cookery School, agrees. "It seems people really do want to eat local these days. Most restaurants in Devon now state the provenance of ingredients on their menus - Exmouth mussels, South Devon beef, Exmoor lamb, Powderham venison, sea bass from local day boats, or whatever. This didn't happen even a decade ago. I'm finding too that there is an increasing interest for me to go into people's homes to teach them how to cook local foods. I shop with them, showing them where and how to shop locally and seasonally. I then teach them how to prepare tasty meals, everything from simple everyday to dinner party or restaurant level, and all using our fantastic Devon produce."

Of course it stands to reason that the desire to buy local only works if local foods are better than those available from outside a region. Caines clearly believes this to be the case when he states that Devon has the best larder in Europe.

Take Devon's famous dairy products. The county has long been known for the rich quality of its milk and cream, the result of a diet of lush grass from rain-fed pastures. At Home Farm in Newton St Cyres, the Quickes family has probably been making cheese from its own herd for nearly 500 years.

Cheesemaking was historically a cottage industry in Devon as in other parts of the country, a means of preserving a bounty of fresh milk in a form that could be stored, aged, and which was able to travel. Much of the local production of cheese ceased, however, when the Milk Marketing Board was set up in 1933 to control milk production and distribution by purchasing milk from dairy farmers. While this guaranteed farmers a minimum price for their milk, it gave them little incentive to use any surplus to make cheese. Rationing after World War II was a further blow to traditional cheesemaking. However when falling milk prices eventually led to the demise of the Milk Marketing Board and the deregulation of the British milk market in 1994, farmers once again turned to the production of cheese as a means of making use of surplus milk.

Today Mary Quicke, the 17th generation of the family at Home Farm, makes traditional farmhouse cheddar with milk from the family's own herd of some 500 dairy cattle. These award-winning cheeses, exported nationally and around the world, are by any standard world class: made by the laborious, traditional method of 'cheddaring', then cloth-wrapped so that they can continue to breathe and develop, the cheeses are matured for periods of months and even years to develop deep and complex flavours that are a direct reflection of the place from where they are made. Here Devon *terroir* translates into not only the unique habitat of lush pastures that feed the cows which produce the milk; *terroir* also means tradition and respect for age-old, timeless artisan hand-methods for the transformation of liquid milk into solid cheese.

The revival of Devon's cheese industry has resulted in a wealth of fine and new farmhouse cheeses. Unpasteurised milk, that is high in fats, from herds of doe-eyed Jersey cattle is transformed into soft, mould-ripened cheeses on the Sharpham estate. Ticklemore Cheese, near Totnes, specialise in the production of hand-made blue cheeses from the milk of cow (Devon Blue), sheep (Beenleigh Blue) and goat (Harbourne Blue). Other notable hard and semi-hard cheeses include Devon Oke and Curworthy. There are smoked cheeses, cheeses with flavourings added, cheeses made from the milk of sheep, goat, cow and even buffalo. What is perhaps most fascinating is to see how tradition and innovation work in harmony, as old cheesemaking methods are utilised or revived to result in a completely new range of Devon cheeses that simply did not exist a few decades ago. It seems certain that the renaissance of Devon farmhouse cheeses will continue.

If Devon's rich dairy products have been revalued in recent decades, local meat from native breeds is also finding favour with consumers, who today value the goodness of naturally reared meat from grass-fed animals such as the Red Ruby breed of cattle, native to Devon. At Pipers Farm, near Cullompton, Peter and Henri Greig work with farmers who raise the cattle on the rugged moorland grasses of Exmoor and the lusher grass of the Somerset Levels before finishing on the verdant pastures of Pipers Farm itself. Once ready, only one or two cattle are taken each week to a small abattoir just a few miles from Pipers Farm where they are killed without stress. The carcasses are left to hang and mature on the farm for at least four weeks. Red Rubies are by nature a slow-growing breed, taking some years to come to maturity. The result is a very finely grained meat with marbling throughout that quite simply has exceptional flavour.

"We began Pipers Farm," explains Peter Greig, "when our own children were growing up. We didn't want to feed them intensively reared meat and so we began to work in a way that is sustainable. We believe that this results in meat of exceptional quality, full-bodied, well-rounded, rooted in our unique *terroir*, and bursting with flavour and goodness."

If food and food culture is rooted to *terroir*, in Devon there is an awareness and appreciation of the need to work in ways that are sustainable, and that protect and enhance a beautiful natural environment.

Brewing has been in the McCaig family for generations. When David and Mary Ann McCaig left a career in brewing with Whitbread to settle with their family in the Blackdown Hills of East Devon, they did not originally plan to start a new brewery. The chance to acquire some old brewing equipment was the early beginnings of a business that is still growing but which is staying true to its family values as well as to its commitment not to harm but to positively enhance the Devon countryside.

Water for brewing comes from the farm's own borehole, and all waste water is filtered through a natural system of willow beds. Spent brewers' malt is fed to local cattle, surplus yeast to pigs, while hops make great mulch for gardens and nurseries. To store the beer in optimum conditions, a new eco-cellar has been constructed. Built into the hill with clay honeycomb block walls, it has excellent insulating properties, maintaining a steady temperature throughout the year without the need for additional heating or cooling. With its sedum roof and striking modern design that fits into the fold of the Blackdown Hills, it sits quite naturally within a beautiful and unspoiled landscape.

Otter Brewery's commitment to the environment and to sustainability has been recognised with important industry awards. In 2011, it won the 'Best Sustainability' category at the SIBA (Society of Independent Brewers) Business Awards in London. In 2009, Otter Brewery scooped top honours at the Devon Environmental Business Awards in the 'Sustainable Devon' category.

Patrick McCaig commented at the time, "This award means the world to us. Since 1990, we have strived to become an exemplar for the brewing industry as a whole whilst providing everyone that drinks Otter with an honest, distinctive and long lasting memory of Devon."

Devon's unique *terroir* makes the region the source of great things to eat and drink that are special to this small corner of England. At the same time, the unspoiled beauty of the landscape encourages people to work in a manner that protects and enhances the environment, not necessarily for commercial reasons, but because it is considered right to do so. The local, indeed the very locality itself, is valued as precious and worth protecting.

In a world that elsewhere seems to be rushing towards globalisation at breakneck speed as McDonalds, Starbucks and other brands proliferate internationally, in Devon there is a sense amongst many of a need to step back, to look around, and to appreciate that which is literally on the doorstep. Out of this, perhaps as a means of fighting the onslaught of the multi-nationals, the supermarkets, the chain shops and chain restaurants, and the international brands, there is a strong and still growing local movement whereby consumers here proactively choose to support and enjoy local food and drink, above all because it gives them pleasure to do so.

Food culture is defined and shaped by many factors, including *terroir*, artisan craftsmanship, a quest for and a dedication to quality, as well as a commitment to sustainability and localism. Perhaps most important of all is the passion and dedication of individuals - food and drink producers; chefs; retailers; food writers; and intelligent consumers who know, value and appreciate the difference between the industrially produced and the artisan and who are prepared to pay for local quality. Here in Devon these combinations of factors mean that its food culture is vibrant, exciting, delicious, and, rather than locked in a straitjacket of centuries-old tradition, still evolving, defining and re-defining itself.

Transylvania Fest:

An itinerant food and culture festival

Pamela Ratiu and Rareş Crăiuţ, with Donald Sloan

Pamela Ratiu is Executive Director for the Ratiu Family Charitable Foundation to Romania, Administrator for Turda Development, President of Transilvania Fest Association, board member of Ratiu Center for Democracy and Chair of the US Ratiu Foundation. She is recipient of the 2007 Woman of the Year Award from Avantage magazine and the Loyalty Medal for Work in Romania by His Majesty King Michael in 2011.

Rareş Crăiuţ is a leading member of the Slow Food movement in Romania, and involved in support for peasant agriculture through arts, food and community initiatives. He regular contributor to Modernism, the Romanian online arts magazine.

'As a new resident of Transylvania, I could see that its unique cultural heritage could hold great appeal to visitors from around the world. But I was also frustrated that local people didn't seem to take pride in their traditions, and that those who held political power failed to champion community interests. My solution – Transylvania Fest. By establishing an international festival focused primarily on local food and drink, I hoped to restore the value of heritage, strengthen community relations, attract large numbers of visitors, and secure valuable publicity. Using gastronomy as a base, I would also stimulate pride in other cultural assets – architecture, music and theatre'.

Pamela Ratiu

The ambitions of Transylvania Fest

Established in London in 1979 by Ion and Elizabeth Ratiu, the Ratiu Family Charitable Foundation initiates and supports educational and cultural projects across Transylvania. Ion Ratiu (1917 – 2000), the elected leader of the World Union of Free Romanians, was a journalist, broadcaster and author, as well as a successful businessman in shipping and property. After studying law and joining the army, he entered Romania's Foreign Service, and his first posting was to London. He obtained political asylum in the UK after Romania's align-ment with the Axis powers – those who fought with Germany against the Allied Forces. After the communist regime came to power in 1947, Ratiu remained in exile in London, from where he became the most consistent voice of opposi-tion to Nicolae Ceausescu. In 1990, after 50 years in the UK, he returned his homeland to contest the presidency. Despite widespread disappointment at his failure to secure power, there is no doubting his impact on political and cultural life in Romania.

Transylvania Fest builds on Ion Ratiu's legacy. Its aims are to empower Romanian citizens to shape a strong future, while also stimulating pride in their unique cultural heritage. By focusing on the traditional foods of Transylvania, albeit adapted for a contemporary audience, it promotes economic development that is inclusive and community-oriented, that respects the natural environment, and that is sustainable. Initially conceived as a means of attracting tourists to a region of Romania that still has relatively few visitors, it has grown to become the country's most prominent food festival that now receives international press coverage and that enjoys the patronage of Her Royal Highness Crown Princess Margarita and of His Royal Highness the Prince of Wales.

The festival operates on two levels: as a three day fair, and as an economic and cultural development tool with projects spread throughout the year, especially in the period prior to the festival itself. The fair brings together approximately 100 food producers and craftsmen in a forum where they can interact directly with the local population, tourists, restaurateurs and retailers. The Transylvania Fest Association also works to improve the tourist infrastructure in whichever location the festival is being staged. In this respect, projects have included consulting on new tourism packages that broaden the appeal of particular destinations, building a communal kitchen (to EU standards) that can be used for product development and commercial production, and the construction of on-line marketing tools. Together with members of local communities, policy-makers and those with specialist expertise, the festival helps to define Transylvania's cultural assets (food, recipes, architecture, literature, art and crafts) and introduce them to new markets.

There is no doubt that partnerships have been key to Transylvania Fest's success and growth. Partners have included local public institutions (city mayors, municipal councils and regional authorities), cultural institutions (European Cultural Routes, The Dimitrie Gusty Village Museum, British Council Romania), academic partners (Oxford Brookes University), NGO representatives (Soros Foundation Romania, Mioritics Association, Adept Foundation) as well as representatives of the business sector (Caprimed, Ippon Med SRL, Meditur, Transgaz) and media partners interested in food and tourism (BBC, The Independent), which have provided both national and international coverage. The festival's participation at tourism fairs like the I.T.B., Romanian National Tourism Association Agencies' Fair and the Ministry of Tourism Touristic Fair, has also helped it to attract additional tourists.

One of the unforeseen benefits of partnerships has been the transformative impact that involvement in the festival has had on the lives of volunteers. While the assistance of US Peace-Corp volunteers and interns from the UK has been invaluable, they have also developed both personally and professionally. Through cultural exposure, assuming high levels of responsibility, and witnessing the value of their contributions, many volunteers have achieved significant personal and professional development that may have a profound influence on their careers.

The context

Transylvania, along with Walachia and Moldova are the three territorial-administrative units that unified at the beginning of the 20th century to form Romania. The region contains Romanians (over 75% of the population), Hungarians (almost 20%), and the remainder a mix of Germans, Roma, Ukrainians and Serbs. This amalgamation of cultural origins is reflected in all aspects of culture, from religious affiliations and social hierarchies, to architecture and cuisine. Literally translated from its Latin roots, Transylvania means 'the place beyond the forest' – appropriate given that much of the region is heavily wooded and enclosed on all sides by the Carpathian Mountains. As an ethno-cultural area it encompasses the counties of Alba, Arad, Bihor, Bistrița-Năsăud, Brașov, Cluj, Covasna, Harghita, Hunedoara, Mureș, Satu-Mare, Sălaj and Sibiu.

This rich cultural diversity does supports some distinctive local speciality dishes, but a hybrid, unifying cuisine has also emerged that has many staple ingredients and recipes. Corn-based *Mămăligă*, similar to polenta, features highly in the Transylvanian diet. As an accompaniment to meat products it often has a thick consistency and can be cut almost like a cake. Its versatility enables it to be used as a key component of other dishes, and to be deep-fried or roasted, often with cheese.

Pork remains the dominant meat and is found, one way or another, in everything from soups to desserts. Pork as a starter (salt-cured pork fat – *slanină*) or as a main, is often accompanied by a strong brandy known as *pălincă*, distilled from fermented plums, which has an alcohol content of over 70%. Though used all year round, dried or preserved in its own fat, pork also forms the centre-piece of celebratory meals, including at Christmas. Beef is rarely served, but after Easter lamb and mutton are relatively common. Poultry, mostly chicken but occasionally duck, is used for soups, of which there is a rich variety.

A typical Transylvanian menu would consist of a sour soup, followed by a pork-based dish served with potatoes and one other vegetable. The most popular pork dish is *sarmale* – cabbage leaves stuffed with pork meat – which could be accompanied by a plain leaf salad of pickled gherkins, peppers and red onions. Tarragon is the main aromatic herb, together with parsley, dill and thyme. Garlic is also favoured, as is smoked or spicy paprika. As dessert, you would often be served a sponge cake with different fruits, often cherries or apricots, or pancakes. *Papanşi*, sweet cheese dumplings, would bring the meal to a close.

Given that local cuisine plays such a central role in rural Transylvanian culture, it's no surprise that there are numerous food festivals in different loca-tions. But given their rather esoteric focus and titles, their capacity to have a comparable impact to Transylvania Fest may be somewhat limited. Examples include: *the Girls Fair* in Alba, *the Pancake Festival* in Arad, the *Acacia Flowers Festival* in Bistriţa-Năsăud, *the Blackberry Festival* in Covasna, *the Stuffed Cabbage Leaves Festival* in Harghita, and, most impressively, *the Sheep Measuring Festival* in Sălaj.

The impact on local food producers and local communities

One of the key challenges faced by the Transylvania Fest Association is to help embed commercial knowledge and entrepreneurial skills in small-scale food producers across the region. While they may be passionate about their products, they rarely know how to drive sales or meet regulatory requirements. So the festival has effectively become a small business incubator, providing a supportive framework focused on start-up, basic management skills, food hygiene, animal welfare and routes to market. It also gives access to valuable networks of experts, such as veterinary medics and city representatives. In this way, Transylvania Fest has helped to launch a wide range of products including raw cheese, gingerbread, jam, pickles, honey and home-baked cakes. In doing so, it has helped maintain the gastronomic heritage, as well as delivering a much needed boost to rural economies.

Understandably, producers have expressed anxiety about the potential costs of their involvement in Transylvania Fest. Fears have been overcome by sharing financial risks, not charging any participation fees, giving free access to the festival's physical infrastructure (such as stalls), covering producers' travelling expenses and providing accommodation, in association with public bodies that have dormitories.

In addition to the festival itself, various complimentary projects operate throughout the year, aimed at maximising positive impacts for producers. One of the most important has been the creation of a Slow Food Convivium, and more recently Slow Food on Campus in association with the University of Agriculture and Vetinary Medicine in Cluj-Napoca. This has enabled producers to form their own mutually supportive collective with fellow small business owners who share similar challenges and ambitions. By establishing them as representatives of Transylvanian cuisine, it has also enhanced their confidence, pride and sense of purpose. Several have been chosen to attend the biennial Slow Food Terra Madre event in Turin, which draws together food and drinks producers from all around the world.

So Transylvania Fest is not only a means of boosting sales. It gives opportunities for producers to interact with consumers, to share their knowledge of food traditions and to advise on cooking techniques. It is helping to stimulate renewed interest in Transylvanian cuisine, encourage knowledge exchange and attract visitors from across Romania and further afield.

Positive attention for Transylvanian culture

The interconnections between food and other important cultural forms, not least the distinctive architecture of Transylvania, is a key dimension of the festival. The Transylvania Fest Association recognises that food can be the catalyst for engagement of individuals in positions of power, by virtue of their job roles or areas of expertise, who have an interest in the region's heritage, as well as its potential. For example, Transylvania Fest 2011, held in Blaj, included an architectural competition focused on the restoration of the city's *Palace of Culture*. Following an exhibition of the winning architectural plans, a dinner for invited guests was held in a partially restored section of the building. The *Royal Cookbook* menu was endorsed by Her Royal Highness Crown Princess Margarita and the event stimulated momentum amongst those who could support the ambitious project, as well as securing valuable press attention.

Publicity also lends credibility and legitimacy to the skills and contributions of local residents, and in doing so strengthens cultural pride and community cohesion. Prior to each festival, members of the press and assorted VIPs are given opportunities to familiarise themselves with the location and, crucially, to experience characteristic dishes and food traditions, all of which helps them form positive images and create interesting stories. Would they like to know how local goats' cheese is made? Can they attend a magical dinner in the forest? Have they tasted bread with *Zacusă* (a traditional pepper and aubergine paste)?

For many outside Romania, the image of Transylvania has been shaped by fiction and is laden with myths. By attracting international media coverage, and presenting stories that reflect reality, the festival is helping to redefine the reputation of the region. In 2010, a dedicated edition of the BBC Radio 4 Food Programme was recorded at Transylvania Fest. Hosted by one of the UK's most prominent chefs, it explored the nature and impact of the festival, set in the context of local food traditions, and in doing so challenged dominant perceptions about life in Transylvania.

Ultimately, Transylvania Fest is driven by the desire to preserve tradition, but in a manner that is appropriate for the modern world. By empowering those in rural communities it enhances the life chances of aspiring food producers and their dependents. And by highlighting the power of grass-roots action, it provides an example to others throughout Romania.

Australia's Culinary 'Coming Out'

Richard Robinson

Richard Robinson is a Senior Lecturer at the University of Queensland, School of Tourism. He joined the School in 2004, after an extended career as a chef, predominantly managing foodservice operations in the prestige club sector. Dr Robinson's research focuses on; tourism and hospitality industry workforce issues, food tourism and the scholarship of teaching and learning. His work has been published in leading academic journals, edited books, international conference proceedings and practitioner periodicals.

Once perceived as a colonial backwater shaped by convicts, bushmen, laconic working class, and ANZACs, Australia has now asserted itself as a nation with strong and admired cultural attributes; home to world-class cities, globally recognised personalities, citizens of growing sophistication and a range of admired cultural institutions. One intriguing observation is that this accumulation of cultural capital has been mobilised by Australia's emerging reputation in the realms of food and drink. Is Australia's cultural 'coming out' indebted to its contemporary food and beverage professionals?

Australia's European heritage, and consequent worldwide exposure, began in the late 18th century. Before European contact, Australia's knowledge of the world beyond its seaboards was limited to visits by the Macassan Indonesians fishing for trepang, or sea cucumber. In 1788, under pressure to alleviate pressure on their groaning penal system, exacerbated by the loss of the American colonies in the previous decade, the British sent Arthur Phillip to Sydney Cove to establish the first permanent European settlement in *Terra Australis*. Within a few decades, penal colonies were founded in all the other current Australian states – in or near their capitals; Hobart, Melbourne, Adelaide, Brisbane and Perth. The military, free settlers and emancipated convicts brought with them their largely Anglo-Celtic heritage, *habitus* and culture – architecture, agricultural and later industrial economies, political, religious and social institutions, clothing, social mores and rituals, and of course food and drink. Many of these, arguably, were ill suited to the remote, sparse and harsh antipodean environment. Yet little changed and the tyranny of distance ensured that what change there was would be tediously slow.

Upon the abandonment of enforced transportation, Australia developed into the pasture and granary of Britain – its vast market garden across the globe! This led to the steady degradation of the landscape, evidenced now by the salination problems confronting Australia's largest waterway network in the Murray-Darling basin, desertification of large tracts of the now deforested inland scrub landscapes, not to mention the displacement and humiliation of the indigenous Australians. More than this, it perpetuated an Anglophile food culture and a long-lasting failure to cultivate a distinctive national cuisine.

Nonetheless, by the turn of the 20th century, coinciding with Australia's federation in 1901, there were signs of an independent and distinctive culture in development. The art of the Heidelberg School, the sketches and publishing endeavours of the Lindsay family, the distinctive balladic poetry of Henry Lawson and Banjo Patterson and Dame Nellie Melba's operatic soprano voice, that charmed audiences across Europe and North America, serve as poignant examples. But stylistically, if not in context, Australia's culture sought inspiration from Western Europe and mimicked the *haute culture* of the aristocracy and bourgeoisie. And so it was in the culinary realm (Abbott, 1970). While indigenous ingredients like emu, turtle, possum, pandanus and yam found their way into the repertoires and cookery books of pioneer Australian cooks like the Beetons and Rawsons (Robinson & Arcodia, 2008) invariably they were subjected to methods of preparation and service according to western recipes and traditions. The Chinese and Greeks, who came to work the Australian gold-fields from the mid-18th century, often turned to foodservice. Paradoxically, instead of cooking their traditional cuisine they buckled to local tastes and predominantly prepared and sold British fare (Addison and McKay, 1985).

Gastronomic theorists have proposed other factors for the slow emergence of a distinctive national cuisine. Symons (1982) has attributed Australia's culinary backwardness to a failure to inherit and develop a peasant cuisine. As is common among the so-called 'settler nations' – Australia together with neighbours New Zealand, and notably South Africa and Canada – the dominant colonial powers largely turned their noses up at the indigenous culinary herit-ages (although granted this is sweeping statement). More than this, in the case of Australia, the first settlers were very slow to establish sustainable pastoral and agrarian practices and so depended on imported food supplies. They turned only fleetingly, in utter desperation, to harvesting and hunting, but not cultivating or domesticating, the indigenous flora and fauna. Compounding this was the fact that vast swathes of Australia's early settlers were from the lower social classes and hence were neither acculturated nor inclined to sophisticated tastes. To be brutally explicit, Australia was an importer not just of foodstuffs but also of culture, and at the same time, much to its dishonour, a destroyer of its original inhabitants' deep, diverse, sustainable and ancient culture and ecology.

It was arguably the two world wars that served as vehicles for exporting Australia's culture. In total over one million men and women served overseas, a great percentage on Europe's battlefields between 1914 and 1945. During this period the archetypical Australian national identity was born, largely revolving around the ANZAC ethos of bravery, mateship, egalitarianism, loyalty, courage, honesty and fortitude, all imbued with a touch of the larrikin. These cultural attributes had been forged in the Australian bush and had been captured in the artistic output of those mentioned before. Yet besides culinary clichés such as billy tea, damper and bully beef, gastronomic distinction remained elusive. This largely mirrored the failure to carve cultural niches in other domains. Even Australia's iconic features were imports. The celebrated Sydney Opera House, built between 1959 and 1973, was designed by a Dane.

During the 1950s Australia experienced an unprecedented influx of migrants, mostly from southern Europe. Their cultural influence was profound. Previously olive oil could only be purchased in a pharmacy. Now wild delicacies – olives, spaghetti, souvlaki, cappuccino and Chianti - jostled with broiled lamb chops, boiled potatoes, canned peas, tepid tea and soapy lager for space on the Aussie post-war table. Even outdoor street dining arrived on Australia's shores. This new found acceptance spurred many resident Chinese to develop suburban market gardens and slowly they opened their own cafes and restaurants, serving acculturated Chop Sui and Chow Mien to the bravest of locals. A new wave of Vietnamese migrants, refugees of decades of war in their homeland, became manifest in new styles of Asian cuisine gracing the tables of suburban cafes. In sum, a polyglot of migrants and a peak in Australian outbound travel (Robinson, 2007), awakened the antipodes from their culinary slumber. It has been argued that these factors, and an emerging social consciousness, perhaps prompted by the horrors of Vietnam, mobilised a leftist-foodie movement. Unlike many of the 'television' chefs of the early 21st century, driven by celebrity, royalties and endorsements as much as their love of food, these so-called 'chardonnay socialists', 'latte liberals' and 'caviar leftists' (Symons, 2007) reinvigorated and reawakened the public palate and consciousness with a flurry of recipes, cookbooks, television programs and restaurant guides. Their bequest and these various other catalysts have left a profound legacy.

Over the past 50 years Australia has developed a number of viticultural and gastronomic industries that have captured the world's attention. Without doubt Australia's wine industry established its food and drink 'beachhead'. Vines were brought to Australia on Arthur Phillip's First Fleet, but plantings proliferated with the various migration booms. Through isolation, good luck and vigilant quarantine management, many of Australia's wine regions survived the global phylloxera scourge that decimated European vineyards in the late 19th century. South Australia's main wine producing regions, including the Barossa Valley, McLaren Vale, the Adelaide Hills and the Clare Valley, and parts of the Hunter Valley, north of Sydney, survived. Since then, Australian wines have garnered international acclaim in competitions and in international markets. Penfolds Grange is recognised as a producer of world-class Shiraz. Its first vintage, produced in 1952, commands prices of AUS$30,000 per bottle on the domestic market. The Semillons of the Hunter Valley, the Pinot Noirs of Tasmania and the Rieslings of the Clare Valley are equally revered and collected by wine aficionados worldwide. Even a sticky Sylvaner from Ballandean Estate, in south-east Queensland's obscure Granite Belt region, has wowed the pundits in Europe. Not satisfied with making outstanding wine with their own grapes, Australia's oenologists are world renowned, and have exported their talents and expertise to both the Old and New Worlds, an exchange eased by the inverted vintages between Australia's southern hemisphere harvest and that of Europe and north America.

Australia also has a number of iconic breweries dating back to colonial times and has enthusiastically embraced the craft and micro-brewery boom. Around 10 major, over 100 micro and nearly 50 craft breweries are located across all Australia's states and territories – and one of these, the Burleigh Brewing Company, just packed a pint-sized punch. With a wheat beer brew they stunned 220 judges from 40 countries, and perennial winners, Germany, by winning their category at the 2012 Brewers Association Beer World Cup (ABC News, 2012) - a far cry from the insipid import Fosters, which competes for shelf-space with equally bland Euro-lagers.

Australia, particularly in the culinary 'meccas' of Melbourne, Sydney and Adelaide, has spawned an enviable number of fine restaurants since the 1970s. Leveraging classical training, diverse influences of the Mediterranean and south-east Asian diaspora, adaptable and innovative technical prowess and a flourishing abundance of produce nurtured by the continent's micro-climes, trademark cuisines such as modern Australian, Pacific Rim and East meets West are now firmly established. Chefs like Cheong Liew, Phil Thompson and Tetsuya Wakuda who champion Asian influences, Stephanie Alexander and Maggie Beer honing more classical styles and Luke Mangan, Neil Perry and Shannon Bennett with cutting edge experimentalism, are just a few iconic Australian chefs who have won as much acclaim for their culinary craft. More than this, not only do Australian restaurants regularly feature in the acclaimed top 50 restaurants in the world, but Australian chefs like Brett Graham from The Ledbury in London, are heading up Michelin star-rated eateries in Europe (*The World's 50 Best Restaurants*, 2012). Australia's finest restaurants are exporting their brands too. For example, Salt, Luke Mangan's independent brand, has launched fine dining establishments in the competitive Tokyo and Singapore markets. At the core of their success is an unassuming diligence, a quiet confidence and perhaps a freedom from influential peasant cuisines (Symons, 1982).

Along the way Australia's agricultural, viticultural and gastronomic pursuits have benefitted from some ingenuity. Australia's agrarian economy benefitted much from the invention of first the mechanised 'grain stripper' and then the 'jump stump plough'. The wine making industry broadened its marketing base significantly with the innovative 'wine cask', facetiously described by some as 'chateau de cardboard'. And the longevity of the food stuffs was greatly enhanced by James Harrison's 'practical refrigerator', which was actually commissioned by a brewery in the 1850s to cool its beer. Later that century, industrial production of ice facilitated the safe export of meat to Britain. Finally, in the early 1900s, a Melburnian developed Aspro (based on aspirin), which has proved an elixir for Australians indulging in its finest (or not) alcoholic beverages.

These scientific achievements aside, Australia's contemporary global cultural presence is ubiquitous. In various fields of popular culture, sport and media, internationally recognised icons abound. The on-screen and stage Blanchetts, Gibsons, Kidmans and Rushs and off-stage Luhrmanns and Weirs, the MacPhersons and Williams of the fashionista, the Minogues and Powderfingers of the hit parade, musical genre exponents Dusty and Urban, comedians like 'gender-bender' Humphries and 'bogan' Hogan, the Freemans, Normans and Evans of the sporting arena and the Murdochs of the tabloids are household names for one reason or the other. Likewise in the 'serious' arts, for example the world of literature, Australia boasts a litany of respected as well as prolific authors; Courtney, Keneally and Nobel Prize winner Patrick White, playwrights like Williamson and poets like Murray. Dame Joan Sutherland, husband Richard Bonynge and compatriot Grainger are legendary in the world of opera, and Seidler's modernist architectural legacy stretches from Austria to France to Mexico. The names Boyd, Dupain, Nolan and Whiteley spruik the interest of the wealthiest Christies' and Sotheby's patrons, while contrarily the challenging works of Greer and Noonuccal send intellectuals ducking for cover.

Despite the acclaim of such luminaries, nowhere is it more apparent that Australians have divested themselves of their collective inferiority complex that through their food and drink. Beyond a national self-confidence, Australia is now exporting its rich and cosmopolitan culture. To conclude on a provocative note, should there be consensus that the production and consumption of food and drink could be associated with, or even responsible for, the cultural 'coming out' of a nation, then the social significance of our food and drink choices demands serious reappraisal.

References

Abbott, E. (1970) 'The English and Australian Cookery Book: Cooking for the many as well as the 'Upper Ten Thousand' by an Australian Aristologist', in A. Burt (ed), *The Colonial Cookery Book,* Sydney: Paul Hamlyn

ABC News (2012) 'Aussie brew beats Germans at their own game', 31st May. Accessed at abc.net.au/news/2012-05-30/aussie-brew-beats-germans-at-their-own-game/4042544 8th August 2012.

Addison, S. and McKay, J. (1985) *A Good Plain Cook: An edible history of Queensland,* Brisbane: Queensland Museum.

Dan Murphy's (2012) 'Penfolds Grange 1952', Accessed at danmurphys.com.au/product/DM_914745/penfolds-grange-1952 8th August 2012.

Head, B. and Walter, J. (eds) (1988) *Intellectual Movements and Australian Society,* Melbourne: OUP.

Horne, D. (1964), *The Lucky Country: Australia in the Sixties,* Melbourne: Penguin Books.

Menzies, G. (2002), *1421: The Year China Discovered the World* London: Bantam Press

Robinson, R.N.S. (2007),'Plain fare to fusion: The impacts of ethnicity on the process of maturity in Brisbane's restaurant sector', *Journal of Hospitality and Tourism Management,* **14** (1), 70-84.

Robinson, R.N.S. and Arcodia, C.A. (2008),'Reading Australian colonial hospitality: A simple recipe', *International Journal of Culture, Tourism and Hospitality Research,* **2** (4), 374-388.

Symons, M. (1982), *One Continuous Picnic: A history of eating in Australia*, Adelaide: Duck Press.

Symons, M. (1998), *The Pudding That Took A Thousand Cooks*, Ringwood: Viking Penguin Books.

Symons, M. (2007), 'The foodie files', *The Australian*, 2nd June. Accessed at theaustralian.com.au/arts/books/the-foodie-files/story-e6frg8nf-1111113635968 8th August 2012.

The World's 50 Best Restaurants (2012). Accessed at theworlds50best.com/ 8th August 2012.

Taking a Light Glass in Soho

Paul Bloomfield

Paul Bloomfield has been a chef for over 26 years. He has been responsible for product development for many leading firms, including Quorn, Covent Garden Soup company, M&S Chinese range, Sharwoods, Moy Park, Jimmy Doherty and Loyd Grossman sauces. He is the author or co-author of *Party Eats*, *Tempting Treats* and *The Brunch Cookbook*.

I have been commissioned to write an autobiography and I would be grateful to any of your readers who could tell me what I was doing between 1960 and 1974.

Jeffrey Barnard

I am taking a light glass in Soho! Standing outside the Coach and Horses (one of my regular haunts), with my newly acquired drinking companion, who is reminiscing about how things have changed. She misses her days with Soho luminaries, not least 'No Knickers Joyce'. She drains the glass of wine that I bought her and goes back inside. She will never speak to me again. Such is the character of Soho – sustained by drink and legends.

Today it's a cosmopolitan quarter of restaurants, pubs, bars, coffee shops and clubs, interspersed with traders, hairdressers, porn shops and media houses. It's here that London's gay 'village' affably co-exists with tourists, hedonists, media-types and epicures.

Soho is comprised of about 130 acres of central London. Oxford Street, Regent Street, Shaftesbury Avenue and Charing Cross Road mark its physical boundaries, and provide a framework for its powerful and enduring symbolic culture. Soho was extolled by a foreign diplomat at the beginning of the 20th Century as a home of artists, dancers and musicians and a sanctuary for foreign refugees. Fifty years later it was condemned by the Daily Mail as a neighbourhood, 'Solely for stinking men, prostitutes, perverts and pimps.' Whatever its perceived failings, its rich diversity placed it at the vanguard of new tastes – particularly in food and fashion. It has remained a case study in cross-cultural acceptance, as well as a theatre of over-indulgence and unruly living.

Soho had its day as a chic residential neighbourhood, albeit short lived. The district's first buildings were erected on Soho Fields in the 17th Century, including a grand house for the Duke of Monmouth, son of Charles II, and a street of houses built by Richard Frith, now Frith Street. More merchant's houses followed, built closely together, creating a strong sense of community. But the area was soon to be deserted by its affluent residents for the more spacious, newly created neighbourhoods of Mayfair and Bloomsbury. Its reputation as a haven for the socially excluded and disenfranchised had begun.

French Huguenot, Jew, Italian and German immigrants have all laid claim to Soho as their home, which has precipitated strong and multiple culinary identities. The French were first to make their mark, notably with the opening in 1867 of *Kettners*, by Auguste Kettner, previously chef to Napoleon III. The French were no longer the black footed terrors who threatened our national liberty. French cuisine and culture were the height of fashion and experimental and unusual food very much on the agenda for the affluent classes. *Kettners* comprised of four houses in Romilly Street and was the 'must be seen at' location of its day. Over the next forty years its reputation was enhanced through patronage by an artistic set, including Oscar Wilde, who was known for his lavish socialising. Its royal seal of approval came from Edward VII, who entertained actress Lillie Langtry in its upstairs apartments. He even had a tunnel dug to *Kettners* directly from the Palace Theatre on Shaftesbury Avenue, to enable more discreet 'comings and goings'.

The latter half of the 19th Century in Europe saw conditions of rural popula-tions steadily deteriorate, in particular in the Italian regions of Piedmont and Lombardy. From the 1890's thousands of migrants from these regions settled in Soho taking whatever work the area could give them – as kitchen hands, porters, cooks and waiters. They also capitalised on the advent of the Great War of 1914 and the exodus of German service staff, who until then had delivered unrivalled hospitality.

During this period Soho re-affirmed its identity as multi-ethnic territory, as new restaurants and cheap eating houses sprang up, taking advantage of lower rents than in more sophisticated neighbourhoods. Berwick Street Market, although a trading area since the 17th Century, became established as a retail destination that played host to a predominantly Jewish clientele who lived in and around Berwick and Rupert Streets. It was a jumble of delis, grocers, butchers and confectioners as well as cheap outfitters and 'clip joints'.

It was possible in the 1950s and 1960s to take breakfast, lunch or supper in an atmosphere of complete respectability whilst surrounded by an assortment of crooks and conmen. Francis Bacon would paint furiously in the morning, and then head for lunch at *Wheeler's* on Old Compton Street, on an almost daily basis, joining the likes of Lord Boothroyd and the Kray twins (notorious London gangsters). Long lunches were usually followed by a visit to The *Gargoyle Club* in Meard Street, a once chic supper club in the 1930s, which had become a drinking den where members of the Soho community could bypass the strin-gent licensing laws.

In contrast, Peppino Leoni had observed affluent English tourists abroad – men dressed in dinner suits, women in evening gowns and fine jewels – confirming their social standing through carefully choreographed public performances, with silent, deferential waiters in supporting rolls. It was a theatre for such conspicuous displays that he created on Dean Street – *Leoni's Quo Vadis* – which became a formative part of Soho's food culture in the inter-war years, and beyond. Such stylised dining did not actually reflect Leoni's own tastes, which were informal and more akin to that offered in contemporary Soho restaurants such as *Polpo, Princi, Barrafina* and ironically, today's *Quo Vadis*.

Soho was more than just a heterogeneous mix of people defined by their dining habits. It was also a hotbed for political discourse on issues affecting its various cultural groups. While in its displaced Italian community the debate raged about fascist politics, discerning British diners ate salami, pasta, cheese and funghi, swilled down with acceptable Chianti, over ten years before the publication of Elizabeth David's *Italian Food*, which is purported to have introduced the British to such delicacies. Indeed it is claimed that two assassination plots against Mussolini were funded by Italian restaurateurs in Soho.

Demographics were not the only influence on Soho's food and drink culture. The arrival of Italian coffee had a significant impact in the 1950s – something that has continued to the present day. Britain may have been recovering from bleak post war austerity but coffee, usually made in huge urns and left to stew for hours, had not moved on. In 1947 Achille Gaggia, in Milan, invented the first modern espresso machine that forced water through coffee grounds at high pressure. Pino Riservato, a travelling salesman who visited the Italian delis and grocer shops in Soho and Clerkenwell, saw potential for the Gaggia machine. But it was slow to catch on as suspicious caterers thought it wasted coffee. In the summer of 1953 he opened the *Gaggia Experimental Coffee Bar* (also known as Risorveto's) on Dean Street. He became the sole importer of Gaggia machines to the UK, making his first sale to Moka on Frith Street, which opened in the same year. Moka was a sensation, selling 1000 cups of espresso a day at its peak. Its greatest significance was that it attracted teenagers, becoming the first to capitalise on this lucrative new market. For teenagers, too young for pubs and no longer interested in ballrooms or youth clubs, the coffee bars became an escape route from parents and a venue where the latest music could be played on jukeboxes. They also became locations where older drinkers could unwind after the pubs had closed. The 2i's club on Old Compton Street (so called because it was originally owned by two Iranian brothers), became a 'Beatnik' mecca for espresso and rock and roll. Showcasing many young musicians, it's where numerous future stars first performed, including Tommy Steele, Cliff Richard and Adam Faith. It sealed Soho's reputation as the music capital of London, and indeed of the UK. The introduction of coffee shops, first in Soho, was a catalyst for changing patterns of social behaviour.

Soho's post-war drinking dens, despite many now having been shut or modernised beyond recognition, have had a lasting impact on the area's reputation. The well-documented exploits of a particular artistic set that included Francis Bacon, Dylan Thomas and Daniel Farson, have assumed mythical status. Jeffrey Barnard, the journalist known for his weekly column *Low Life* in the *Spectator* (described by Jonathan Meades as 'a suicide note in weekly instalments') was defined by his alcoholism. Tom Conti, the actor who portrayed him in Keith Waterhouse's play *Jeffrey Barnard is Unwell*, claims that Barnard's enduring appeal is not only built on his wit and way with words. He suggests 'There is an envy, I think, that people have for… the idea of someone who just has relinquished all responsibility. It is a seductive idea.' Asked if drinking ever got in the way of his work, Barnard replied "The situation is very much the reverse. Work frequently interferes with my drinking". There also seems to be an acceptance that for some, drinking could be not only a source of humour, but also of inspiration, that to produce great works you have to have sunk to the lowest depths.

It was also some of those who provided hospitality who achieved iconic status, none less so than Muriel Belcher at the Colony Room Club on Dean Street. She secured an all-day license, enabling her to continue serving while other pubs had to shut from 2.30pm until early evening. The club became known as much for Belcher's foul language as it did for the eccentric clientele. She provided Bacon with a weekly allowance of £10, in return for him frequenting the Club along with his entourage of wealthy and influential patrons, as well as his hard core drinking partners. In her canny way, Belcher was reinforcing the image of the Colony Room as Soho's most avant-garde venue.

The strengthening association of Soho with youth, fashion, artistic and drinking cultures went hand-in-hand with its image as the most sexually liberated enclave of London. Soho in the 1950s was seen to be at the centre of a new wave of consumption, not only of food, drink, clothes and music, but also of sex for pleasure, in both consensual and exploitative ways. This contributed to a sense of moral anxiety, fuelled by the popular press, which reported society being, 'in the grip of the twin vices of male homosexuality and prostitution'

(Mort, 1990: 889). It was not the city in its entirety that was viewed as being morally corrupt, but particular quarters, most notably Soho. In response to the forces of conservatism, the government commissioned the Wolfenden Committee – or the Home Office Committee on Homosexual Offences and Prostitution, 1954, to use its correct title, to advise on policy. Ironically, it promoted greater visibility for particular groups and the partial decriminalisation of homosexuality. However, police evidence on records of offences served to map out a 'sexual geography' of the area, which reasserted its connection with 'illicit' sexuality.

Soho's connection with the gay community has continued, and indeed strengthened. As legislation and social attitudes have progressed, gay men have become one of the area's most culturally visible groups, and the consequent impact on drinking culture has been profound. Catering to different 'tastes', there is now a plethora of gay bars, centred on Old Compton Street. They create a postmodern environment in which identity is achieved and communicated through participation and the adoption of style. This might imply a utopian, democratised existence, but this emphasis on aesthetics can also be alienating. The gay bars of Soho have become theatres of consumption in which young gay men learn the rules of acceptance, or not.

So there we have it. Soho was and remains the capital's playground for those on the edge – for those who may operate in the mainstream, but who just occasionally need to feel more at home.

Now, time for another light glass ... !

References

Mort, F. (1998) 'Cityscapes, consumption, Masculinities and the mapping of London since 1950', *Urban Studies*, **35**: 889-907

Sloan, D. (2004) *Culinary Taste: consumer behaviour in the international restaurant sector*, Oxford: Elsevier

Give a Dog a Bad Name:

British cooking and its place on the culinary leader board

Charles Campion

Charles Campion is a food critic, writer and broadcaster. He has written in The Times, The Independent *and other leading newspapers and magazines. His books include* Eat Up! *about the excellent home cooks of Britain. His radio and TV work includes regular appearances in MasterChef. Charles is a patron of Oxford Gastronomica, at Oxford Brookes University.*

Ask any American, particularly those who have not yet visited Europe, and they will tell you that French food is magnificent while British food is ghastly. Visitors from the other side of the Atlantic long to be as glam as Gene Kelly or Leslie Caron, and they long to be that American in Paris – or better still a rose-tinted version of that city where the weather is always perfect and the food is always ambrosial.

Somewhere along the time line between the Battle of Agincourt and the present day, British cooking has ended up pigeon-holed as a culinary also-ran to the French and there's a widely held, if erroneous, view that the food in Britain is very poor indeed. This assessment may have been valid for a few impoverished decades after the Second World War but when it comes to cooks and cooking, things change quickly and today's reality is very different.

The rivalry between British cooking and French cuisine is deep-seated, in the 19th Century French gastronomes were jealous of the British mastery of the arcane skills of roasting and baking meats (they also made a distinction between 'roasting' – which was cooking before an open fire, often using a spit – and 'baking', referred to a dish cooked in a closed oven, which to confuse matters we would now call roasting). Meanwhile in the one-upmanship circles of the English aristocracy the 'must-have' accessory was a French chef. In 1816 when George, the Prince Regent, hired Marie-Antoine Carême (a French chef who had worked for Talleyrand and was known for his elaborate and architectural banqueting dishes) he had to stump up £2,000 a year, a sum that would be footballer or rock star money today. But this royal patronage added momentum to a myth that the best chefs were always French, a view that underpinned the success of Auguste Escoffier in the latter part of the 19th Century.

It was the sea change from 'Service à la Française' (serving all the dishes at once) to 'Service à la Russe' (serving dishes in succession) that enabled Escoffier to turn the dining room at London's Savoy Hotel into what we would now recognise as a restaurant. For the first time you could book your own table and choose the dishes that you wanted from a 'Carte'. This era also saw the first appearance of 'menu French' – as well as 'pêche Melba' in honour of Australian chanteuse Nelly Melba, the Savoy menus were sometimes graced with 'Cuisses des nymphes Auror' an inspired re-naming of a dish that did not sell well under the original rather laconic descriptor – 'Frogs' legs'.

Alarmingly, French culinary supremacy was to go unchallenged for the next fifty years, decades that included both World Wars. During the Second World War – while dreaming of a free Europe, golden butter, plenty of sugar and a world without ration books – British cooks were at their most pragmatic. Francis Latry, the head chef at the Savoy in wartime, put aside the French notions of his predecessor Escoffier and devised the infamous Woolton Pie, named after his Lordship the Minister of Food. This pie was a formidable and heavy-pastried affair filled with potatoes, carrots and sometimes parsnips. The constraints of rationing brought with them an austere diet and perversely the British people have never been healthier than in those years of hardship.

As the 1950s, dawned the balance of power between British chefs and French chefs was holding steady; the French were aloof and the British cowed. It didn't help that the next great mover and shaker, although British, came down heavily on the side of French cooking. Elizabeth David returned from Cairo to the rather grey and thoroughly drab world of post-war Britain, as she put it: 'There was flour and water soup seasoned solely with pepper; bread and gristle rissoles; dehydrated onions and carrots; corned beef toad in the hole. I need not go on.' Her first job was writing for Harper's Bazaar and it paved the way for a steady stream of books – *Mediterranean Food*, *French Country Cooking*, *Italian Food*, *Summer Cooking*, and *French Provincial Cooking*. Much has been written about the concision and precision of her writing. She bagged a CBE, a couple of honorary degrees, a fellowship of the Royal Society of Literature and the 'Chevalier de l'Ordre du Mérite Agricole'– But it is irksome that the cookery writer many people would class as Britain's greatest should have been so resolutely Francophile.

Meanwhile some of the diners faced by those 'bread and gristle rissoles' decided to take things into their own hands and 1951 they welcomed the publication of the *Good Food Guide* which 'tells you of 600 places throughout Britain where you can rely on a good meal at a reasonable price, recommended by members of the Good Food Club.' It was edited by Raymond Postgate and the objects of the Club were:

1   To raise the standard of cooking in Britain and keep prices reasonable

2   To encourage the drinking of good wine and the proper care of beer

3   To earn foreign currency by improving British hospitality and offering overseas visitors honest guidance and not official puff

4   To reward enterprise and courtesy

5   To do ourselves a bit of good by making our holidays, travels and evenings out in due course more enjoyable.

Postgate's rules look pretty sensible even after all this time. He also decided to take the fight to the French, 'Yet there is no reason in nature why British cooking should be worse than, say, French. We have no worse materials than the French have; indeed in some cases our materials are undeniably tastier, as for example, strawberries, tomatoes, apples, asparagus, lowland beef and mountain mutton.' Postgate's thesis was that the quality and quantity of respected restaurant guide books in France kept Continental chefs up to the mark and he set out to fulfil the same function in Britain.

During the 1960's cooking in Britain segued from the kind of 'hotel' food that desperately wanted to be French to a few lonely dishes that had a British provenance – in the 1963 *Good Food Guide* the Great Eastern Hotel on Liverpool Street, London EC2 lists as specialities: 'scampi Niçoise'; 'filets de sole Veronique'; 'côtellettes d'agneau Reform' and then rather encouragingly 'Lancashire Hot-pot'. British cooking was starting to speak up for itself.

When you read the 1971 menu from Robert Carrier's eponymous, and well thought of, restaurant at Camden Passage in Islington, London, you can see the first signs of what will later become Modern British cooking. Yes, there are some classical French dishes – 'oeufs à la Russe'; 'côte de Veau Mornay'; 'ragout d'agneau à la Ancienne' – but then there are also dishes in the British tradition 'trio of baby lamb chops with fresh mint and garlic'; 'prawn and bacon tart'; 'barbecued chicken with fresh herbs'; and even some quirkier exotic combinations 'truffled chicken Kiev'; 'Turkish kebab of beef, sauce Diable'; 'Souvlakia of turbot, sauce Mousseline'. Carrier also divided the main courses into two subsections 'Your main course from the open fire' heads up the grills, while 'Great dishes of the day' gathers together the French dishes and everything else from 'gratin of quail with sage' to 'sauté of prawns Duchesse'. Although he was an American, Carrier's show-casing of the 'open fire' harks back to the traditional British strengths of roasting. On a more wistful note, in 1971 a four course dinner at Carrier's could be had for £3.75!

Meanwhile on the other side of the channel three highly respected restaurant critics and guide book writers were hatching a plot to redefine all that was best in modern French cuisine. The conspirators were André Gayot, Henri Gault and Christian Millau and their brainchild was 'Nouvelle Cuisine'. This was a codification of the cooking style of many leading French chefs – stellar names such as Paul Bocuse, Alain Chapel, Michel Guérard, Roger Vergé and the

Troisgros brothers. In their original manifesto the three guidebook men set out ten commandments, and even today most of them make perfect sense. Chefs should use the freshest possible ingredients. Over -complexity was to be avoided. Cooking times should be reduced to conserve flavour. More use to be made of the technique of steaming. Out with heavy, classical, flour-thickened sauces, in with reductions, butter sauces and fresh herbs. Use regional dishes for inspiration rather than turning to venerable recipes.

These are all sensible points and you would think that such an initiative would be a force for good. Unfortunately the short journey across the Channel turned Nouvelle Cuisine from a commentary on the nuances of haute cuisine into a frightful parody. British chefs adopted those elements that were easiest to copy and Nouvelle Cuisine quickly became a byword for portions that were too small, presentation that was too fussy, and freakishly inappropriate combinations of random ingredients. (The dishes 'Liver in Lager' and 'Saveloy with Lychees' served at the 'Regrette Rien' restaurant in the Mike Leigh film *Life is Sweet* were all too close to reality). It is no surprise that the British dining public never warmed to Nouvelle Cuisine– they saw it as paying more and getting less. The hospitality industry's attempt to foist this new style onto the public made even sophisticated diners wary and was a major setback to the development of Modern British Cooking.

There is one sector of Britain's restaurant business that has never faltered, and has always been head and shoulders above its French equivalent – the Indian restaurant business. In 1955 there were ten Indian restaurants in London and by the end of the 1960's that figure had risen to 800. Today the U.K. figure is over 10,000 and the Indian food industry has annual sales that have been estimated at £3 billion. Some commentators would have it that Britain has embraced all manner of foreign cuisines so avidly simply because traditional British cooking is so poor, but this is a rather harsh view. A good many of the staple ingredients of dishes typical to Indian restaurant food – for example chillies and tomatoes – were introduced to both India and Britain at around about the same time, circa 1580, so if you were able to attend a formal dinner in the 16th Century you would have been faced with very similar spicing whether you were in England or India – dishes would feature cinnamon, cloves, nutmeg, pepper and mustard. Perhaps the unstoppable rise in popularity of Indian food in Britain reflects nothing more complex than a search for the once familiar spices which have fallen out of favour in European cooking? That, and an overwhelming love of chilli heat. If you seek out the highest-rated Indian restaurants in Paris you will be amazed by the lack of fresh spices and the poor standard of the cooking in general. Broadly speaking, none of the top ten Indian restaurants in Paris would get into a UK top 50.

One of the most attractive characteristics of British diners is their open-mindedness and their willingness to try new dishes. British chefs can, and do, get inspiration from an enormous spectrum of restaurants that represent the majority of world cuisines while French chefs are the prisoners of tradition. The ability to eat the food of Myanmar, Nigeria, Italy, Sichuan, Vietnam, Pakistan, Ethiopia and even France – to name but eight of the reputedly 80 different cuisines available in London alone – is the perfect foundation for a genuinely inclusive modern cuisine.

Only recently – say 1990 – the term 'Modern British' food was valued as a useful label that journalists could use for any restaurant, chef, or cuisine that was not pigeon-holed elsewhere. 'Modern British' was an umbrella for French food cooked in Britain; Tuscan dishes from English chefs; South East Asian spicing – it's hard to forget 'galangal custard' a dessert spotted in Chelsea at the turn of the century. If a dish was modern and British it was welcome aboard. Then almost overnight things changed, and unlike Nouvelle Cuisine which came with its own rulebook, Modern British Cooking grew out of a single premise. Chefs started to place a great emphasis on fresh, seasonal and care-fully-sourced ingredients. Leading the pack were men like Fergus Henderson at St John whose quirky love of offal was finally taken seriously. When Mark Hix left Caprice Holdings behind and set up his own restaurants, his menus revelled in the seasons and revelled in British culinary history. Richard Corrigan brought Irish blarney to the party. Jeremy Lee has added a Dundonian lilt to Quo Vadis. Tom Pemberton has made an off the beaten track success of Hereford Road. These restaurants are packed, and deservedly so.

Now the UK can offer excellent British cooking that is the match for any cuisine in the world. The only difficulty lies in Britons avoiding any trace of smugness as French cuisine sinks into the morass of burgers in polystyrene boxes and pizzas taking over from the table d'hote that so charmed Elizabeth David. What a brilliant fight back Britain ... this show will run and run.

Index